A Crack in the Mirror

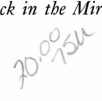

"Imagine mankind as dwelling in an underground cave with a long entrance open to the light across the whole width of the cave; in this they have been from childhood, with necks and legs fettered, so they have to stay where they are. They cannot move their heads round because of the fetters, and they can only look forward, but light comes to them from fire burning behind them higher up at a distance. Between the fire and the prisoners is a road above their level, and along it imagine a low wall has been built, as puppet showmen have screens in front of their people over which they work their puppets."
. . .

"Now consider," said I, "what their release would be like, and their cure from these fetters and their folly; let us imagine whether it might naturally be something like this. One might be released, and compelled suddenly to stand up and turn his neck round, and to walk and look towards the firelight; all this would hurt him, and he would be much too dazzled to see distinctly those things whose shadows he had seen before. What do you think he would say, if someone told him that what he saw before was foolery, but now he saw more rightly, being a bit nearer reality and turned towards what was a little more real? What if he were shown each of the passing things, and compelled by questions to answer what each one was? Don't you think he would be puzzled, and believe what he saw before was more true than what was shown to him now?"

"Far more," said he.

Plato, *The Republic,* Book VII

Description is revelation. It is not
The thing described, nor false facsimile.

It is an artificial thing that exists,
In its own seeming, plainly visible,

Yet not too closely the double of our lives,
Intenser than any actual life could be,

A text we should be born that we might read,
More explicit than the experience of the sun

And moon, the book of reconciliation,
Book of a concept only possible

In description, canon central in itself,
The thesis of the plentifullest John.

Thus the theory of description matters most.

—Wallace Stevens
("Description Without Place" vi–vii, 122–33)

A Crack in the Mirror

Reflexive Perspectives in Anthropology

Jay Ruby *editor*

University of Pennsylvania Press · Philadelphia · 1982

Illustrations on pp. 71 and 77 by Janis Essner
Interior designed by Adrianne Onderdonk Dudden

Library of Congress Cataloging in Publication Data
Main entry under title:

A Crack in the mirror.

    Bibliography: p.
    Includes index.
    Contents: Introduction / Barbara Myerhoff and
Jay Ruby — Collective reflexivity / Richard
Schechner — Dramatic ritual/ritual drama / Victor
Turner — Life history among the elderly /
Barbara Myerhoff — [etc.]
    1. Ethnology—Methodology—Addresses, essays,
lectures.   2. Ethnology—Philosophy—Addresses,
essays, lectures.   I. Ruby, Jay.
GN345.C73   306   81–51147
ISBN 0–8122–7815–1   AACR2

Printed in the United States of America

CONTENTS

PREFACE

Clyde Kluckhohn's book *Mirror for Man* is one of the most widely read introductions to anthropology, known by thousands of people who have never set foot in an anthropology classroom. The title was Kluckhohn's metaphor for anthropology—a mirror held before us to allow a better understanding of ourselves through the study of others. What Kluckhohn never mentioned is that one can also examine the mirror. The purpose of this book is to point out some of the cracks in the mirror and to suggest a new metaphor—a paint-by-number realist painting. On the surface these paintings appear to be ideologically neutral renderings of reality. Upon more careful examination, one can see that an underlying structure was provided for the artist by the manufacturer, leaving the artist the task of filling in the schema with appropriate colors.

Jay Ruby

ACKNOWLEDGMENTS

Edited volumes of essays are, by definition, group efforts. I wish to begin by acknowledging the participants in the original American Anthropological Association symposium for beginning the process. The ones who hung on through the conversion of the symposium into a book deserve additional thanks. But most of all I wish to express my thanks to Barbara Myerhoff, who guided me through the process and taught me that it is possible to write an article with someone who is 3,000 miles away. There are many people who have affected and influenced my ideas on reflexivity and who have read various drafts of various papers. Without them it would not have occurred to me to put this book together. I would like to dedicate the book to two of them: to Sol for teaching me to see and to Janis for teaching me to feel.

INTRODUCTION

BARBARA MYERHOFF *and* JAY RUBY

I. Reflexivity and Its Relatives

There is a thick tangle of terms clustered around the central idea explored in these essays: reflexivity.[1] Such confusion often accompanies a technical term used in many disciplines and in everyday language as well. In this case it is worsened by the very nature of the activity indicated by the term: consciousness about being conscious; thinking about thinking. Reflexivity generates heightened awareness and vertigo, the creative intensity of a possibility that loosens us from habit and custom and turns us back to contemplate ourselves just as we may be beginning to realize that we have no clear idea of what we are doing. The experience may be exhilarating or frightening or both, but it is

---

1. Portions of this essay were published elsewhere (Ruby 1980).

generally irreversible. We can never return to our former easy terms with a world that carried on quite well without our administrations. We may find ourselves like Humpty-Dumpty, shattered wrecks unable to recapture a smooth, seamless innocence, or like the paralyzed centipede who never walked again once he was asked to consider the difficulty in manipulating all those legs. Once we take into account our role in our own productions, we may be led into new possibilities that compensate for this loss. We may achieve a greater originality and responsibility than before, a deeper understanding at once of ourselves and of our subjects.

Though reflexivity takes on different shades of meaning in various disciplines and contexts, a core is detectable. Reflexive, as we use it, describes the capacity of any system of signification to turn back upon itself, to make itself its own object by referring to itself: subject and object fuse. A long tradition exists in which thought has been distinguished from unconsidered experience: where life is not merely lived naively without being pondered but regarded with detachment, creating an awareness that finally separates the one who lives from his history, society, from other people. Within the self, detachment occurs between self and experience, self and other, witness and actor, hero and hero's story. We become at once both subject and object. Reflexive knowledge, then, contains not only messages, but also information as to how it came into being, the process by which it was obtained. It demonstrates the human capacity to generate second-order symbols or meta-levels—significations about signification. The withdrawal from the world, a bending back toward thought process itself, is necessary for what we consider a fully reflexive mode of thought. To paraphrase Babcock (1980), in order to know itself, to constitute itself as an object for itself, the self must be absent from itself: it must be a sign. Once this operation of consciousness has been made, consciousness itself is altered; a person or society thinks about itself differently merely by seeing itself in this light.

Reflexivity can be individual or collective, private or public, and may appear in any form of human communication: arts, natural science, the science of humanity or any other contrived uses of, or comments on, experience. Though it may seem modish and new, the idea of reflexivity is indeed very old, existing in the natural as well as the social world. As an example, consider storytelling, an ancient and apparently universal human occupation. In all cultures and times we find embedded tales, stories about storytelling. Scherezade's *1001 Nights* is a famous example; Sinbad's version of Scherezade's exploits is a story about a storyteller telling stories. And usually there is a satisfying replication between stories and their frames; we learn about Sinbad by observing Scherezade and vice versa. Lest one is inclined to regard reflexivity as confined to the intelligentsia, it should be noted that Norman Rockwell, a popular artist, was fond of using this technique. One of his *Saturday Evening Post* covers shows him painting the cover in which the magazine itself appears with a picture of him painting the cover.

Reflexivity is found in the universal activity of dreaming, a story the unconscious tells to the conscious mind. (Among the Dinka of Africa, the word dreaming is translated as a story the self tells to itself.) It is not unusual to dream about dreaming; we awaken wondering not only what the dream meant to say but also what it says about dreaming itself.

"Reflective" is a related but distinguishable term, referring also to a kind of thinking about ourselves, showing ourselves to ourselves, but without the requirement of explicit awareness of the implications of our display. Without the acute understanding, the detachment from the process in which one is engaged, reflexivity does not occur. Merely holding up a single mirror is not adequate to achieve this attitude. The mirrors must be doubled, creating the endless regress of possibilities, opening out into infinity, dissolving the clear boundaries of a "real world." Babcock refers to this as "identity with a difference" (ibid.: 2):

> Narcissus' tragedy then is that he is not narcissistic enough, or rather that he does not reflect long enough to effect a transformation. He is reflective, but he is not reflexive—that is, he is conscious of himself as an other, but he is not conscious of being self-conscious of himself as an other and hence not able to detach himself from, understand, survive, or even laugh at this initial experience of alienation.

All societies have created occasions for reflecting upon themselves: regularly engineered crises, collective ceremonies, celebrations, rites of passage, rituals, public performances, and the like; times when the society tells itself who it is (or how it would like to be or should have been). But these interpretations do not necessarily call attention to themselves as interpretations. Often they parade as other versions of "reality," no matter how fabulous. They masquerade as different versions of truth into which individuals may come and go without realizing how contrived it all is. Rituals in particular may generate sentiments that mostly discourage reflexivity, requiring a mindless and frenetic, repetitive activity that keeps the body too busy to allow the mind to criticize. This occurs even while the event may be precariously fiddling with the frames, mirrors, masks, reversals, screens, clowns, transvestites, and all the other commentators that threaten the sanctity of the order of things being presented. Precariously, a ritual may march along the edge of discovery of its own contrivances, producing not reflexiveness but reflections. These two ideas are capable of coexisting without penetration. The sleep of the unexamined life is one extreme, the achingly clear realization of the nature and process of understanding the other. No doubt most people and events range in between. For both attitudes the devices we call metacommunication are necessary. Markers, frames, keys, clues, and disruptions remind us not to be content with how things seem; something more important is going on. The world as it is being presented is not to be taken at face value.

The term reflexivity is in need of many fine distinctions. We have touched on the fact that it may be public or private, collective or individual, displayed openly or pondered introspectively. Cultures have moments of self-commentary as do people; these moments may be performed in a fully exposed fashion or quietly noted almost sotto voce. The commentary may be sustained or abbreviated, mere moments or protracted examinations. When in a film, conventions of realism are mocked, as, for example, when the main character is a film director making a film (François Truffaut's *Day for Night* or Mike Rubio's documentary on Viet Nam, *Sad Song of Yellow Skin*), we are thus reminded that we are seeing a film, not reality or even a pretend version of reality. But this can be merely an aside, read as a comment on the film's character and the director's work. We can proceed to forget that illusion and reality have been severed and return to the conventional suspension of disbelief, enjoying the film as if we had not been told it was not what it pretended to be, or was pretending not to be what it, in fact, turns out to be.

In more protracted reflexive works, we are not allowed to slip back into the everyday attitude that claims we can naively trust our senses. We are brought into a different reality because the interplay between illusion and reality continues. The frame is repeatedly violated, and the two stories, commenting on each other, travel alongside, simultaneously commanding our attention and creating a different world than either represents by itself.

In this collection of essays, these distinctions are not always maintained; they are logical possibilities but not (or perhaps not yet) the conventional devices used in discussions of the topic. That is, readers will not always find the authors of these essays being reflexive while discussing reflexivity.

Since reflexivity is a term used by many people to stand for a variety of concepts, it is essential that we attempt a formulation that includes the various usages which are both implicit and explicit among the authors in this book. Let us examine the idea from a communications viewpoint using terms borrowed from Fabian (1971)—PRODUCER, PROCESS, and PRODUCT. We chose general terms applicable to a range of phenomena because the issues raised here are general ones not confined to anthropology. By producer, we mean the sender of the message, the creator of the sign. Process is the means, methods, channel, mode, code, and the like, whereby the message is shaped, encoded, and sent. The product is, of course, the text—what the receiver or consumer gets. To be reflexive is to conceive of the production of communicative statements as interconnecting the three components thusly:

PRODUCER	PROCESS	PRODUCT

and to suggest that knowledge of all three is essential for a critical and sophisticated understanding.

Furthermore, we argue that a reflexive producer must be aware that the conditions of consumption predispose audiences/readers to infer particular meanings from a product (Sekula 1975; Ruby 1977). It therefore becomes incumbent upon producers to control the conditions and contexts in which the product appears if a specific meaning or signification is to be implied.

Significant distinctions exist between reflexiveness and related attitudes such as self-regard, self-absorption, solipsism, self-reference, self-consciousness, and autobiography. Reflexiveness does not leave the subject lost in its own concerns; it pulls one toward the Other and away from isolated attentiveness toward oneself. Reflexiveness requires subject and object, breaking the thrall of self-concern by its very drive toward self-knowledge that inevitably takes into account a surrounding world of events, people, and places.

In an autobiography the producer—the self—is the center of the work. Obviously the author has had to be self-conscious in the process of making the product, but it is possible to keep that knowledge private and to simply follow the established conventions of the genre. In fact, few autobiographies are truly reflexive. To be reflexive is to be self-conscious and also aware of the aspects of self necessary to reveal to an audience so that it can understand both the process employed and the resultant product and know that the revelation itself is purposive, intentional, and not merely narcissistic or accidentally revealing.

Self-reference, on the other hand, is neither autobiographical nor reflexive. It is the allegorical or metaphorical use of self as in Woody Allen's *Stardust Memories* or Janis Ian's song "Stars." The maker's life in these works becomes symbolic of some sort of collective Everyman —all filmmakers, all pop stars, for example. It is popularly assumed that self-reference occurs in virtually all art forms; an artist uses personal experience as the basis of his or her art. The devotees of a particular artist try to ferret out biographical tidbits in order to discover the hidden meaning in the artist's work. Again, there is the cultural fact that we believe it is quite common for producers to be self-referential. What we wish to stress is that self-reference is distinct from reflexivity; one does not necessarily lead to the other.

Being self-conscious has become a full-time occupation among many Americans. However, it is possible, and indeed common, for this kind of awareness to remain the producer's private knowledge, or at least to be so detached from the product that all but the most devoted are discouraged from exploring the relationship between the maker and the work. Only if a producer makes awareness of self a public matter and conveys that knowledge to an audience is it possible to regard the product as reflexive. Otherwise, audiences will not know whether they are reading into the product more or other than what was meant (Worth and Gross 1974).

Being reflexive is structuring communicative products so that the audience assumes the producer, process, and product are a coherent whole. To be more formal, we would argue that being reflexive means the producer deliberately, intentionally reveals to an audience the underlying epistemological assumptions that caused the formulation of a set of questions in a particular way, the seeking of answers to those questions in a particular way, and finally the presentation of the findings in a particular way.

Until recently it was thought inappropriate, tasteless, unscientific, overly personal, and trivial to include information about process and producer in a product. Moreover, it confused the audience and kept it off balance by destroying illusion and rupturing the suspension of disbelief assumed to be vital. Of late, we have grown to recognize our science, and indeed, ourselves, as imaginative works and have become less threatened by the dissolution of barriers between works of imagination and reality. Disbelief is not so often suspended, and backstage (to use Erving Goffman's term) proves to be considerably more alive and full of possibilities than the domains of well-engineered, cosmetic front regions to which we were previously confined.

II. Reflexivity as a Cultural Phenomenon

In contemporary America, the public examination of the self and its relationship to the ways in which meaning is constructed is becoming so commonplace as to be modish, ironically conventional. To many this is cause for concern. The distinction between true reflexiveness and self-centeredness is not always maintained by social critics who sometimes decry the "Me Generation"—a degenerate society wallowing narcissistically in empty self-preoccupation (Lasch 1978). Mark Sennett locates the demise of public responsibility in this turning inward toward private realms of personal experience. Other social critics remark that we have become a hedonistic, indulgent, and solipsistic lot, escaping self-consciousness by turning to gurus, authoritarian religious cults, and the simplifications of extreme right- or left-wing politics. There is perhaps an area where reflexivity and self-centeredness touch, possibly the point from which they both originated: the restoration of subjectivity as a serious attitude, a basis for gaining knowledge and evaluating it, a ground for making decisions and taking action.

When Thomas Kuhn published *The Structure of Scientific Revolutions* in 1962, he recognized scientific knowledge as the product of a particular paradigm and argued that science changes through the process of discovery of the inadequacy of previous paradigms and the subsequent construction of a new one. Kuhn's argument detached science from reality. Like Berger and Luckmann's *Social Construction of Reality* (1966), it drew attention to the sociological and cultural bases of *all* knowledge. Science was no longer privileged or pure. This recognition has deeply penetrated everyday consciousness (though not as a direct result of public interest in the writings of the likes of Kuhn,

Berger, and Luckmann). The secularization of science has been evident for some time. The collapse of yet another authoritative ideology seemed to encourage the turning away from an idealized realm of facts and objectivity toward the recognition that the individual was in it alone. Personal experience seemed to be all that was left to throw into the breach where fixed ideological structures had once been. As we have shown, alienation and self-knowledge are tightly linked, if not causally connected, and reflection, introspection, hedonism, anomie, reflexiveness are all likely to occur under these conditions. A Kuhnian-like change in paradigm has occurred in the popular taste and has appeared in general cultural products, going far beyond the scope of a scientific revolution.

It is now a commonplace to recognize the relativity of experience. Students have heard of "cultural relativity" before they take anthropology courses! That positivism in science buckled close in time to the collapse of confidence in the authority of government augmented the sense that the world was not what it seemed to be. Added to this was the slow democratization of access to the engines of truth: every citizen could afford tape recorders, still and movie cameras, then videotape equipment. Reality could be fooled with: speeded up, played backward, stopped, excised, and rearranged. The truth values once imparted to these aloof and utterly neutral records, "the really out-there," were shown to be mere imaginative products. Slowly, then, it became apparent that we do not dwell in a world that continues without our attention or active participation. As a socially-made arrangement, it is a story in which citizens find themselves to be among the chief actors. Inevitably subjectivity in such circumstances must return to favor.

Examples of reflexivity abound in all of the arts, sciences, and humanities. Often they are associated with what Clifford Geertz calls "blurred genres" (1980), a confusion about what were once discrete categories for making statements. As examples of blurred genres, he cites "Harry Houdini and Richard Nixon turning up as characters in novels, . . . documentaries that read like true confessions (Mailer), parables posing as ethnographies (Castenada), theoretical treatises set out as travelogues (Lévi-Strauss); . . . one waits only for quantum theory in verse or biography in algebra. We cannot tell literature from criticism, treatise from apologetic. . . . Something is happening to the way we think about the way we think." This, he points out, is a redrawing of the cultural map, wherein we see fewer fixed types divided by sharp boundaries. "We more and more see ourselves as surrounded by a vast almost continuous field of variously intended and diversly constructed works we can order only practically, relationally, and as our purposes prompt us" (ibid.). Social science turns out to be built on models taken more from aesthetics, gaming, theater, literature, play, and the like than the earlier principles, laws, and facts of science (Schechner, this volume).

Geertz sees the major branches of social science as falling into three groups: those which see social life as a game (Erving Goffman); as social drama (Victor Turner); and as "texts" (Geertz and others). All have in common an emphasis on interpretation, a view of the world as basically constructed and symbolic. Reality is not discovered by scientific tools and methods but is understood and deciphered through a hermeneutic method. A profoundly different world view is implied, "a refiguration of social thought."

In the arts reflexiveness and its relatives may describe the literary characteristic that is apparent in the *Odyssey,* in figures such as Cervantes and Wordsworth, and in modern writers such as Gide, Joyce, Proust, Mailer, Updike, Barth, and Borges. Autobiography has been perhaps the strongest mode for postwar minority expression in the United States *(The Autobiography of Malcolm X, Coming of Age in Mississippi).* Increasingly writers have turned to autobiography as an avenue for self-expression (Margaret Mead's *Blackberry Winter*), as a technique for inquiry, and as material for study (the popular books by Oscar Lewis, Erik Erikson's study of Ingmar Bergman's *Wild Strawberries*); and psychiatrists report that narcissism has become a familiar presenting symptom. We find recurring films about filmmakers, prints of printmakers making prints, photographs of photographers and their equipment, plays about playwrights.

Scientists, philosophers, and social scientists have also been engaged in reflexive activities. Psychoanalysts have been concerned with the ways in which the act of observation affects the results of the doctor-patient relationship, philosophers with the necessity of thinking about thinking, sociologists with the ways in which the investigator's culture alters the methodological process itself. Historians have applied the techniques of historical analysis to examine and revise the historical method, and scientists continuously test their own assumptions and procedures. Computers are used to check computers, and systems analysis is applied to systems analysis.

The phenomenon of the process of creation as the subject of creation, the mode and meaning of research as the subject of research,
thought as the subject of thinking—in short, the inalienability of the self
in cognitive and creative acts—may become, in turn, the subject of
study.

To chronicle and describe these manifestations—modern and historical—would require a book-length treatment. We have merely cited
a few examples in order to suggest that anthropological reflexivity is not
unique nor is the interest in it merely the newest fad.

≫ MUSIC

Self-consciousness, self-reference, autobiography, and reflexiveness appear in the lyrics of popular songs and in performances, recorded and
live. (The remarks that follow reflect personal interest in and knowledge
about popular music and jazz. Similar examples undoubtedly exist in
other musical forms.)

Lyrics.

It is popularly assumed that composers and performers, like most Western artists, write and sing about their own personal experiences and
convictions. Hence most popular song lyrics are thought to be by
definition autobiographical or at least self-referential. The lyrics are
regarded as a symbolic system, and young people spend much time
trying to ferret out the true meaning of a song's lyrics: was "Mr. Tam-
bourine Man" Bob Dylan's connection? Who was Carly Simon singing
about in "You're So Vain"? Some of the personal references in lyrics
are so arcane and obtuse (such as Bob Dylan's "Sad-eyed Lady of the
Lowlands") they resemble South American myths and require a Lévi-
Strauss to untangle them. Others are self-referential, like Janis Ian's
"Stars," and still others overtly autobiographical, such as Dylan's
"Sara."

The balladeer tradition of telling stories through song is an old
Anglo-American musical form. At least since the emergence of rock
music in the sixties, audiences have held composer/singers personally
responsible for the content of their lyrics. Audiences expect these artists
to believe in the personal, social, and political implications of their songs.
It's very much like the song gospel singer Mahalia Jackson used to sing:

"I'm Going to Live the Life I Sing About in My Songs." The personal lives of artists are critically examined by their fans to see to what degree they match the sentiments expressed in their work.

While autobiographical and self-referential statements abound, lyrics which are truly reflexive are rare. One clear exception is to be found in Carole King's song "So Far Away" *(Tapestry):* "One more song about moving along the highway / Can't say much of anything that's new. . . ." These lines clearly acknowledge that the song is an example of a song type (actually the reference is much more complicated, but for our purposes we can leave it there).

Performances and Records.

If any act that deliberately attempts to test an audience's assumptions about the parameters of an art form is a reflexive act, all of John Cage's performances are reflexive. Most recordings are from a realist tradition that seeks to provide audiences with the illusion of firsthand experience. However, backstage moments, when the performer reminds the audience it is listening to a recording and not participating in a live performance, are reflexive. For example, Dylan, in the *John Wesley Harding* album, begins one song by asking the engineer/producer Bob Johnson if he is ready to record: "Are you rolling, Bob?" This type of patter exists on the heads and tails of all studio tapes. It wasn't planned. The only explanation for the inclusion being intentional is the assumption that Dylan or someone connected with the release of the record (the problem of authorship with records is a complex one) decided to include that which is normally excluded. In the album *We're Only in It for the Money,* one hears Frank Zappa musing about the engineer and his activities in the sound booth. These musings are not part of the normal backstage of recording. They constitute a deliberate attempt by Zappa to remind audiences they are listening to a recording.

Zappa's reflexive concerns are also found in the liner notes of his albums. "This is an album of greasy love songs and cretin simplicity. We made it because we really like this kind of music (just a bunch of old men with rock and roll clothes on sitting around a studio, mumbling about the good old days). Ten years from now you'll be sitting around with your friends someplace doing the same thing if there's anything left to sit on" *(Ruben and the Jets,* Bizarre Records, V6 5055-X, 1971).

And, "Note: All the music heard on this album was composed,

arranged, and scientifically mutilated by Frank Zappa (with the exception of a little bit of surf music). None of the sounds are generated electronically . . . they are all the product of electronically altering the sounds of NORMAL instruments. The orchestral segments were conducted by SID SHARPE under the supervision of the composer" (*We're Only in It for the Money*, Bizarre Records, V/V6 5045X, 1967).

And, "The music on this album was recorded over a period of about five months from October 1967 to February 1968. Things that sound like a full orchestra were carefully assembled track by track through a procedure known as overdubbing . . ." (*Uncle Meat*, Reprise Records, 2024, 1968).

≫ ART

Self-portraits and self-reference in painting make their appearance by at least the fifteenth century. Jan Van Eyck's *Giovanni Arnolfini and His Bride* (1434) may be one of the earliest paintings to carry these ideas into a reflexive stance. In the middle of the canvas Van Eyck painted a mirror with the reflections of three people peering into the room—one of them being Van Eyck. Lest anyone not know his face, he wrote "Van Eyck was here" over the mirror.

One can easily characterize the entire Modernist movement as having a reflexive concern. The Dadaists, Surrealists, Pop, Funk, Conceptual, and Minimal artists, as well as those involved in Happenings and Performance art, all ask their audience/viewers to become self-aware about their definitions and expectations about art. (The Photorealists belong in this category and indeed the entire recent return to realism in painting, but that argument is too long and tangential to be useful here.) Among the more obvious artists whose works abound in reflexivity are DuChamp, Magritte, and Warhol.

Leo Steinberg, in his brilliant introductory essay to a catalog on "Art about Art" (1978), has examined the concepts of borrowing, citing, referencing, commenting, and other means whereby one artist will explore another's work. As Steinberg points out, the primary message of these paintings and indeed of many paintings is a comment about art, that is, a reflexive communication.

In attempting to explain his Neon art, Annson Kenny, a Philadelphia artist, said, "Let me make an analogy. If I were an architect, I guess I would insist on exposed beams, and maybe I carry this sensibility too far. For if there were no beams I would insist they be installed. And if that were impossible then I would insist we construct artificial beams so that we have something to expose."

≫   JOURNALISM

"New Journalism," according to one of its chief practitioners, Tom Wolfe, is the writing of "accurate non-fiction with techniques usually associated with novels and short stories" (Wolfe and Johnson 1973:15). Wolfe suggests that new journalism is the direct descendent of the realist novel and the chief proponent of literary realism in the sixties and seventies.

While Wolfe looks to reporting and novel writing as the major sources of new journalism, there are two he overlooked—movies and social science, particularly anthropology and sociology. Scene by scene construction and realistic dialogue, as Wolfe points out, are found more frequently in films than in novels, particularly in the last twenty-five years. Secondly, it is possible to argue that the recognition of the need for detailed descriptions of the cultural settings and artifacts comes as much from anthropology and sociology as it does from the novel. The new journalism can be viewed as a popular manifestation of the same set of ideas that spawned the work of Erving Goffman (1959), the ethnomethodologists, and the phenomenologists, that is, a concern with accurate, realistic descriptions of the everyday life of ordinary people. Viewed from this perspective, new journalism is perhaps the widest spread of the concept of culture as a means of understanding human existence. In addition, new journalists, like ethnographers, are more concerned with "common" folk than with super stars. This interest clearly separates new journalists from their more traditional brethren.

While the new journalists have been influenced by social science, the reverse is less true. Few anthropologists have experimented by attempting to incorporate stylistic features borrowed from journalists or novelists. Oscar Lewis is a rare exception. Compare his book, *Five Families* (1959) with chapter one of Albert Goldman's *Ladies and Gentlemen, Lenny Bruce!* (1974). Both employ the composite "day-in-the-life" construction.

Without doing violence to the connotation of the term, it is possible to see new journalists as "folk" or naive ethnographers. We call them this (although it is hard to imagine Tom Wolfe in his ice cream suits belonging to any folk) for several related reasons: they seem to lack a self-awareness of the implicit epistemological basis for their activities; they do not appear to understand the folk models of description and explanation they employ in their writings; they have no desire or ability to go beyond their intuition and become rigorous, that is, social scientific. Wolfe and others like him are behaving *like* ethnographers and producing writings that clearly *resemble* ethnography, but we are not suggesting that they are ethnographers doing ethnography.

Their need to understand the scenes, dialogs, characters, artifacts, and settings of human activities forces them to become participant-observers and, like the ethnographer, to actually hang out with the people they are writing about. "They developed the habit of staying with the people they were writing about for days at a time, weeks in some cases" (Wolfe and Johnson, 1973:21). The new journalists' methods are quite unlike the "literary gentlemen with a seat in the grandstand" school of journalism and the "wham-bam-thank-you-Ma'am" approach to interviews by reporters.

So-called "investigative" reporting made popular by Woodward and Bernstein of the *Washington Post* is obviously related to new journalism in the sense that both employed participant-observation as part of their methodology and fiction devices in their presentational styles. Wolfe would like to disassociate new journalism from investigative reporting on the basis that investigative reporting comes from the tradition of politically motivated advocate reporting, and new journalism has no such overt political tradition (ibid.:42–43).

Regardless of how these two are related historically, it is clear that a large number of people who call themselves journalists, nonfiction writers, and reporters have discovered the need for participant-observation and employ styles of presentation that make their writing resemble ethnographies.

Pop sociology and anthropology have come of age. Unfortunately when one examines new journalism more closely, one discovers a naive concept of realism. Wolfe describes new journalism as an amalgam of several devices: "The result is a form that is not merely *like a novel*. It consumes devices that happen to have originated with the novel and mixes them with every other device known to prose. And all the while, beyond matters of technique, it enjoys an advantage so obvious, so built-in, one almost forgets what a power it has: the simple fact that a reader knows all *this actually happened*. The disclaimers have been erased. The screen is gone. The writer is one step closer to the absolute involvement of the reader that Henry James and James Joyce dreamed of and never achieved" (ibid.:34).

Wolfe seems to be saying that the literary conventions of social realism, originated by nineteenth-century novelists such as Dickens, Balzac, and Zola and now employed by the new journalists to deal with "real life" situations (as opposed to their original intended use, which was to create a fiction of verisimilitude), are not merely conventions with socially agreed upon significance and meaning but devices that provide readers with "what actually happened."

Novelists have made a disastrous miscalculation over the past twenty years about the nature of realism. Their view of the matter is pretty well summed up by the editor of the *Partisan Review*, William Phillips: "In fact, realism is just another formal device, not a permanent method for dealing with experience." I suspect that precisely the opposite is true. If our friends the cognitive psychologists ever reach the point of knowing for sure, I think they will tell us something on this order: the introduction of realism into literature by people like Richardson, Fielding and Smollett was like the introduction of electricity into machine technology. It was *not* just another device. It raised the state of the art to a new magnitude (ibid.).

This naive belief in realism serves to perpetuate several unfortunate folk beliefs that must be destroyed or at least discredited in order for any social science purporting to be reflexive to achieve general acceptance or even comprehension. Wolfe's simple faith in realism has to be based on the discredited idea that "the world is as it appears to be" (called phenomenal absolutism by Segall, Campbell, and Herskovitz 1966:45). The logical corollary of this idea is that it is possible to make bias-free, value-free descriptions of the world that are accurate and realistic.

If one shares Wolfe's view, it is logical to posit a particular role for the new journalist. If the world is objectively describable, the journalist's ethical and professional responsibility is to become as transparent as possible, that is, to allow the reality of the situation to predominate. From this point of view (one shared by many social scientists and filmmakers), opinions, characterizations, views of the world are never the property of the author. The author is merely the vehicle for the people he or she writes about.

In some respects new journalism is antithetical to a reflexive social science. However, its popularity helps to create a useful tension and ambivalance among readers—to confuse and confound audiences in ways similar to the confusion experienced with all blurred genres. The neat and simplistic division into fiction and nonfiction or reality and fantasy clearly cannot be used to evaluate these works.

This creative confusion is obviously not confined to the printed word. There is a similar tradition in documentary film. Jim McBride's *David Holzman's Diary* and Mitchell Block's *No Lies* follow the conventions of documentary realism. They are in fact fiction films. There is a major difference between these films and the writings of new journalists. Once the credits appear, members of the audience know they have seen a fiction film that merely fooled them into thinking it was a documentary. With new journalism one can never know which is which. The fiction film disguised as a documentary makes one aware of the conventions of documentary realism and therefore establishes the possibility of one being "fooled" by films that are not what they purport to be. This filmic confusion has reached an apex with the so-called docudramas, which follow the conventions of fiction yet apparently cause some people to believe they are documentaries because they deal with recent history.

New journalism can make one aware that the entire system dividing mediated messages into nonfiction or documentary or real versus fiction or fantasy is misleading and not particularly useful. To read something that is concerned with real people engaged in actual behavior and discover that it reads like a novel can cause readers to question their assumptions about narrativity, fiction, documentary, and even the conceptual basis of their version of reality. It can also lead them to ponder the role and responsibility of the authors/creators of mediated messages.

Some contemporary fiction writers, as we have already suggested, are expressing reflexiveness in their works. We think it is significant that such different sorts of writers as John Updike, Kurt Vonnegut, Bernard Malamud, Philip Roth, and John Irving have been writing fiction in which the writer confronts himself in the act of writing or in his role as an author. If in some ways this can be seen as a throwback to the eighteenth century self-conscious narrator of Fielding, it is also a very modern reaction against the well-known dehumanization of art in this century.

The novel has had an interesting history, which in many respects parallels the development of ethnography (Edgerton and Langness 1974; Rabinow, Marcus, and Parssinen, this volume). It is therefore not surprising to discover that novelists and anthropologists are both concerned with the implications of reflexiveness. To further complicate the relationship between these two forms, one can find novelists such as Vonnegut and Saul Bellow trained in anthropology.

One formal feature separating the novel from the ethnography is the fact that realistic novels, at least, employ a narrative form, while ethnographies are seldom, if ever, written as narratives. Narratives, particularly in the first person, are considered by most anthropologists and social science writers to be too personal and too subjective to be vehicles for scientific communication. It is ironic and also symptomatic of the set of problems fundamentally related to this book that first-person narrative is perhaps the most natural way of describing experience—including the experience of doing fieldwork (Jay 1969). It is difficult to express your self-awareness and reflexiveness to others without employing some first-person narrative. Once the need to be reflexive is more widely recognized, narrative form will become more acceptable as the rhetorical form most logical for the communication of anthropology.

We have only touched on the range of examples of reflexive consciousness in our culture. Its fadishness may pass, but the consequences of being reflexive are permanent. Once you enter into the process, it is not possible to return to the naive assumptions of the past.

III: Reflexivity as Anthropological Praxis

Reflexivity is used in anthropology in a number of different ways. It can be a means of examining a field problem, that is, to refer to the study of the "Natives' " reflexive acts, those events wherein, as Victor Turner puts it, "The community . . . seeks to understand, portray, and then act on itself, in thought, word and deed . . . public reflexivity takes on the shape of a performance." This is what happens when a group formally steps out of itself, so to speak, to see itself, and is aware of so doing. Clifford Geertz's explication of a Balinese cockfight is a classic case, in which we clearly see the Balinese playing with their most serious conceptions. They are performing a story about their society intentionally and, it might be said, literally, rather than metaphorically, since they enact rather than merely refer to the interpretation involved.

Reflexivity is also a means of examining anthropology itself. Anthropology, as a branch of science, is required to be explicit about its methods. Science is reflexive insofar as its findings refer back to the system in which they are explained, making clear the means by which they were assembled. Labrot (1977) puts it this way:

Science is not static. Its development is determined to a great extent by the body of science as it stands at any given moment. This determination is not one of a natural progression to a greater and greater number of known facts built on those previously discovered. It is rather one in which the fundamental principles, the structures in a broad sense, determine the nature of search for the facts and finally to some extent, the facts themselves. So science, which describes the world, also determined the world which it described.

This interpretation is becoming, as we indicated, widespread in all branches of knowledge. The radical objective/subjective dichotomization of experience disturbed many scientists long before reflexivity became popular. Gunnar Myrdal warned against the trap of believing in a "disinterested social science," which he insisted for logical reasons could never exist. It could only confuse and leave the researcher unaware of the operations of his or her biases.

All social sciences deal with human beings as subjects of study, but in anthropology special problems arise because of the complex relationship between the ethnographer and the subject of study. It is through the understanding of self-to-other that the investigator comes to examine culture. Often the collective, impersonal portrait of a culture is penetrated. Key informants may jump out, however briefly, standing apart from the generalized picture of the group—truly idiosyncratic people—ones who demand to be reckoned with on their own terms. Because the ethnographer is enjoined to use immediate experience to "verstehen" (borrowing Weber's term), that is, intuitively understand and empathize, he or she must project and identify. These are invaluable but not universally shared abilities that can only be employed by an individual with a finely honed sense of self. It was not mere partisan ideology that caused the early theorists in Freudian anthropology to recommend that ethnographers' studies would be improved if they undertook to be psychoanalyzed. These days we are more ecumenical; we would recommend not five years on the analyst's couch but any personal study that develops the anthropologist's self-awareness of his or her own culture. With increased self-awareness, studies can be not only more penetrating but also more reliable.

The anthropologist, as a data-generating instrument who must also make explicit the process by which he or she gathers data, is an integral part of the final product: the ethnography. The anthropologist must take his or her behavior into account as data. To quote Lévi-Strauss (1976), participant-observation, the basis of fieldwork methodology, makes this essential.

To Rousseau we owe the discovery of this principle, the only one on which to base the sciences of man. . . . In ethnographic experience, the observer apprehends himself as his own instrument of observation. Clearly he must learn to know himself, to obtain from a *self* who reveals himself as *another* to the *I* who uses him, an evaluation which will become an integral part of the observation of other selves.

Thus the public examination of the anthropologist's response to the field situation, the inclusion of methodology, and participation in constructing the final report is reflexive in anthropology. The examination of the *form* in which ethnographic data are reported also becomes a reflexive act, that is, creating an ethnography of anthropology, as some of the authors in this book have done.

To refer to our earlier paradigm, producer, process, and product may be fully included. The process or methodology is made overt, the investigator portrayed. But in anthropology another layer may be entered into this equation: the effect of the anthropologist looking at the native looking at the anthropologist (cf. Michaels, this volume). We enter the hall of mirrors, the infinite regress, yet it is undeniably necessary. The subject changes by being observed, and we must observe our impact on him or her and the resultant impact on ourselves and. . . . To refer again to the Balinese cockfight, we first see the anthropologists looking at the Balinese, and the Balinese looking back at them; then a change occurs as the Balinese alter their attitudes toward the anthropologists, who in turn begin to see the Balinese differently.

Ethnographer-filmmaker Jean Rouch has some thought-provoking comments on this matter. Borrowing Vertov's term "cinema-eye" (used to describe a way of seeing with the camera eye that is different from seeing with the human eye), it can be said that the ethnographer also alters his ordinary modes of perception in the field.

In the field the observer modifies himself; in doing his work he is no longer simply someone who greets the elders at the edge of the village, but—to go back to Vertovian terminology—he "ethno-looks," "ethno-observes," "ethno-thinks." And those he deals with are similarly modified in giving their confidence to this habitual foreign visitor they "ethno-show," "ethno-speak," "ethno-think."

It is this permanent ethno-dialogue which appears to me to be one of the most interesting angles in the current progress of ethnography. Knowledge is no longer a stolen secret, devoured in the Western temples of knowledge; it is the result of an endless quest where ethnographers and those they study meet on a path which some of us now call "shared anthropology" (1979:8).

Rouch does not go to the extreme of calling his native subject an ethno-person, but it would not be unreasonable to do so. The anthropologist and the subject of study together construct an interpretation of a cultural feature, an understanding of the interpreter, that would not have come into existence naturally. The study is an artifice and resembles nothing but itself, a collusion of two viewpoints meeting in a middle terrain, created by the artificial circumstances of the foreigner's visit and project, disappearing when the foreigner departs. Both the portrait of self at work in the field (if it includes the impact of the natives' vision of self) and, equally, the impact of the native on the ethnographer are constructions arising out of the ethnographic enterprise, studies of ethno-persons.

The human scientist has had to learn how to relate self-knowledge of him- or herself as a multisensory being with a unique personal history as a member of a specific culture at a specific period to ongoing experience and how to *include* as far as possible this disciplined self-awareness in observation on other lives and in other cultures (Mead 1976:907).

We now wish to explore an apparent paradox within anthropology, which both reveals the need for a reflexive anthropology and explains its absence. It can be expressed as follows: Why do most anthropologists identify themselves as scientists and their work as scientific yet often fail to describe adequately the methods employed in their research and to account for the possible effects of the researcher on the research? Why is Malinowski's fifty-year-old-admonition so seldom followed (1922: 2–3)?

The results of scientific research in any branch of learning ought to be presented in a manner absolutely candid and above board. No one would dream of making an experimental contribution to physical or chemical science, without giving a detailed account of all the arrangements of the experiments; an exact description of the apparatus used; of their number; of the length of time devoted to them; and of the degree of approximation with which each measurement was made . . . in Ethnography, where a candid account of such data is perhaps even more necessary, it has unfortunately in the past not always been supplied with sufficient generosity, and many writers do not ply the full searchlight of methodic sincerity, as they move among their facts, but produce them before us out of complete obscurity.

A general examination of ethnographic literature reveals a fairly consistent lack of systematic, rigorous statements on method and discussions of the relationship between research and the researcher. Recently this trend has shifted with the publication of works like Berreman's *Behind Many Masks* (1962). While this and other books may signal a change, Bellah is unfortunately still accurate when he states that, "Rarely have anthropologists regarded fieldwork as a serious object of study, it is tacitly accepted as their major activity" (Rabinow 1977:ix).

In an unpublished study of reflexive elements in written ethnography, Miller (1977) has suggested two places where they are most likely to be found outside of the work, one of them being in introductory remarks or prefaces or postscripts. The tradition appears to have begun with Malinowski (1922). Yet in spite of his admonition to others, Malinowski's own methodological statements were rather perfunctory. As Young (1979:11) points out,

Despite his incorrigible self-dramatisation and his claim that "the facts of anthropology attract me mainly as the best means of knowing myself," (Malinowski 1932:xxv), Malinowski did not propose any theory which included the observer in its frame of reference. . . . He mentions the "personal equation" of the investigator only to caution against selectivity in observation and recording, and he counsels the keeping of an "ethnographic diary" of events as a corrective measure (1922:20–21). Paradoxically, however, the field diaries which Malinowski himself kept (1969) constitute an entirely different form of document—one which, in laying bare his prejudices, gives the lie to his public image and puts his sincerity severely to the test.

Other examples of "reflexive" instructions in ethnographies include Bateson's *Naven* (1936), in which the work is bracketed with reflexive statements in the preface and postscript (cf. Marcus, this volume).

The other location of reflexive elements Miller found was in travelogue-like, popularized or anthropological accounts of fieldwork. For example, Maybury-Lewis in his introduction to *The Savage and the Innocent* states that,

This book is an account of our experiences, it is not an essay in anthropology (emphasis ours). Indeed I have tried to put down many of those things which never get told in technical anthropological writings—our impressions of Central Brazil, our personal reactions to the various situations in which we found ourselves, and above all, our feelings about the day-to-day business which is mysteriously known as "doing fieldwork" (1965:9).

Other examples of this form of reflexivity would include Lévi-Strauss's memoir, *Tristes Tropiques,* Alex Alland's account of his fieldwork in Africa (1975), and Hortense Powdermaker's professional autobiography, *Stranger and Friend* (1966).

Perhaps the most extreme form of separation of reflexive elements from the ethnography is to be found in the writing of a novel about fieldwork under a pseudonym (Bowen 1954). While we have not systematically examined the question, it is our impression that more anthropologists than any other social scientists write novels, plays, poems, and science fiction. We believe they do so because of the strictures imposed by traditional science on the reporting of experience. They cannot do it in their ethnographies so they seek other outlets.

Further, anthropologists who want to be reflexive and still report on their fieldwork in a "scientific" manner have found it difficult to locate an acceptable form. "*The Jungle People* has a plot because the life of the Kaingang has one. Yet, since behavioral science views life as plotless, *The Jungle People* violates an underlying premise. Moreover, in behavioral science, to state that life not only has a plot but must be described as if it did is like spitting in Church" (Henry 1964:xvii). Hymes states the conflict between the reporting of experience in ethnography and the scientifically acceptable communicative forms quite well (cf. Parssinen, this volume): "There is an inescapable tension in ethnography between the forms, the rhetorical and literary forms, considered necessary for presentation (and persuasion of colleagues), and the narrative form natural to the experience of the work, and natural to the meaningful report of it in other than monographic contexts. I would even suggest that the scientific styles often imposed on ethnographic writing may produce, not objectivity, but distortion" (1973:199–200).

In addition to an anti-narrative tradition within the canons of scientific communication, there are two additional strictures that further conflict with reflexivity. Scientists are supposed to use the passive voice and the third person—for example, to say, "The Bushman makes bows and arrows," not, "I saw some Bushmen make a few bows and arrows." Both literary devices cause statements to appear to be authorless, authoritarian, objective, and hence in keeping with the prevailing positivist/empiricist philosophies of science.

As Marcus (this volume) argues, ethnography is virtually an un-analyzed literary genre. The art and craft of producing an acceptable ethnography is learned indirectly and accidentally. The question of the relationship between ethnography and other literary forms is seldom discussed. Langness (in Honigman 1976:254) points out that ". . . the whole question of the relationship of ethnography to poetry and play-wrighting, as well as to the short story and the novel, has never been carefully examined. What, for example, are the similarities and differences between ethnography and literary 'realism?' What is the relation of the novelist's quest for verisimilitude and the task of the ethnographer? Could an ethnography be both anthropologically acceptable and at the same time a work of art?"

The following statements constitute the paradox we have been discussing:

1) Most anthropologists consider themselves social scientists and their work as being scientific;

2) To be scientific means the scientist is obligated to systematically reveal research methods and any other factors which might affect the outcome of the investigation;

3) Most ethnographies lack an adequate and integrated methodological statement; and

4) Those methodological statements that do exist are most frequently attached to the ethnography.

Some social scientists do not see the situation as being paradoxical. They feel that being reflexive is actually counterproductive to their goals. Honigman, while advocating the acceptance of a "personal" approach in anthropological research, states that

Critics demanding a high degree of self-awareness of investigators using the personal approach are unrealistic. It is chimerical to expect that a person will be able to report the details of how he learned manifold types of information through various sensory channels and processed it through a brain that can typically bind many more associations far more rapidly than the most advanced, well-stocked computer. . . . Some of the individual factors operating in description can be brought into awareness and controlled, but a high degree of self-conscious attention to the process of description can only be maintained by scaling down the number and range of events that are to be studied, thereby possibly impoverishing the results while gaining a comparatively explicit account of how information was collected (1976:243–46).

We would agree that excessive concern with either the producer or the process will obviously cause the focus of the product to turn inward; total attention to the producers creates autobiography, not ethnography. However, anthropologists have largely denied the need for reflexivity and ignored the scientific necessity for revealing their methods. As a consequence, perhaps we need a brief period of overcompensation. We need several extensive attempts to explore the implications of doing reflexive anthropology before we can establish conventions for "how much is enough." Questions of narcissism, of turning oneself into an object of contemplation, of becoming a character in your own ethnography are very fundamental and complex. Until we have a tradition, albeit a minor one, of the ethnography of anthropology (Scholte 1972), we think that a concern over excesses is a bit premature.

What anthropology has to offer is primarily a systematic way of understanding humanity—ours as well as everyone else's. Therefore, the processes we evolve to accomplish that task may be our most significant contribution, that is, teaching others to see human beings from an anthropological perspective. Geertz has said it well (1973a:16):

Anthropologists have not always been as aware as they might be of this fact: that although culture exists in the trading post, the hill fort, or the sheep run, anthropology exists in the book, the article, the lecture, the museum display, or sometimes nowadays, the film. To become aware of it is to realize that the line between mode of representation and substantive content is undrawable in cultural analysis as it is in painting; and that fact in turn seems to threaten the objective status of anthropological knowledge by suggesting that its source is not social reality but scholarly artifice.

It does threaten us, but the threat is hollow. The claim to attention of an ethnographic account does not rest on its authors' ability to capture primitive facts in faraway places and carry them home like a mask or a carving, but on the degree to which he is able to clarify what goes on in such places, to reduce the puzzlement—what manner of men are these?—to which unfamiliar acts emerging out of unknown backgrounds naturally give rise. This raises some serious problems of verification, all right—or if "verification" is too strong a word for so soft a science (I, myself, would prefer "appraisal"), of how you can tell a better account from a worse one. But that is precisely the virtue of it. If ethnography is thick description and ethnographers those who are doing the describing, then the determining question for any given example of it, whether a field journal squib or a Malinowski-sized monograph, is whether it sorts winks from twitches and real winks from mimicked ones. It is not against a body of uninterpreted data, radically thinned descriptions, that we must measure the cogency of our explications, but against the power of the scientific imagination to bring us into touch with the lives of strangers. It is not worth it, as Thoreau said, to go round the world to count the cats in Zanzibar.

Anthropology has too long suffered from the popular assumption that it is "the study of oddments by eccentrics." As such we are, at best, sources of trivial information and cocktail-party conversations like, "Do the Eskimos really live in igloos?" The concept of culture as a means of understanding our humanness is a powerful idea. Too bad we haven't conveyed it to more people in a form that they can apply to their own lives. To hide our personas and our procedures from the public clearly lessens our impact.

Regardless of whether or not one is convinced by arguments pro or con for a full reflexive statement in every ethnography, there can be little argument that anthropologists tend to be remiss in fulfilling their scientific obligation to specify their methods. We believe the reasons for this apparent self-contradictory behavior are to be found in the implicit, taken-for-granted philosophical position of many American anthropologists, which we would characterize as naive empiricism and/or positivism/pragmatism. By naive empiricism we simply mean someone who "tends to believe that the world 'out there' is isomorphic in every respect with the image the detached observer will form of it" (Nash and Wintrob 1972:529). By positivism, we mean the idea "that, since experience is the sole source of knowledge, the methods of empirical science are the only means by which the world can be understood" (Stent 1975:1052).

Joined together into a philosophy of science, one that dominated the development of social science, they produce the major cause of the paradox. This point of view causes the social scientist to strive to be detached, neutral, unbiased, and objective toward the object of study; to withhold value judgments; to disavow political, economic, and even moral positions. In other words, the social scientist must attempt to negate or lose all traces of his or her culture so that someone else's culture can be studied. As Nash and Wintrob put it, "to turn the field worker into a self-effacing creature without any reactions other than those of a recording machine" (1972:527).

The procedures developed to insure the neutrality of the observer and the control necessary for this type of research were evolved in a science of subject/object relations and not an anthropological science of subject/subject relations. Setting aside any political or ethical considerations, one cannot make another human being into an object of study in the same way that one can control animals or inanimate objects.

This conceptualization of science may be possible if one assumes that researchers exclusively use quantitative methods in controlled experimental settings. While anthropologists do employ quantitative methods (although seldom in labs), our chief claim to methodological fame and the primary method for doing ethnography is the most involved, nonstandardized, personal version of qualitative methods: participant-observation. We recognized quite early that, "The first means to the proper knowledge of the savages is to become after a fashion like one of them . . ." (Degerando 1800:70). While anthropologists seldom talk about it publicly, all fieldworkers know that, "In the field the researcher becomes trapped in the role of power broker, economic agent, status symbol, healer, voyeur, advocate of special interest, manipulator, critic, secret agent, friend or foe" (Konrad 1977:920).

Anthropologists who subscribe to a naive empiricist/positivist view of science and practice participant-observation in their fieldwork find themselves in a bind. "Since participant observation causes the researcher to become the primary instrument of data generation, his own behavior, his basic assumptions, the interactional settings where research is conducted, etc., all now become data to be analyzed and reported upon" (Honigman 1976:259). One is almost forced to conclude that ". . . an ethnography is the reflective product of an individual's extended experience in (usually) an exotic society mediated by other experiences, beliefs, theories, techniques (including objective procedures when they are used), personal ideology, and the historical moment in which the work was done" (ibid.).

The more the ethnographer attempts to fulfill a scientific obligation to report on methods, the more he or she must acknowledge that his or her own behavior and persona in the field are data. Statements on method then begin to appear to be more personal, subjective, biased, involved, and culture bound; in other words, *the more scientific anthropologists try to be by revealing their methods, the less scientific they appear to be.*

Given that dilemma, it is not too difficult to see why most anthropologists have been less than candid about their methods. They are justifiably concerned that their audience will realize that, as Sue-Ellen Jacobs has said, "Perhaps the best thing we learn from anthropological writings is how people who call themselves anthropologists see the world of others (whoever the others may be)" (in Chilungu 1976:469). It is asking anthropologists to reverse their traditional assumption about the ultimate goals of anthropology, and to suggest instead that what anthropology has to offer is a chance to see the native through the eyes of the anthropologist. Hence, most anthropologists would rather live with the dilemma than explore the implications of being reflexive.

Some anthropologists retreat behind slogans like, "Anthropology is a soft science," or "Anthropology is actually a humanities with scientific pretentions." Kurt Vonnegut, Jr., has summed up the position nicely in a recollection of his own graduate student days at the University of Chicago (1974:176):

> I began with physical anthropology. I was taught how to measure the size of a brain of a human being who had been dead a long time, who was all dried out. I bored a hole in his skull, and I filled it with grains of polished rice. Then I emptied the rice into a graduated cylinder. I found this tedious. I switched to archaeology, and I learned something I already knew; that man had been a maker and smasher of crockery since the dawn of time. And I went to my faculty adviser, and I confessed that science did not charm me, that I longed for poetry instead. I was depressed. I knew my wife and father would want to kill me, if I went into poetry. My adviser smiled. "How would you like to study poetry which pretends to be scientific?" he asked me. "Is such a thing possible?" I said. He shook my hand. "Welcome to the field of social or cultural anthropology," he said. He told me that Ruth Benedict and Margaret Mead were already in it—and some sensitive gentlemen as well.

Some anthropologists, particularly in the last fifteen years, have begun to seek a solution to the problem (e.g., Honigman 1976, and Nash and Wintrob 1972, represent two recent attempts to survey the literature). The reasons for this renewed interest (renewed in the sense that Mead and others actually started in the 1930s, but the interest died out) are complex and probably have their origins outside of anthropology in the culture at large. Nash and Wintrob list four factors for the emergence of what they call "self-consciousness" in anthropology: 1) An increasing personal involvement of ethnographers with their subjects; 2) the democratization of anthropology (a polite way of saying that in the sixties some lower-middle-class students who didn't share some of the "gentlemanly" assumptions of the older anthropologists got Ph.D.s; 3) multiple field studies of the same culture; and 4) assertions of independence by native peoples (1972:529). To that we would like to add: 1) The influence of other disciplines, particularly the effect of phenomenological and symbolic interactional sociology, ethnomethodology, and structural linguistics; 2) the development of Marxist criticism of anthropology in the United States—a criticism aimed at an examination of anthropology as an ideology; and 3) the rise of an urban anthropology concerned with doing ethnography in the United States, the complexity of the subject matter having caused some researchers to question such fundamental ideas as culture.

We have articulated a view of reflexivity as it pertains to anthropological praxis. To summarize what should be obvious now, we have argued that anthropologists behave like scientists to the degree that they publicly acknowledge the role of the producer and the process in the construction of the product, or, simply, that being reflexive is virtually synonymous with being scientific. Moreover, we have suggested that the lack of reflexive statements on methods is a consequence of a particular view of science espoused by many anthropologists.

In some ways we have said nothing novel. Social scientists have been discussing these problems and ideas for a long time. Because of the domination of participant-observation field methods, anthropologists have been particularly occupied with creating a science that allows for both quantitative and qualitative methods that can justify qualitative procedures as being scientific.

For a variety of reasons discussed earlier, the elements are now present for the emergence of a new paradigm for anthropology and perhaps for science in general. Margaret Mead in her 1976 presidential address to the American Association for the Advancement of Science noted this development (1976:905):

Both the methods of science and the conflict of views about their more general applicability were developed within Euro-American culture, and it is never easy to break out of such deeply felt but culturally bound conceptions. Because of the clarity which has been achieved I believe we can move from conflict toward a new kind of integration. As a first step in this direction I suggest that it is necessary to recognize that our knowledge of ourselves and of the universe within which we live comes not from a single source but, instead from two sources—from our capacity to explore human resources to events in which we and others participate through introspection and empathy, as well as from our capacity to make objective observations on physical and animate nature.

The problem stated in its simplest form is to find a way to be scientific, reflexive, and do anthropology—to resolve the conflict between what anthropologists say and what they do. Most of the authors in this book address themselves to the resolution of this conflict.

IV: The Editors' Confessions

To be consistent with the position espoused in this introduction, we should reveal ourselves as producers and discuss the process employed in the construction of this work, that is, be reflexive about our ideas of reflexivity. What follows is a brief confessional aside.

Jay Ruby.

My interest in these ideas stems from what began as an elitist fascination with "backstage" (Goffman 1959). I was convinced that if I could understand how someone made something and I knew who they were, that that knowledge would make me an "insider." In time the interest broadened and became more sophisticated. It caused me to admire the novels of Kurt Vonnegut, Jr., and Tom Robbins, the music of Frank Zappa, the photography of Lee Friedlander and Duane Michaels, the films of Jean-Luc Godard and Woody Allen, the paintings of René Magritte, and the comedy of the Firesign Theatre and Monty Python. Whatever else these people were doing, they were trying to raise the critical consciousness of their audiences by being publicly, explicitly, and openly self-aware or reflexive. "I have become an enthusiast for the printed word again. I have to be that, I now understand, because I want to be a character in all my works. I can do that in print. In a movie, somehow, the author always vanishes. Everything of mine which has been filmed so far has been one character short, and the character is me" (Vonnegut 1972:xv).

Two other factors figured in the development of my interest. For the past fourteen years I have been engaged in exploring the theoretical possibility of an anthropological cinema (Ruby, this volume). In this process I discovered an apparent conflict between the scientific necessity for the anthropologist to reveal his or her methodology and the conventions of documentary film, which until recently have virtually prohibited such a revelation. In seeking a solution to this dilemma, I was drawn to the literature on reflexivity. In 1974 during the Conference on Visual Anthropology at Temple University in Philadelphia, I organized a series of film screenings and discussions on autobiographical, personal, and self-referential films. In doing so, I began in a more formal and systematic way to explore the relationship between what I am now calling reflexive film and reflexive anthropology.

Finally, like many anthropologists, I have felt a progressively widening ethical, political, and conceptual gap between the anthropology I learned in graduate school and the world as I have come to know it.

Among the wedges, I would note the publication of Malinowski's diary (1967) and the public disclosure of the clandestine use of social scientists in Latin America and Southeast Asia. These revelations produced a crisis of conscience and loss of innocence for many of us and gave our personal dilemmas about the role of the researcher a moral and political perspective (Hymes 1969). It should be difficult if not impossible for us now to continue to defend our naive assumptions about our responsibilities toward the people we study and toward the intended audiences for our work. We should stop being "shamans of objectivity." After the involvement of anthropologists in Viet Nam, it is an obscene and dishonest position.

It should be obvious by now that I am partisan. I strongly believe that anthropologists have ethical, aesthetic, and scientific obligations to be reflexive and self-critical about their work. I would, in fact, expand that mandate to include anyone who uses a symbolic system for any reason.

Lest the reader be led to believe that what follows are some hackneyed political and moralizing sermons on the sins of objectivity and value-free science, I wish to reassure you that having exposed myself sufficiently to make you aware of my motivations, a more reasoned exploration of these ideas follows.

In 1977 I became aware that reflexivity was being used to explore the social construction of self and those social rituals designed for people to be reflective and reflexive. Through the works of Barbara Myerhoff, Victor Turner, Richard Schechner, Barbara Babcock, and others, I saw how social dramas, ceremonies, rituals, and fieldwork could be reflexive moments in an individual's life.

One of the functions of these performances is to give definition to self by seeing the self alongside or in opposition to "the other." Then the act of doing anthropology provides our collective self—culture—with a chance to examine itself through the other that exotic cultures represent. We are able to see ourselves anew when we experience other vicariously through the experience of being an ethnographer. The ethnographer becomes audience for a performance so that he or she can be a performer for us, the audience. Furthermore, fieldwork can be a reflexive experience, because ethnographers are trying to acquire social identities not their own. In one sense the success of ethnographers is measured by how well they can become not themselves while at the same time retaining their original identity.

Barbara Myerhoff.

My interests in reflexivity go far back into my childhood, though, of course, I had no such term to apply to them. The fascinating play with alternate realities came naturally out of an unhappy childhood in which books were a great consolation, providing an alternative world, more real and better in every way than the one in which most mortals spent their time. But even before reading, I recall some of my earliest moments of private play occurred as I lay in bed during a long illness and stared at the ceiling, which I found I could make into the floor. I then entered a realm of space and privacy all my own, where strange appurtances that others called lamps jutted abruptly into the air, asking to be used in surprising ways, as tables, chairs. I looked pityingly at the upside down mortals (all adults) living mindlessly in an unreal world below me, a Platonic shadow of the true world that I inhabited.

The play with the notion of the "real" versus the "pretend" shadow world, one actual, the other an upside-down reflection, was a theme that continued to haunt me. Many years later, I understood that this fascination was more than an idiosyncracy, that it had religious counterparts. Working among the Huichol Indians, I participated in their experience of visiting their sacred land, a kind of Paradise, in which everything was reversed. Sacredness was the obverse of the normal or mundane, and as many actions as possible were done backwards. The suggestion of an alternative opposite realm that somehow exchanges attributes with its counterpart, blurring the clear lines between actual and imagined, was a source of continuing fascination, which I fully understood during a camping trip in 1977 when I witnessed a perfect reflection of the scene I inhabited in a still mountain lake that lay before me. So clear was the reflection that the two images were indistinguishable save that one was upside down. It was not necessary to choose between them. The image and reflection were fused, completing a reality between them, a totality that achieved a unification and state of perfection. Dream and the waking life, unconscious and conscious, the above and the below, the hidden sacred domain and the palpable ordinary one were the same. The mending of those splits was a numinous experience that told me clearly, for the first time, why I had always been so attracted to and disturbed by the problem of reflected realities.

When I grew into the world of words, my life was dominated by a storytelling grandmother, an illiterate woman of European origin, whose passion for storytelling transformed my life. Each day she told me a different story about one of the houses on the hill behind our house. We imaginatively entered each in turn, making their stories into a commentary on our own lives. One day I wept because the kitchen window was covered with frost. I thought there would be no story since we could not see out. My grandmother laughed, warmed a penny in her palm, pressed it against the glass to make a peephole in the frost, then informed me that I had all I needed there. An opening big enough to glimpse the street outside, transformed by this frame, this tiny aperture, providing the sharpest possible focus; the ordinary scene without became a spectacle, separated from the ebb and flow of mundane life around it. It was the first time I clearly understood that something magic happened when a piece of nature was isolated and framed. It was the beginning of some comprehension of the seriousness of paying attention to a selected aspect of one's life or surroundings.

Alienation came naturally to an unhappy, not too healthy child, who happened, as well, to be raised in a neighborhood and time when children of immigrants were not fully human beings. Alienation is one precondition for a reflexive attitude, but is not reflexivity itself. This private sense of separateness was transformed into a useful sensibility when I began to study the social sciences. I recall being immensely amused and reassured by encountering a Feiffer cartoon. A small boy was not allowed to play baseball with his friends. He stood on the sidelines, excluded, and, for lack of anything better to do, began to observe the rules of the game. He discovered "baseball" as a code, and in the last square was shown somewhat smugly commenting, "It's a good thing the other kids wouldn't let me play. Otherwise I never would have noticed (the rules of the game)."

An extended period of travel also paved the way for my interest in reflexivity. I recall being confused and fascinated by the sense of somehow being a totally different person as I traveled from country to country. Something about how people saw me clearly altered the way I saw myself.

These vague interests and proclivities came into sharp focus during my first fieldwork, when I had an extreme sense of being a stranger. It was clear that I was more a nonperson to the Indians than they were to me. This was brought home to me painfully and dramatically when my key informant visited my home. With pride I showed him the things he and others from his group had given me, displayed in my home. Then I showed him pictures of my family, assuming he would be as interested in my mother's brother's son as I was in his. Nothing of the kind. The relationship between us, though strong and deep, was not symmetrical. It was not friendship, therefore, what was it? Neither of our cultures provided a suitable category. Enforced thought about how we saw each other ensued, though a term to call what we meant to each other never did appear.

Another significant experience that encouraged reflexive thinking occured when I began to turn my dissertation into a book. I had the good fortune of working with an excellent editor who required that I specify at every point how I knew what I was reporting. She deleted all the impersonal forms, the third person, the passive voice, the editorial "we," and insisted on responsibility. "How did you know this?" "Who saw that?" "What was seen?" "Who is 'one?'" Her insistence on an active and personal voice was extremely difficult but eventually invaluable. By requiring me to insert myself and my verified observations *into* the manuscript, the editor was requiring the methodological rigor that we are simultaneously trained to value and avoid. After this bout with the editor, I found I had written a book I trusted more, that was clearer and more reliable (and, I think, more readable as well), and I had received a lesson in anthropological methods better than many I had been offered in the course of my formal training.

The last, clearest experience of reflexivity occurred in my more recent fieldwork among my own people. Required by political and personal circumstances to work at home, and among my own people (Eastern European Jews who were also very old), I found myself doing a complex enterprise that involved ceaseless evaluation of the effects of membership on my conclusions. I have written about this at some length elsewhere (1979) and will only adumbrate the high points here. It was soon evident that I knew more than I needed to, or sometimes wanted to, about the people I was studying, that at every juncture, I was looking at my own grandmother, which was to say a variation of myself-as-her, and as I would be in the future. We even looked alike. I responded with embarrassing fullness to my subjects' uses of personal mechanisms of control and interpersonal manipulation, such as guilt and tacit obligatedness, spontaneously (even involuntarily) acknowledging over and over that indeed we were one. In time I began to realize that identification and projection were enormously rich sources of information but often painful and often misleading, requiring my constant monitoring.

Another push toward reflexivity occurred when I made a film about this group. I began to understand the impact on them of being seen and saw eventually how my view of them, and my production of this view in the form of a film, affected them, and in turn affected the world in which they lived, that is, how they were seen by others (who, by the way, had previously largely ignored them). The group, it must be added, was a naturally performative one, always enacting an interpretation of themselves on which the outside world did not agree. They persisted and ultimately succeeded in convincing themselves—and anyone they managed to corral as an audience—that this was a true picture. It became that by virtue of being performed. As Geertz put it in another context, their self-interpretation came into being as it was formulated. It did not exist clearly or in a coherent fashion until it had been publicly demonstrated. "Subjectivity does not properly exist until it is thus organized, art forms generate and regenerate the very subjectivity they pretend only to display. Performances are not merely reflections of a pre-existing sensibility analogically represented; they are positive agents in the creation and maintenance of such a sensibility" (Geertz 1980). A consummately self-commenting and self-conscious people (as pariah people often are), the group I studied completed my conversion to reflexivity as one of the most interesting and generative attitudes possible.

≫

In 1977 we began to discover our mutual interest in reflexivity and to exchange drafts of papers and ideas. We decided it would be a good idea to organize a symposium bringing together some of the people who were working out their views of reflexive anthropology. So, in 1978 we organized a day-long symposium for the American Anthropological Association meetings entitled, "Portrayal of Self, Profession, and Culture: Reflexive Perspectives in Anthropology."[2] This book grew out of that symposium.

2. The original symposium consisted of the following participants and papers: Stephen Lansing (University of Southern California), "An island in the liminal zone"; Paul Rabinow (University of California, Berkeley), "Observer and observed: New forms of anthropological presentation"; Dennis Tedlock (University of Massachusetts), "Between text and interpretation: Toward a dialogical anthropology"; John Szwed (University of Pennsylvania), "Ethnography—a meditation"; Denise O'Brien (Temple University), "Images of women in the South Seas"; Carol Ann Parssinen (Institute for the Study of Human Issues), "Social explorers and social scientists: The dark continent of Victorian ethnography"; Barbara Babcock (University of Arizona), "The dangers of 'delight-making' and the difficulties of describing it"; Victor Turner (University of Virginia), "Performative and reflexive anthropology"; Jay Ruby (Temple University), "Ethnography as trompe l'oeil: Film and anthropology"; Ira Abrams (University of Southern California), "A reflexive view of anthropology through its film"; Richard Chalfen (Temple University), "Ethnofilm and docudrama: Constructing and interpreting ambiguous realities"; Eric Michaels (University of Texas), "Looking at us looking at the Yanomami looking at us"; Dan Rose (University of Pennsylvania), discussant.

A Crack in the Mirror is a collection of essays that explores the relationship between reflexivity and anthropological theory and practice. Some essays will concentrate on the question of how the form of an anthropological presentation (publication) might shape, influence, or create content. Anthropology contains a dominant ideology (and several contra-ideologies) with appropriate or accepted forms through which its concepts are communicated. Those forms, once acknowledged, can be examined for the ways in which they regulate the messages. Taking a cue from cross-cultural studies, we suggest that a cross-modal comparison might be productive. By trying to communicate anthropology using nontraditional forms, such as film, one becomes aware of the ideology of anthropology. These ideas are explored in essays that deal with life history as performance (Myerhoff); anthropological cinema (Ruby and Michaels); the relationship between the novel and ethnography (Parssinen, Babcock, and Rabinow); the ethnography as a literary form (Marcus); ethnography as theater (Turner and Schechner); the written transmission of oral tradition (Tedlock); and ethnography as autobiography (Rose). We seek to join together in this book the concepts of performative and communicative reflexivity; to explore cultural and methodological self-awareness.

Looked at another way, this book is about ethnography from the "inside" as the primary means of anthropological expression; from the "outside" in comparison to other written forms such as the novel and as an entity performed as theater, seen as a film, or heard as a poem. The book challenges the alphacentric bias of ethnography. It disputes the idea that ethnography as a written form is adequate by itself to deal with the varieties of human experience. Our goal is to renew ethnography by going outside its traditional boundaries to discover essences and limitations.

Part One

Performing Experience

1 COLLECTIVE REFLEXIVITY: RESTORATION OF BEHAVIOR

RICHARD SCHECHNER

Restored behavior is living behavior treated as a film editor treats strips of film. These strips can be rearranged, reconstructed; they are independent of the causal systems (psychological, social, technological) that brought them into existence: they achieve a life of their own. The original "truth" or "motivation" of the behavior may be lost, ignored, contradicted. How the strip of behavior was made, found, developed may be unknown or covered over and elaborated by myth. Originating as a process, used in the process of rehearsal to make a new process— a performance—the strips of behavior are not themselves process, but things, items, "material." The strips can be of long duration as in some

The work that led to this essay was supported partly by my Guggenheim Fellowship in 1976. An early draft of "Restoration of Behavior" was prepared for the Burg Wartenstein Symposium No. 76, sponsored by the Wenner-Gren Foundation for Anthropological Research.

rituals or of short duration as in some dance movements or mantras.

Restored behavior is used in all kinds of performances from shamanism, exorcism, and trance to ritual theater and aesthetic theater, from initiation rites to liminal social dramas, from psychoanalysis to newer therapies like psychodrama, transactional analysis, and primal. In fact, the use of restored behavior is the main characteristic of performance. The practitioners of all these arts, rites, and healings assume that some sort of behavior—organized sequences of events, scripted actions, known texts, scored moves, strips—exists separately from the performers. The performers get in touch with, recover, remember, or even invent these strips of behavior and then re-behave according to these strips either by being absorbed into them (playing the role, going into trance) or by existing side-by-side with them (Brecht's *verfremdung Effekt*). The work of restoration is carried on in rehearsals and/or in the transmission of behavior from master performer to novice. Understanding the work of rehearsals and the subjunctive mood used there is the surest way to link ritual process to aesthetic process.

Restored behavior is "out there," distant from me in time, as in the psychoanalytic abreaction; or in sphere of reality, as in the encounter between Rangda and Barong in Balinese dance-drama; or by aesthetic convention, as when Hamlet rejects his mother, Gertrude; or by tradition, as in the brave way a Gahuku boy during his initiation accepts the ordeal of having sharp, jagged leaves cut the inside of his nostrils, bringing much blood; or in the shy way a New Jersey "blushing bride" behaves at her wedding even though she and her groom have lived together for three years.

Restored behavior is symbolic and reflexive. These difficult terms are reducible to the same principle of self-in/as-other: the social or transindividual self. Symbolic and reflexive behavior is the hardening into theater of social, religious, medical, educational, and aesthetic process. Performance means: never for the first time; it means: for the second to the nth time; reflexive means to see the self in the self-and-other.

Neither painting, sculpting, nor even writing, uses behavior in actual flow. But thousands of years before movies, rituals were made from strips of restored behavior so that action and stasis could coexist in the same act. Great comfort flowed from ritual: the deeds of people, gods, ancestors participated simultaneously in being and becoming, in having been and will be. These strips of behavior were replayed many times. Mnemonic devices insured that the performance was "right"— as rehearsed or as received—and some performances have been transmitted across many generations with few accidental variations. Even now the terror of the first night is not the presence of the public but that mistakes are no longer forgiven.

This constancy of transmission is all the more astounding when you realize that restored behavior involves choice. Animals repeat themselves and so do the cycles of the moon, but only when the actor can say "no" to an action is there the possibility of restored behavior. Even the shaman or the trancer falling into trance gives over or resists; and there is general suspicion of he who too easily says yes.

≫

Put in personal terms, restored behavior is "me behaving as if I am someone else." But this someone else may also be "me in another state of feeling/being": performing my dream, re-experiencing my childhood trauma, showing what I did yesterday. Also social actions: the enactment of events whose origins cannot be located in individuals, if they can be located at all. Sometimes these events are attributed to collective individuals like the Books of Moses, the Iliad of Homer, the Mahabharata of Vyas; sometimes they belong anonymously to folklore, legend, myth. Restored behavior offers to both individuals and groups the chance to become someone else "for the time being," or the chance to re-become what they once were. Or even, and most often, to re-become what they never were.

Three performative systems are shown in Figure 1-1. In 1→2, I become someone else, or myself in another state of being. There is only moderate displacement, few rehearsals, sometimes none, and my performance is a solo. Two or more individuals can perform 1→2 simultaneously, as when several people fall into trance together. The astonishing thing about Balinese sanghyang is that each individual dancer has so incarnated the collective score that solo dances cohere into a group performance. Upon recovering from the trance, dancers are often not aware that others were dancing; sometimes they don't remember their own dancing.

Many traditional performances are 1→3→4. The score of a Noh play—not just its text, but its mise-en-scene—is transmitted within a school or family from one generation to the next with only minor variations. During his lifetime a Noh *shite* moves from one role to another in a fixed progression. He accepts the score of the role he

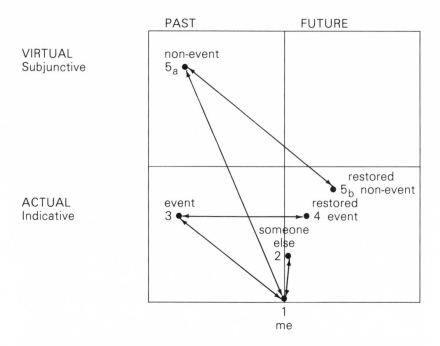

FIGURE 1-1.   *Restored events are placed in the future because rehearsals are a means of collecting behavior and "keeping" it for the performance-to-be. Once performances begin, these are, of course, in the present.*

approaches and leaves behind the score of his earlier role, which is taken over by another. Only the greatest masters of Noh are permitted to change the score, and these changes then become part of the tradition; they are passed on. The roles, and their place within the mise-en-scene, and the mise-en-scene itself, remain fixed. But, surprisingly, each Noh performance also includes a good deal of surprise. The groups who come together to do a Noh play include shite and chorus, waki, kyogen, drummers, flutist. Each of these learns the score separately. True to its Zen roots, a Noh drama staged traditionally will occur only once, with little or no rehearsal, as each group gathers, interacts, and departs. The particular constellation of participants, text, and mise-en-scene happen once only. Those Noh troupes assembled for touring to foreign lands where they do the same repertory over and over complain of the boredom and lack of creativity in this kind of rote playing. Traditionally each performance of Noh, and every variation in the roles, each change in personnel—each single performance—is the leading edge of a long tradition formed during the thirteenth and fourteenth centuries. But in those days, when Noh was being performed, and in flux, it was more $1 \to 5_a \to 5_b$.

$1 \to 5_a \to 5_b$ is a performance based on a previous performance—even if this previous performance claims to be an "original event." $1 \to 5_a \to 5_b$ is theater in which the mise-en-scene is developed during rehearsals; it is rituals that enact or commemorate myth or folklore, as most rituals do; it is ethnographic films most definitely; it is neoclassical or ancient traditional forms "recovered" for modern audiences. In $1 \to 5_a \to 5_b$ the event to be restored is either forgotten, never was, or is overlaid with other material, so much so that its historicity is irrelevant. What is recalled are earlier performances: history not being what happened but what is encoded and transmitted. Performance is not merely a selection from data arranged and interpreted; it is behavior itself and carries with it a kernel of originality, making it the subject for further interpretation, the source of further history. That is why ritual is so much more powerful than myth. Ritual lives—is performed—or it isn't, while myths die and lie around libraries. Sometimes whole artistic forms are reinvented, as was the case of Indian Bharatanatyam, whose history was invented—a new history suitable to the program of cultural renewal of which the "classical Bharatanatyam" is a part.

$1 \to 3 \to 4$ is unstable. Many performances that start out as, or seem to be, $1 \to 3 \to 4$ are really $1 \to 5_a \to 5_b$. Sometimes masters of an art reconstruct the scores they receive; these changes enter the score and become part of the tradition. This ability to accept change is a characteristic of a living tradition. Noh drama is fixed, but performers who achieve *hana* ("flower," or mastery of their roles) introduce changes, some of which are passed on to their successors: Noh actors are also Noh directors and teachers. But $1 \to 5_a \to 5_b$ is not restricted to these kinds of changes.

It is the work of rehearsals to prepare the behavior of performers so that it seems spontaneous, authentic, unrehearsed. I don't mean only in the psychological way familiar to Western naturalism. Authenticity is a question of harmony/mastery of whatever style is being played—Chekov or Chikamatsu. For the Brechtian actor to show that he is acting is no less difficult than for the Stanislavskian actor not to show he is acting. During rehearsals a past is invented or assembled out of bits of actual experience, fantasies, historical research; or a known score is recalled. Earlier rehearsals and/or performances quickly become the reference points, the building blocks of performances. Useful recollections are not of "how it was" but of "how we used to do it." The "it" is not of the event but of an earlier rehearsal. Soon reference back to the original—if there is an original—is irrelevant. How Christ offered his disciples wine and matzo at the Last Supper is irrelevant to the performance of the Eucharist. The church ceremony has its own history. The language of church ceremony has never been the language Christ spoke, Aramaic-Hebrew. Nor are the gestures or costume of the priest modeled on Christ's. And if the Church had chosen another of Christ's gestures as the keystone of the Mass—say, the laying on of hands to heal the sick —this would have developed its own traditional script. Indeed, in some pentacostal churches the laying on of hands or the handling of serpents is the key representation of Christ, the demonstration of his presence. And each of these gestures has developed its own way of being performed. What happens over the years to the various church services happens much more quickly during rehearsals.

This is not just a thing of the West. John Emigh reports an example of $1 \rightarrow 5_a \rightarrow 5_b$ from the Sepik River area of Papua New Guinea. In the village of Magendo, sometime before the performance Emigh saw, an uninitiated boy named Wok wandered into the House Tamboran (men's house, forbidden to the uninitiated) and was killed. The story goes that a bird came to the boy's mother in a dream and told her what had happened and where to find Wok's body. The mother accused her brother of causing Wok's death. She said her brother had painted a dangerous spirit image in the House Tamboran. The brother accepted the blame, the House was torn down, a new one built, and the spirit of Wok resided in the new house. Wok is also credited by the villagers with teaching them how to build better canoes, how to catch fish, and how to plant crops: he is a full-blown culture hero. Emigh goes on: "Now there are several things about this story and its preparation for the event at hand that I find fascinating. First is the immediate and physical sense of relationship between past and present. The old House Tamboran stood *there* across the swamp. The reeds the child was found in were over *here*—people are very specific about the geography involved, and also about improvements in the village life made possible by the intervention of Wok's spirit. Performing the dance at this time would be an act of renewal, of reconnection of past and present."[1]

1. All Emigh citations from a letter he distributed to several people concerning his 1975 work in West Irian. Emigh has made very important observations relating Balinese performance to Papua New Guinea and West Irian performance.

But what is rehearsal at Magendo like? How does it use the material of Wok's story?: "As the rehearsal proceeded an old man would stop the singing from time to time to make suggestions on style or phrasing, or, just as often, just as much a part of the event being rehearsed, he would comment on the meaning of the song words, on the details of the story. The rehearsal was at once remarkably informal and absolutely effective." Questions of performing style are combined with interpretations of the story. The historical-legendary Wok is being transformed into his dance. A virtual or non-event in the past, which, I grant, may have been itself based on something that happened, a dead child, is made into a concrete, actual present. But this is rehearsal: the present is something being made "for tomorrow," for the future when the dance will be danced: "As the rehearsal proceeded men and women would occasionally drift by. The assembled singers, drummers, and witnesses practiced the movements of the dance that accompanies the mother's lament. Lawrence, a school teacher who spoke English, explained that this was an "imitative" dance, a dance in which both men and women imitated the movements of birds performing activities that loosely correlated to the events described in the mother's lament."

Wok is represented by his mother's lament, and the lament is represented by dancers, both men and women, and they are dancing as birds: "The dancers imitate birds because the clan the story is significant to is a bird clan, has a bird as its totem. The story is at once distanced— put in an artistic remove—by the translation of the women's lament into gestures performed by both men and women acting as birds and made more immediate in its impact to all the people of the village by this artistic displacement." More immediate because the bird clan exists now. A woman's lament for a murdered son is transformed into a dance of men and women imitating birds. A non-event of the past—the killing of Wok (by a spirit?)—is used as the jumping-off place for a theatrical event of the future: a bird dance commemorating a mother's lament. I say "non-event" because the killing of Wok, however it happened, even if it happened, is not what makes him significant to Magendo. It is as if the role of hero culture-bearer was there waiting for someone to play it, and Wok was selected. Wok's spirit taught the people how to fish, plant, build ceremonial houses. We don't know whether Wok's murder was the precipitating event or whether his role as culture-bearer meant that he had to be killed. It doesn't much matter. It can't be found out. And the Wok who is the hero bears no necessary relationship to that other Wok who was murdered: except that by now they are both part of the same script, the same strip of behavior. The important event— the event that Magendo needs—is not Wok's death, nor his skills, nor his mother's lament, but the performance of the dance that is none of these yet brings them all together. The performance is itself the text.

The rehearsal Emigh saw, like so many performances elsewhere, is doubly reflexive. The scheme of time is worked with as a single fabric, to be rewoven according to needs uncovered during rehearsals. And the attention during rehearsal is as much toward the technique of the dance as it is toward what the dance signifies. The rehearsal looks backward to Wok and forward to its finished performance. Rituals disguise themselves as restorations of actual events when, in fact, they are restorations of earlier rituals. The ritual process as rehearsal is a shuttling back and forth between the non-event and the restored event to be performed, between the significance of the event (as story, obligatory act, prayer, etc.) and the details of technique that make up the performance as performance. The rehearsals create the non-event even as the non-event is apparently creating the rehearsals. It is not because of Wok that the people of Magendo dance, but because of their dance that Wok (still) exists.

Look again at Figure 1-1. The fetch, or distance traveled, increases so that the trip $1 \rightarrow 5_a \rightarrow 5_b$ is greater than either $1 \rightarrow 2$ or $1 \rightarrow 3 \rightarrow 4$. This increase is in scope of time as well as scope of mood. $1 \rightarrow 5_a \rightarrow 5_b$ links past, rehearsal time, and performance time both in the subjunctive and indicative moods. (I use "$5_a \rightarrow 5_b$" because the non-event and the restored non-event are versions of one another, not independent events.) Doing a known score is $1 \rightarrow 3 \rightarrow 4$. But even this known score has behind it a $1 \rightarrow 5_a \rightarrow 5_b$: a time when the score was being invented, being put together, in flux.

The model has implications for a unified theory of ritual. The repetition of individual or social facts in the future indicative ($1 \rightarrow 2$) is ritual in the ethological sense. The repetition of a given or traditional performance ($1 \rightarrow 3 \rightarrow 4$) is ritual in the social and religious sense. It is also those aesthetic performances—Noh drama, a performance of medieval music on original or facsimile instruments by the Pro Musica Antiqua —that share in a necessity of unchangeability. The collective invention of new performances or the substantial revision of traditional performances that draw together all times and modes ($1 \rightarrow 5_a \rightarrow 5_b$) is ritual in the symbolic sense. A particular performance can combine or be between modes, especially between $1 \to 3 \to 4$ and $1 \to 5_a \to 5_b$. The model is meant to provide guideposts in a dynamic system. Performances of the type $1 \to 5_a \to 5_b$ may seem to be recollections of the past, but they are actually conjunctions whose center cannot be located in any time or mood but only in the whole bundle, the full and complex interrelation among them all. As performances they are played in the indicative mood, but as performances of something they are in the subjunctive mood. The difference between animal ritual and human ritual is that animals are always performing what they are, while humans almost always perform what they are not.

»

A very clear example of a restoration of behavior of the $1 \to 5_a \to 5_b$ type is the agnicayana that Frits Staal and Robert Gardner filmed in 1975 in Panjal, Kerala, India. Staal writes:

This event, which lasted 12 days, was filmed, photographed, recorded, and extensively documented. From 20 hours of rough footage, Robert Gardner and I produced a 45 minute film, *Altar of Fire*. Two records are planned with selections from the 80 hours of recorded recitation and chant. Photographs of the ceremonies were taken by Adelaide de Menil. In collaboration with the chief Nambudiri ritualists and other scholars, I am preparing a definitive account of the ceremonies, which will appear in two illustrated volumes entitled: *Agni— The Vedic Ritual of the Fire Altar*. . . . Vedic ritual is not only the oldest surviving ritual of mankind; it also provides the best source material for a theory of ritual . . . . Hubert and Mauss . . . used the Vedic animal sacrifice as source material for a construction of a ritual paradigm. However, they did not know that these rituals are still performed, so that many data were inaccessible to them.[2]

This was written in 1978; by now most of Staal's program has been executed. Note also that he regards the agnicayana as a chief source of ritual paradigm: the performance exists to feed scholarship. Indeed, in his work Staal develops a theory of ritual based on the 1975 performance. I am not concerned here with that theory because of an irony: were it not being filmed, photographed, and recorded, the agnicayana would not have been performed. The impetus for the 1975 agnicayana came from America, not India; and most of the funding originated outside India. I doubt that various agencies would have responded with cash to pleas by Nambudiri Brahmins for support of a ritual that was too expensive for them to mount unaided. In fact, it was the threat of

2. Staal, unpublished essay, "The Meaninglessness of Ritual," 1978. Staal bases his theoretical assertions on the 1975 agnicayana.

extinction, the sense that "this is the last chance to record this event," that created the event.

The film's narrator proclaims that the viewer is seeing "probably the last" of its kind. But actually the 1975 agnicayana was either the one after the last of a series or the first of a new series. Before 1975, agnicayana was last performed in the 1950s. Behind that is an undocumentable but safely presumed set of performances reaching back maybe the 3,000 years Staal-Gardner claim. But maybe not: it is not clear when agnicayana was performed before the 1950s. The transmission of the ritual—both its mise-en-scene and its text—was largely oral, from man to boy, older Brahmin priest to younger, employing a number of mnemonic devices used by Vedic reciters.

The ritual is very expensive by Kerala Indian standards. Many priests are employed, a ritual enclosure has to be built, an altar of fired brick assembled, implements gathered, and so forth. The rite itself is archaic: long ago Vedic ritual gave way to later forms of Hinduism. Brahmin priests had to reconstruct the agnicayana from a variety of sources: memory, Sanskrit texts, local opinion. Also, and decisively, the agnicayana involves animal sacrifice, now repugnant to many, if not most, Indians in Kerala. A great row erupted over whether or not to include the required sacrifice of fourteen goats. The debate was sharp, often political, with local Marxists being most strongly in opposition to blood sacrifice. Finally, the goats were spared, and rice wrapped in leaves was substituted. It is therefore ironic when Staal speaks of "Vedic animal sacrifice . . . still performed."

Thus the whole contextual situation of the performance of the agnicayana in 1975 is more multiplex than Staal discloses (figure 1-2). The 1975 agnicayana is between an original event—an authentic continuation of the oral tradition—and a media event. In restoring the agnicayana, considerations of how best to document the ritual were always in the minds of Staal-Gardner. Their shooting script shows this. They did not just set up their cameras and let the machines look on passively. Like many rituals, the agnicayana involves a great deal of simultaneous action. But the camera and the microphone are instruments of single focus. Even when panning, the camera and microphone select less quickly and adjust less easily than the human eye and ear. The agnicayana itself as performed in 1975 took more than 120 hours, plus many hours of preparations. Staal-Gardner were able to shoot only twenty hours, and their shooting script indicates that for "numerous

Time	ORIGINAL EVENTS	MEDIA EVENTS	SCHOLARSHIP
"Then" 1	Agnicayana, 1950s and earlier: oral tradition		
2	Agnicayana, 1975		
2	Deciding how to do the ritual: consultations with priests, scholars, locals, filmmakers, etc.		
2		Rough footage Still photos Recorded sound	
2	People who came to see the ritual		
2		People who came to see the filming	
2	Row over sacrificing the goats		
3			Finished film Finished book Finished recording
4 "Later"			Theory of ritual

FIGURE 1-2

episodes filming depends on remaining quantity of raw stock."[3] The twenty hours of raw footage were edited into a forty-five-minute movie. The shooting script breaks the twelve-day ceremony into numerous episodes convenient to the camera. And the script is very specific about who the main performers are, and what is of interest:

Advaryu 1 (chief priest): as stage manager he performs most of the rites and commands the others. He is where the action is.
[. . .]
The final killing of the goat within the Camitra will not be filmed on this

3. The shooting script was obtained by me in India. The script gives detailed instructions to camera people, technicians, and others. It also includes drawings of the altars, etc.

occasion (day 1) since this would upset many people; but hopefully on a later occasion.
[. . .]
(For day 2) No more than 30 minutes of filming for the entire day.

These procedures are only faintly included in *Altar of Fire*. Edmund Carpenter, one of a number of visiting scholars invited to comment on camera, says that there are three kinds of events going on simultaneously: the agnicayana, the social event surrounding the ritual, and the media event. *Altar of Fire* spends almost all its time on the agnicayana. But in India every ritual performance attracts onlookers, merchants, beggars, and crowds of curious. Media events, especially in rural areas, are more rare, making the filming of the agnicayana a powerful media attraction around Panjal. But *Altar of Fire* is carefully non-reflexive. Except for a few feet here and there—concentrating on the visiting Western scholars—Staal-Gardner used the old fly on the wall technique: "Gosh, it sure is lucky we got here in time to shoot this."

Nothing in the film indicates the controversy surrounding the sacrifice of the fourteen goats. It is mentioned in the shooting script: the killing "would upset many of the people." Can there be an agnicayana without blood sacrifice? How did the priests feel about the issue? What were the political questions surrounding the argument, that is, were "progressive" Marxists pitted against "reactionary" ritualists? Did the "ugly American" come in for a beating? Kerala has long had a Marxist government; Kerala's literacy rate, 80 percent, is the highest of any Indian state. The issue of the goat sacrifice was debated hotly in the area and its press during the filming.

Altar of Fire does not hint at any out-of-sequence filming, but the script indicates the sacrifice was put off from day one to a later time; then effigies were used instead of goats. Was the ceremony using these effigies filmed out of sequence and later edited into sequence? The film is mute on this; everything seems to be "in place in time." And, most importantly, except for the shots of the visitors, there is no sense that a film is being made. *Altar of Fire* is designed to make the viewer feel "I am here at the enactment of a rare, ancient ritual." But after seeing the movie several times, even deeper questions arise. There is an old priest—a Walter Huston of a man, with a scraggly beard, a canny sparkle—a casting director's dream of a "wise old folksy priest," who explains in English much of what is going on. But he isn't the chief priest, who is much younger and to American eyes doesn't look the part. Why was the old man picked to explain?

Such procedures raise important questions. We need no new educating to the idea that the instruments and means of observing and recording things so deeply affect what's being observed that a new situation arises, one where the observer is included in the same bundle as the observed. And we are used to questioning the authenticity of performances like the 1975 agnicayana, as Robert A. Paul did in the *American Anthropologist* (1978, 80:197–99, answered by Staal 1979, 81: 346–47). But if the discussion stops here, we miss a chance to recognize in the Staal-Gardner film another harbinger of an important shift toward the theatricalization of anthropology. I mean this in a double sense. First, by replacing the notebook with the tape recorder, the still camera with the movie camera, the monograph with the film, a shift occurs whereby we understand social life as narrative, crisis and crisis resolution, drama, person-to-person interaction, display behavior, and so on. As Staal-Gardner say succinctly in their shooting script: "the advaryu 1 as stage manager . . . is where the action is." More than that, it creates action.

Second, this shift of paradigm has direct consequences in the world it maps. The shift in anthropology is part of a larger intellectual movement in which understanding of human behavior is changing from clear differentiation between cause and effect, past and present, form and content, and so forth—and the literary, linear modes of discovery, analysis, and presentation—toward the theatrical paradigm. The theatrical paradigm uses editing, rehearsal, deconstruction/reconstruction of actuality: the creation and organization of strips of behavior. These techniques blur temporal and causal systems, creating in their stead bundles of relations attaining only relative clarity, and that only within contexts themselves needing definition. An effect may precede its cause: something that happened later in the shooting of a film or in the rehearsal of an event may be used earlier in the finished performance, as when effigies of goats are edited into the sequence of the agnicayana so that they appear earlier than when the decision was actually made to use them.

Look at Figure 1–2 mapping the time scheme of the agnicayana. The original events—the ritual as performed in the 1950s and earlier— and the scholarship purporting to interpret this ritual are separated by a cluster of performance events. The ritual was not a function of Kerala culture in 1975 but of Euro-American culture. Scholars now writing on Vedic ritual, however, will turn to *Altar of Fire* and the book and recordings. Probably scholars will assume that original events of the class $1 \to 3 \to 4$ are being discussed. But actually the 1975 agnicayana is a $1 \to 5_a \to 5_b$ event. It was restored in order to be filmed. It exists liminally between the original series that ended in the 1950s and the media events of the Staal-Gardner project. *Altar of Fire* ends with the narrator announcing that the viewer has seen what is probably the last performance of agnicayana. Not true. The viewer has seen the first of a new series of performances—one where the event will never change because it is "on film." When people want to "see" the agnicayana, they will not go to Kerala, they will rent *Altar of Fire*. Scholarship using the agnicayana will not be based on the series that ended in the 1950s—about which very little is known—but on the material gathered by Staal-Gardner. And few, if any, scholars will examine the raw footage, the full set of tapes; they will instead look at the movie, listen to the recordings released by Staal-Gardner. Theories will be built on items extrapolated from strips of restored behavior.

Is this any different than building theories on writings? Writings are more easily recognized as interpretations than are restorations of behavior. Theories are presented in the same bundle as the data on which these theories rest. References are freely made to earlier interpretations and theories. Often writing is clearly reflexive. I don't prefer writings to restorations of behavior as a way of scholarship, but restorations are not yet understood as thoroughly as writing. Therefore, at present, restorations leave more mess than writing. People use restorations and consider them $1 \to 2$ or $1 \to 3 \to 4$, when actually they are $1 \to 5_a \to 5_b$. $1 \to 5_a \to 5_b$ is hard to deal with, ambivalent, with no clear temporal sequence, no fixed causal system.

Why not think of Staal-Gardner as film producers-directors? Their work in India is more easily understood when seen in performative terms. An earlier event is "researched" and/or "remembered"—actions equivalent to rehearsals. A performance is arranged that presumably duplicates this earlier event. An event created in the future (the film, *Altar of Fire*, 5_b) is projected backward in time (the "original" agnicayana, 5_a) and restored "now" in order to be filmed (what happened in Kerala in 1975, 1). The items in this bundle cannot be separated; they must be considered as a unit. The so-called prior event (the "original" agnicayana is not strictly prior) certainly doesn't "cause" the 1975 performance. The 1975 performance is caused by the project of making a film. So in a sense the future is causing the present, which, in turn, makes it necessary to research, remember—rehearse—the past. But this past—what is turned up by the rehearsal process—determines what is done in 1975, and those events are used to make the movie. The movie then replaces the "original" event; the movie is what we have of the past.

≫

Restorations need not be exploitations. Sometimes they are arranged with such care that after a while the restored behavior heals into its presumptive past and its present cultural context like a well-set bone. In these cases "tradition" is rapidly established and judgments about authenticity are hard to make. Let me give an example from India.

Bharatanatyam, the classical Indian dance, is traced back not only to the ancient text on theater, *Natyasastra* (ca. second century B.C.– second century A.D.), that describes dance poses but also to temple sculptings that show these poses. The best known of these sculptings is the group at the fourteenth-century temple of Nataraja (Siva, king of dancers) at Cidambaram, south of Madras. Most writings assume a continuous tradition connecting *Natyasastra*, temple sculptings, and today's dancing. According to Kapila Vatsayan, India's leading theorist and historian:

Bharatanatyam is perhaps the oldest among the contemporary classical dance forms of India. . . . Whether the dancer was the devadasi of the temple or the court-dancer of the Maratha kings of Tanjore, her technique followed strictly the patterns which had been used for ages (Vatsayan 1974:15–16).

Whenever the contemporary forms of Bharatanatyam and Manipuri and Odissi evolved, two things are clear: first, that they were broadly following the tradition of the *Natyasastra* and were practicing similar principles of technique for their inception, and, second, that the stylization of movement began as far back as the 8th and 9th century. . . . Some contemporary styles preserve the characteristic features of this tradition more rigorously than others: Bharatanatyam uses the basic adhamandali (postures) most rigorously (Vatsayan 1968:325, 365).[4]

In fact it is not known when the "classical" Bharatanatyam died out, or even if it ever existed as described by scholars and danced by contemporary dancers. The old texts and the sculptings surely show that there was some kind of dance, but nothing was remembered of this dance when moves were made to "revive" it at the start of the twentieth century, not even its name.

There was a temple dance called *sadir nac* danced by women of families hereditarily attached to certain temples. According to Milton

4. Vatsayan's opinion is not unique; it is the common opinion.

Singer, from whom I draw this account (1972:14): "The dancing girls, their teachers, and musicians performed not only on the occasion of temple festivals and ceremonies, but also for private parties, particularly weddings, and at palace parties. Special troupes of dancing girls and musicians were sometimes permanently attached to the courts." Some dancing girls were prostitutes: temple prostitution was widespread. The British and some Indians campaigned from the start of the twentieth century to stop temple dancing. In 1947 Madras State outlawed it. Long before that the number of *devadasis* (dancing girls) dwindled. Along with the campaign to outlaw *sadir nac,* Dr. V. Raghavan, scholar and critic, coined the term Bharatanatyam to describe the dance he and dancer Rukmini Devi were developing. They wanted to use *sadir nac* but not be identified with its bad reputation. They cleaned up *sadir nac,* brought in gestures based on the *Natyasastra* and temple sculptings, and developed standard teaching methods. They claimed that Bharatanatyam was very old. And, of course, a conformity to ancient texts and art could be demonstrated: every move in Bharatanatyam was measured against the sources it presumed to be a living vestige of. The differences between *sadir nac* and the old sources were attributed to degeneracy. The new dance, now legitimized by its heritage, not only absorbed *sadir nac,* but attracted the daughters of the most respectable families to practice it. Many study Bharatanatyam as a kind of finishing school. It is a major export item.

The "history" and "tradition" of Bharatanatyam—its roots in the ancient texts and art—are actually restorations of behavior of the $1 \rightarrow 5_a \rightarrow 5_b$ type. 5_a = the "ancient classical dance." But this dance is a construction based on the restoration work of Raghavan, Devi, and others. They used *sadir nac* not as a dance in its own right but as a faint image of some ancient glory. That "ancient classical dance" is a projection backwards in time: we know what it looks like because we have the Bharatanatyam. Soon people believed that the ancient dance led to Bharatanatyam when, in fact, the Bharatanatyam led to the ancient dance. An original ancient dance is created in the past in order to be restored for the present and the future. There is no single source for Bharatanatyam, only the whole bundle $1 \rightarrow 5_a \rightarrow 5_b$.

In Bharatanatyam a modern version of an old art is born through the intervention/invention of one or a few dedicated persons from outside the class of those they are leading. This is, maybe, a version of the Moses myth or the Marxist fact: revolution comes to a group from outside, typically brought by a lost member of the tribe who rediscovers his origins. As Indians, Raghavan and Devi were not outsiders the way Staal and Gardner were, but Raghavan and Devi were not from devadasi families.

I see nothing amiss in the restoration of behavior called Bharatanatyam. It is analogous to French dramatists of the seventeenth century conforming to what they thought were the rules of Attic Tragedy. Or to Renaissance architects restoring what they thought were Greek and Roman building styles. These people had at hand Aristotle, the Greek plays, architectural ruins, and Vetruvius. Today we have at hand relics of behavior, ancient texts, sculptings, and the memories of Hindu priests. "Nativistic movements" seek to restore the old ways. I'm talking about something else. There is something postmodern in restoring behavior.

Scholars and specialists fear a disruption of historical variety brought about by world monoculture. Just as physical well-being depends on a varied gene pool, so social well-being depends on a varied culture pool. Restored behavior is a way of guaranteeing a varied culture pool. It is a strategy that fits within, and yet opposes, world monoculture. It is not the natives who practice restored behavior. The devadasis were content to dance their *sadir nac*, even if it was doomed. But the moderns want to bring into the postmodern world "authentic cultural items." Within the frame of postmodern information theory—that all knowledge is reducible/transformable into bits of information (and therefore potentially reconstructible in new orders, new beings in fact) —an illusion of diversity is projected: backward in time to 5_a, forward to 5_b. This illusion is artful because it is art itself, pure theater. The underlying idea that information, not things, is the basic material of nature as well as culture is at the root of such recent explorations as recombinant DNA, gene-splicing, and cloning. What is created through these experiments is a liminal existence between nature and culture. It suggests that "nature" and "culture" might be a false dichotomy, representing not opposing realms but different perceptions of identical processes.

When Raghavan and Devi find vestiges of a classical dance in *sadir nac*, is what they find incomplete? Only with reference to a presumed past and a rehearsed-restored future is it incomplete; only when measured against the whole bundle $1 \rightarrow 5_a \rightarrow 5_b$. The restorers view the behaviors they restore through a wider time lens, a wider conceptual lens, than the dancers of "native" *sadir nac*. Restored behavior is not a process of scraping away dead layers of paint to reveal the original

artwork; it is not discovering an unbroken—dare I day, unconscious?
—tradition, but of research and fieldwork, of rehearsals in the deepest
sense.

There is more of this kind of thing coming. Already the past fifty
years are available on film. Waves of styles return regularly because of
this availability. We are not going to "lose" behavior from the 1920s,
for instance, in the same way or to the same extent as we lost previous
epochs. We live in a time when traditions can die in life, be preserved
archivally as behaviors, and later be restored.

❯

Although restored behavior seems to be founded in the past and
follows a linear chronology—"Bharatanatyam is perhaps the oldest
among the contemporary dance forms in India," "Vedic ritual is . . . the
oldest surviving ritual of mankind"—it is in fact a synchronic bundle,
$1 \to 5_a \to 5_b$. The past, 5_a, is recreated in terms not simply of a present,
1, but of a future, 5_b. This future is the performance being rehearsed,
the next showing, the "finished thing" made efficient, graceful, and
perfect through rehearsals. Restored behavior is both teleological and
eschatological. It joins original causes and what happens at the end of
time. It is a model of destiny.

❯

Restorations of behavior are not limited to New Guinea or India,
that world of the non-Western other. All over America restorations of
behavior are common, popular, and making money for their owners.
Maurice J. Moran, Jr., has written an account of theme parks and
restored villages (1978). Their diversity is undeniable: Renaissance
Pleasure Faires, restored villages in almost every state, Disneyland and
Disney World, safari and wildlife parks, amusement parks organized
around single themes, Land of Oz, Storyland, Frontierland, Ghost
Town in the Sky, even L'il Abner's Dogpatch. The Marriott Corpora-
tion, operators of parks and owners of hotels, describes the parks as "a
family entertainment complex oriented to a particular subject or historical area, combining a continuity of costuming and architecture with
entertainment and merchandise to create a fantasy-provoking atmosphere" (quoted in Moran 1978:25). These places are large environmental theaters. They are related to get-togethers like the Papua New
Guinea kaiko, the Amerindian pow-wow, and the Indian kumbhmela:
pilgrimage centers where goods, services, and ideologies are displayed,
performed, and exchanged.

This essay will concentrate on only one kind of theme park, the restored village. As of 1978 there were more than sixty of these in the United States and Canada and, it seems, more are coming. Millions of people visit them each year. Typically they restore the colonial period of the seventeenth and eighteenth centuries; they reinforce the ideology of rugged individualism as represented by early settlers of the Eastern States (Colonial Williamsburg, Plimoth Plantation); the shoot-'em-up West (Buckskin Joe, Cripple Creek, Cowtown, Old Tucson); or romanticized heroic industries like mining and whaling. Some, like Amish Farms and Homes, are a spectacle of people actually living their lives; a few, like Harper's Ferry, commemorate historical confrontations. The scope of the architectural reconstructions and the behaviors of the persons who work in the villages makes these restorations more than museums. For example, at Plimoth Plantation in Massachusetts (Moran 1978:64–70):

In each building a member of the household that would have resided there (in 1627) greets you and asks "How be ye?" Within a few minutes you find yourself responding in a language that was foreign only moments ago. "I be well, thank ye." One little girl is asked, "Where be ye from?" "New Jersey," she answers. "I'm afraid I don't know that place." A parent intervenes. "You see, Susie, New Jersey isn't invented yet." . . . As the day proceeds, the villagers go about their work. Food is prepared in black kettles over hot coals, while they explain to their visitors the difference between pottage and ragout. . . . One young lad is helping build Mr. Allerton's House. With Irish brogue he explains: "I was in a shipwreck on my way to Virginia Colony. When I washed ashore the Indians took me here. I was surprised to find anyone speaking English in these wilds." . . . One goat insisted on coming into the Standish household, only to be shooed away by the maid. The houses are all hand constructed, some with wooden floors, some with clay (damp in the spring thaw). The streets are uneven, rocky . . . . Many special events continue the theme of historic reenactment. There is the opening of the Wampanoag Summer Encampment, staffed by native Americans in the style of the 17th century. There is a village barn-raising and a reenactment of a typical wedding in the colony and also in the Indian camp. But the classical attraction, and one of the chief fundraisers for the village, is the Harvest Festival held in October. . . . Here the villagers renew 17th century harvest customs with cooking and feasting, songs, dances, and a general show of high spirits. Native Americans from the summer settlement join in friendly challenges of skill and chance.[5]

5. The exchange between centuries is sometimes seasoned with nice ironies. A visitor at Plimoth apologized for interrupting a craftsperson and asking questions. "As many as you like, sir," the performer responded, "I have a few questions meself about your time period." See also Hess 1974; Kyriazi 1976; McKay 1977:27ff; and James H. Bierman, Department of Theatre Arts, University of California, Santa Cruz, has a great deal of information on the Disney enterprises.

What a mix of categories at Plimoth! The architecture of the Village is totally recreated indoors and out; nothing survives from the original colony. But it is known who was there, and background information has been researched, so that performers have some sense of who they are playing. Each performer receives a "personation biograph" that includes specimens of dialect, some notes about the character's personality, a wardrobe design, and other details that will help in playing the role assigned. Thus an unusual situation obtains at Plimoth: the characters have a kind of authenticity the architecture lacks. The buildings and furnishings are "typical" of the period, but the people are "actually from" 1627.

Inside the fenced-in Village a seventeenth-century atmosphere is kept up. But a visit to the whole complex—reception center, orientation center, recreated and restored environments and behaviors—is a thoroughly anachronistic experience, a theatrical experience, made even more sharply so by the use of restored behavior as the key element of the whole place. Everything is as authentic as possible, but the day ends for visitors at five, and the season runs from April through November. Maybe the village is closed for the winter because those early Pilgrim winters were hard. The ordeals of hunger and cold, of death, cannot yet be shown—or, rather, recreated. The limits of theater end with Thanksgiving. During the winter the Plimoth Plantation runs special programs and gears up for spring. The contradictions and anachronisms—framed and carefully kept separate (all gifts and books, restaurants and toilets, are outside the Village proper)—are what give Plimoth, and its sister restored villages, their special kick. The people who make Plimoth are aware that what they're doing isn't "just" presenting static exhibits à la the American Museum of Natural History. Plimoth Plantation is a mix of $1 \rightarrow 3 \rightarrow 4$ and $1 \rightarrow 5_a \rightarrow 5_b$.

But what of villages that specialize in re-creating fantasies? More than one Old West town features regular *High Noon*-style shoot-outs, or an attack by Indians. These events are not taken from history but from the movies. Sometimes, curiously, they double-back into film. Buckskin Joe, Colorado, was created by Malcolm F. Brown, former art director at M.G.M. The town has been the setting for more than one movie, including *Cat Ballou*, a parody of Westerns. At Buckskin Joe a shootout takes place in front of the saloon, and the spectators, who are actual customers at the bar or other stores, duck for cover. At King's Island in Cincinnati a passenger train is held up, the conductor taken hostage, and passengers asked to intervene to save the day. Audience participation, on the decline in the theater, is increasing at theme parks and restored villages.

Considered theoretically, restored villages, even those built on fantasies and/or movies, raise hard questions. How are they different from the Staal-Gardner agnicayana? Staal-Gardner based their Vedic ritual on a reconstruction of an "Old India" as distorted, and as true, as the Old West of America, where Amerindians attacked settlers and shoot-outs happened in front of saloons. The Brahmin priests went to texts, their own memories, and what old people could recall of the agnicayana, just as architects, performers, and craftspeople of restored villages research their stuff. No, the difference between the American restored villages and the agnicayana is that the performers and spectators in the restored villages know it's all make-believe. In Figure 1-3 there is a move from frame A into frame B resulting in a special consciousness, AB. AB is another way of stating the subjunctive mood of restored behavior: the overlaying of two frames that cannot coexist in the indicative: "being in" the seventeenth and twentieth centuries simultaneously, "being" Rama and Ravana and two village persons, "doing" a Vedic ritual before cameras and tape recorders. What happens is that the smaller subjunctive frame temporarily and paradoxically expands and contains the indicative frame. Everything is "for the time being." Figure 1-4 illustrates how the indicative world is temporarily isolated, surrounded, and penetrated by the subjunctive: on the outside is the environment of the performance, on the inside is the special consciousness of performing and witnessing/participating in a performance. The famous "suspension of disbelief" is the agreement to let the smaller frame AB become the larger frame AB'.

For the 1975 agnicayana there were two audiences: an immediate

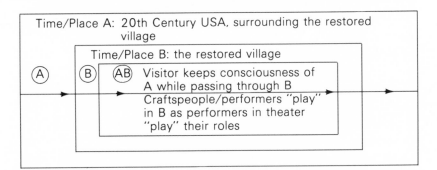

FIGURE 1-3

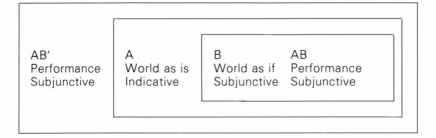

FIGURE 1-4

one of locals, many of whom treated the ritual as a media event (this happens whenever a film is shot on location, even outside my window on Sullivan Street in Manhattan); and an audience of Americans who see *Altar of Fire* mainly as a documentary of an actual ritual. But ritual with a difference: ritual for study, for entertainment: a "specimen." The inversion is ironic. The audience in Kerala sees the agnicayana as media; the audience in America sees the media (version of agnicayana) as ritual. Both audiences are alienated from the "pure" agnicayana. But was there ever a pure agnicayana? Isn't every instance of it $1 \rightarrow 5_a \rightarrow 5_b$? The narrator of *Altar of Fire* tells the audience the performance it is seeing is probably the last ever of this ritual. This adds a P. T. Barnum flavor. And at Plimoth nothing (new) is going to happen, life there is finished. These examples of restored behavior are very much like theater in a theater: the script is set, the environment is known, the actors play set roles. But Bharatanatyam is different. This restoration has healed seamlessly into its cultural surround: it is living art. As such, this dance will change; its future is not predictable. Plimoth Plantation either continues as it is or ceases to be what it is: its very existence is knotted into its specific historicity. Each production of aesthetic theater is like Plimoth, but "the theater" as a genre is like Bharatanatyam. The similarities and differences among various performance systems are summarized in Figure 1-5.

One of the big differences among performance systems is the physical environment—what contains what. In ordinary theater the domain of the spectator, the house, is larger than the domain of the performer, the stage, and distinctly separate from it. In environmental theater there is a shift, in that the spectator and performer often share the same space, sometimes exchange spaces, and sometimes the domain of the performer

Performance Systems: A Comparative Chart

	A	B
1.	ARTS Theater, dance, etc.	RESTORED ARTS Bharatanatyam

Between these there is little or no phenomenological distinction, making it very hard to tell 1A from 1B without doing historical research—1B heals seamlessly into 1A. Both 1A and 1B have "lives of their own." In both, performers know they're "in a show" and audiences know they're "watching a show."

	A	B	C	D
2.	MEDIA FICTION Regular movies	MEDIA SIMULATION Recreated especially for media	MEDIA "PUSH" Without media there would be no event, as the 1975 agnicayana	MEDIA "THERE" Documentaries, news

A move to the right = decreasing dependence on media to make the event—though news items are edited, creating a feedback between what "is" news and what media "makes into" news. Also a move to the right = an increase in narration—in suggesting an independent event that needs an observer outside "objectively" explaining it. There 2B, 2C, and 2D merge into one another. Only in 2A is the performer sure he is "in a show" and the spectator sure he is "watching a show." A recent form, "docudrama," combines 2A and 2D.

	A	B	C
3.	THEME PARKS Disneyland, Land of Oz, Dogpatch, etc.	RESTORED VILLAGES MADE FROM FANTASY AND HISTORY Buckskin Joe, Frontierland, Columbia Historic Park, etc.	RESTORED VILLAGES MADE FROM HISTORY Plimoth, Smithville, Louisbourg, etc.

In 3A people know they are "in a show" as spectator-participants or performers. In 3B and 3C even the performers begin to feel they are "in life." But paradoxically, 3B and 3C are very close to 1A and 1B where the event begins to have a "life of its own." In 3A most of the machinery—mechanical and human—is hidden from the spectator, creating a fictive environment. In 3B and 3C there is an attempt—as at museums—to show as much as possible. But these days even museums are fictionalizing. For example, the Ice Age Art exhibit at the American Museum of Natural History (1978–79) was made mostly from simulated items.

FIGURE 1-5

is larger than that of the spectator, enclosing the spectator within the performance. This tendency is taken even further in restored villages and theme parks where the visitor enters an environment that swallows him. Every effort is spent on transforming the spectator into a participant. And while the visitor keeps a consciousness of this own time and place, he simultaneously enjoys a temporary surrender of these. The 1975 agnicayana combines the qualities of film with those of a restored village. There are two frames working: that of the ritual and that of the film being made of the ritual. The Brahmin priests are performers of the agnicayana and "visitors" absorbed into it (Vedic ritual being older and different from brahmanic Hindu ritual); the local people watch both the ritual and the filming of it, neither of which is familiar. If the priests had been totally absorbed into the agnicayana, they would have insisted on sacrificing the goats, or they would have stopped the performance because in Vedic terms the goat sacrifice is essential. But the priests, too, wanted the film to be made. The priests acted in regard to animal sacrifice not as Vedic priests but as modern Indians. More: they acted as performers in a film with a big stake in seeing that the shooting came off well. Using their authority as priests, they devised the substitute effigies as a way of making the film, performing the agnicayana, and not offending the values of modern Kerala Indians. Thus the priests played three roles: Vedic ritualists; Brahmin priests arbitrating a living tradition; film performers. In a way the film performers convinced the Brahmin priests that it was okay to tamper with the Vedic tradition. Or: as film performers Brahmin priests were asked to play the role of Vedic ritualists. This double, or triple, life is typically that of theater actors; it is the theatrical brand of truth. And between the frame of the agnicayana and the frame of the filmmaking stood the local audience, enjoying both spectacles.

But is it fair to say that the priests were play-acting? From the perspective of Euro-American conventions, "acting" means make-believe, illusion, lying. Even Erving Goffman, who has studied acting in ordinary life, identifies it most directly with con men and others who must maintain a "front" separate from their "true" selves. This understanding of acting derives from our Platonic view of a hierarchy of realities, in which the most real is the most distant from experience, and our Aristotelian view of art, which is an imitation of a reflection. From the perspective of Indian conventions, and the system of maya/lila underlying them, acting is playful illusion but so is the world itself; so that in India acting is both false and true.

I might think the priests were acting; and Kerala villagers might think they were doing what priests always do: mediating between ordinary and nonordinary experience, both of which need acting. The priests are trained/prepared by birth and education to restore the behavior of the agnicayana. It is not accurate to call them actors, and it is not accurate not to call them actors. They were between "not actors" and "not not actors"—a realm of double negativity that precisely describes the process of theatrical characterization, a liminal realm.

As for American restored villages, anyone with proper training can demonstrate colonial crafts and speak English in a seventeenth-century Yankee dialect. At the end of the work day, craftspeople and performers take off their costumes, put down their tools, and go home. The visitors assume this divestiture of roles is taking place even if they don't see it with their own eyes. At Plimoth some of the conventions ordinarily followed in an American theater are dropped. The performers are not on a stage, not rewarded by applause, and not required to follow strictly a word-by-word script called a drama. In some of the villages the actors interact with spectators, making the visitor enter into the world of the village and thereby further blurring the seam between the performance and its nonacting surround. The performers at Plimoth are acting, but they may not seem to be acting. In America we say someone is "only acting" when we detect the seams between the performance and the nonacting surround. We also say someone is acting when they are performing on a stage. We say someone is not acting when they are doing what they ordinarily would do were there no audience. Documentary film imposes an acting frame around a nonacting situation. But documentaries like Edward Curtis's *In the Land of the Head Hunters* or Robert Flaherty's *Nanook of the North* combine people sometimes going about their ordinary tasks, sometimes restoring behaviors of a recent past, and sometimes acting for pay in fictive situations in an "on location" set wearing costumes and saying lines written for the occasion.

In some cases, in restored villages, and because of people like Curtis, matters have gotten more complicated. Some performers at restored villages have become permanent residents of the village, live off the income from their crafts, eat the food they cooked that day in the presence of the visitors. Their "lived lives" mesh with their "performed lives" in so strong a way that it feeds back into their performances. Their roles become their "ordinary life," supplying their restored behavior with a new source of authenticity. When this happens, the residents of the restored villages can no more comfortably be subsumed under the category of "play actors" than can the Kerala Brahmin priests.

In T. McLuhan's 1974 film, *The Shadow Catcher,* a few of the original participants in Curtis's 1914 *Head Hunters* explain how Curtis's interest in the "old ways" rekindled their own interest and led to restoring some ceremonies previously abandoned. Thus the value frame of the new dominant culture encouraged the enactment as fiction of what was previously performed in fact; while other actions—masked dancing, shamanic healing—were done in fact but before the rolling camera. Later a new cultural whole emerged, combining fiction and fact, and including performances invented for tourists. Younger Kwakiutls said Curtis's movie helped them learn about the old life, because seeing something "really being done" is so much more powerful than just hearing about it. But what was "really being done" even the old-timers didn't do any more by the time Curtis arrived. Who knows if they ever did it the way he filmed it. Curtis paid performers fifty cents an hour, and five dollars when there was danger, like rowing the huge war canoes or hunting sea lions.

Increasingly American theater of all kinds is like *Head Hunters* (whose title was changed to *Land of the Long Canoes* because Curtis thought American audiences would find head-hunting repulsive; the movie failed commercially anyway), combining documentary, fiction, history: in other words, restored behavior, $1 \rightarrow 5_a \rightarrow 5_b$. From the seventies into the eighties experimental theater puts acting and nonacting side by side, as in the work of Spalding Gray, Leeny Sack, Robert Wilson-Christopher Knowles, and Squat Theater.[6] On the other side, such factual strongholds as network news programs are anchored by people selected for their ability to perform, not to gather or edit news. A suitable aesthetic theory doesn't exist to handle these crossovers and juxtapositions. They are all $1 \rightarrow 5_a \rightarrow 5_b$.

Taken as a whole the performances discussed here belong to the subjunctive and not the indicative mood. And the spectators, too, by virtue of their being physically inside the action instead of standing outside looking in, give over to the subjunctive, to behaving "as if" they

6. Much has been written about the work of these people, especially in *The Drama Review* and *Performing Arts Journal.* Gray deals directly with events from his own life, unmediated by a fictive frame (such as Eugene O'Neill uses). Wilson develops pieces with Knowles, who is—depending on your style—"brain damaged," "nonordinary," "directly creative." In any event, Knowles isn't acting—any more than a circus bear is. Squat has used Twenty-third Street in New York—the avenue one windowpane away from their theater—as backdrop, stage, and source of inadvertant performers.

were really there in that negotiated space-time-event I call restored behavior. Negotiated because it takes an agreement among all parties to keep the thing up in the air, moving, alive. The restored village and Curtis's half-restoring, half-inventing for the sake of his feature film are performances intermediate in type between the Brahmin priest restoring an archaic and nowadays unperformed ritual for the benefit of the cameras and Olivier playing Hamlet on the orthodox Euro-American stage. Intermediate also are performances like Wilson-Knowles, Gray, and Squat. The most interesting work of the past ten years is intermediate, liminal: work that illuminates its own ambivalence, that is, explicitly reflexive, and very difficult to categorize. In orthodox theater the domain of the spectator ("the house") is larger than and separate from the domain of the drama ("the stage"). This framing helps maintain the objectivity and critical/aesthetic distance of the orthodox theatergoer. But in restored villages, as in environmental theater, the domain of the performance surrounds and includes the spectator. Looking at becomes harder, being in, easier. There is no house, and spectators are thrown back on their own resources for whatever assurance they need to maintain who and where they are. How to behave, what to do or not to do, are definite troubling questions in this situation. Although work like Wilson-Knowles's and Gray's does not include the spectator physically, it undermines his psychic distance by presenting nonacting as performance. The same uneasiness results.

≫

The theory explaining all this will come from theater specialists or from social scientists learned in theater. Theater is the art specializing in the concrete techniques of restoring behavior. Victor Turner's theory, like Goffman's, is actually a theatrical one generalized to suit social process. Working in the same field are Clifford Geertz, Roy Rappaport, and Barbara Myerhoff. The field is fertile because individual cultures and world monoculture are increasingly theatrical.

Preparing to do theater includes either memorizing a score of gestures, sounds, and movements and/or achieving a mood where apparently "external" gestures, sounds, and movements "take over" the performer as in trance. This basic theatrical process is universal. Everywhere, behavior that is other is transformed into the performer's own; alienated or objectified parts of the performer's self—either his private self or his social self—are reintegrated and shown publicly in a total display. The process has two parts and a conclusion; these are strictly analagous to what Arnold van Gennep and Turner describe as the ritual process. First there is the breaking down, where the performer's resistance is overcome, he is made open and vulnerable, "ready"; then there is the building up, or the filling up, where at first short and then increasingly long and integrated strips of behavior are added to what the performer can do. At a certain point in the process —a point that differs widely from culture to culture, artistic form to form—a public is required before whom, or in collaboration with whom, the new behavior is displayed.

Theater is an "artificial species" of ritual, a hothouse version often created by individuals or temporary groups. Turner calls the arts and some other leisures of modern society "liminoid," suggesting that they share some of the functions and processes of liminal acts, but that they are also characterized by a voluntariness—a conscious subjunctivity— that is not present in liminal actions. In theater the performer induces in himself, or has induced for him, replications/restorations of those life-crises most people avoid or undergo only when pressed by necessity. Comedy as well as tragedy deals with difficult, anxiety-ridden crises. The pleasure comes because of the subjunctive mood of the activity— the learned ability to experience an action without suffering its consequences. Hamlet dies, not Olivier. Of course, as I've noted, contemporary theater skirts or even crosses the boundaries, and some of our recent Hamlets have suffered a real wound or two.

The workshop-rehearsal phase of performing, the "pre-performance," is designed to make the performer a *tabula rasa* with regard to what is going to be performed. The performer is stripped of his everyday identity, or he learns how to put it aside. Then, once cleaned, the performer brings out of himself, or is inscribed upon, or filled up with, another, a "character," or some special aspect of himself, his "persona." Workshop-rehearsal passes through three distinct steps that coincide with the ritual process: 1) separation, or stripping away, reducing or eliminating or setting aside "me"; 2) initiation, or revelation, or finding out what's new in "me" or in/from another, or what's essential and necessary; and 3) reintegration, or building up longer and longer meaningful strips of behavior; making something for the public—preparing to re-enter the social world but as a new and/or different self. The time spent in these three steps and the place where this work is done are liminal. Not the finished performances but this multiphasic process of "making up" performances is what needs to be compared to ritual. Little comparative work of that kind has been done because few anthropologists have participated in, or closely observed, the workshop-rehearsal process.

How do workshop-rehearsals work? There are two basic methods. In the first, actual items of performance are passed on directly from master to neophyte. There is no technique separate from parts of the performance to be learned. In "direct acquisition" by manipulation, imitation, and repetition, there is the paradox that the creativity of the performer comes only after he has mastered a form by rote learning. Experimentation, which literally means "going outside the boundaries," is reserved for the most experienced, most respected, and often the oldest performers. In Euro-American theater experimentation is mostly the work of the young, because the initial phases of workshop-rehearsal are the freest; and it is the youthful performer who is encouraged to do something new. In the method of direct acquisition, there is no reference during training to any generative grammar of performance. Nor do training or exercises stimulate creativity or encourage experimentation or the discovery of new material or patterns. I have watched the *vyas* (director) of the Ramnagar Ramlila employ direct acquisition in teaching the texts and gestures to the teen-aged boys who perform the *swarupas* (the gods Rama, Bharat, Lakshmana, and Satrughna). Learning the score prepares the boys to be entered by the gods during moments of the actual performance. The last thing a vyas wants of such performances is creativity. The swarupas must be receptive, even passive. When the boys are not wearing the crowns that signify the activation of the godhead within them, they are just boys, lectured by the vyas, scolded by their mothers. At the same time, however, they are fed a special diet of godly foods: pure milk, sweet rice, fruit, nuts, yogurt. This diet not only gives them strength but makes them feel like gods. Through the method of direct acquisition, two tasks are accomplished simultaneously. Performance texts—I mean not only the words but the whole mise-en-scene—are passed on from generation to generation; and particular performances are made ready for the public. There is no way to separate these tasks, for the texts are both written and oral; the libraries where these texts are kept are the bodies of the performers.

The second method of workshop-rehearsal is to teach a grammar, a set of "basic exercises" out of which, through transformation, the particular, and often very different, mise-en-scenes will come. Some great texts do not exist as performances but only as words. There is no one way to play *Hamlet,* nor even 250 ways. There is no continuity of performing *Hamlet* from 1604 to now. Not only were the theaters closed during the Cromwell era, but the Euro-American modern tradition located continuity in the written text and innovation in the performance. Recent violations of this tradition—for example, my collaging and rearranging classical texts or the attempt to build in theater "performance texts" as seen in the work of Brecht or Mabou Mines— have had tough going. In the "learn a basic alphabet/grammar" method, students learn how to use their mind-bodies in order to invent the particular gestures that will make up this or that production. A radical separation of written text and performance text has occurred. The written text is preserved separately from any of its performances. A large body of criticism arises dealing with the written text, and this criticism tends to dominate the field. There is also a separation between training and rehearsal. Training is generalized in that techniques are learned that can be applied to any number of performances. Schools brag that their graduates can act in any number of styles. In the "alphabet method" an actor pants not in order to be able to pant in performance, but in order to strengthen his diaphragm, get in touch with the different ways the voice can resonate, control his breathing so that difficult physical exertions can be accomplished without losing breath, and so on. Or scenes from plays are practiced in training not because they will be played soon or in a certain way, but so that the student can learn to "build a character," evoke genuine emotions or effectively feign them on stage, or deal with his fellow actors.

But just as there are intermediate or liminal performance styles, so there are some training methods that occupy a position in between these extremes, combining elements of both. In Kathakali, the dance drama of Kerala in southwest India, training begins with a series of massages administered by the guru's feet to the student's whole body. These massages literally erase old body stances and help bring the student's body to a new alignment. The massage period coincides with a series of rigorous exercises that are later used with some variations in Kathakali itself. The exercises are not the basis for invention; they are there to help the student use his body in the necessary way. Thus the exercises can be looked at as part of the breaking down phase of training. They do not help a student grasp the underlying logic of the performance. That can come only after years of experience as the student deciphers for himself what he is doing. Many excellent performers never come to this kind of theoretical knowledge, but some do, and those are the ones most likely to introduce changes.

In the Euro-American method, rehearsal is not a matter of transmitting a known performance text but of the invention of a new text. This new text is arrived at during rehearsals. It is necessary to teach performers a generative code. In the method of direct acquisition, rehearsals involve not inventing a new performance text but mastering a known one. But performance itself can be extremely flexible. Noh drama appears very formal, but during performance subtle cues pass between the shite (principal actor) and musicians, chorus, and waki (second actor). These cues tell the others that the shite has decided to repeat a section or increase the tempo, or slow it down, and so forth. Euro-American method rehearsals are "explorations" that lead to a "fixed score" during performance. Only shows advertised as improvisatory change markedly from night to night. And most improvised shows are mere rearrangements of fixed routines. The physical details of shows can vary greatly as long as the written text is recognizable. Shakespeare has been done in period costume, modern dress, eclectic mixed dress, and the like, yet when I staged plays environmentally and introduced audience participation, journalists publicly demanded to know, "Is this theater?"

During rehearsals of the Euro-American type the grammar of techniques is used to discover and "keep" items that will later appear in the performance. That which is already known through the direct acquisition method is discovered or invented. Something happens that is "right" and the director says "keep that." What he means is not to do it again, but to put it ahead in time: literally to throw it forward in the hope that the item of action will be used later, that it will provide a clue as to what the finished mise-en-scene will look like. During rehearsals the shape and feel of the performance being discovered/invented/restored lies in a liminal area between present and future, and between past, present, and future, as personal associations from performers and director are added to the scheme. Thus a $1 \to 5_a \to 5_b$ situation happens. To the outside observer, the bits of performance being "thrown forward," being "kept," may appear haphazard. But sooner or later a pattern emerges, as when, through a fog, a coastline is first sensed ("I smell land"), then vaguely discerned as a darkness, then seen as a blurred image, and finally resolved with increasing detail. So, too, in this method the performance evolves out of rehearsals. It is, as Brecht said, that the performance is the least rejected of all the things tried.

Early rehearsals are not only jerky and disjointed, but also laden with anxiety. The actions of the rehearsal have a high information potential but a very low goal orientation. "What are we doing?" "What are we looking for?" "I don't understand why we're doing this" are the common questions. The director doesn't know, he, too, is hunting. A director may maintain confidence by imposing order in the guise of known exercises or by introducing new basic techniques, expanding the range of the group's generative grammar. But if, by a certain time, a target is not visible (not only a production date but a vision of what is to be produced), if not enough has been thrown forward to provide an outline, a goal, the project falters, then fails. The possibilities for failure are great enough when, as in the case of *Hamlet*, the task is to generate a performance text that suits a written one. Where there is no preexisting text whatsoever—as with some experimental theater—the likelihood of failure is greater still.

During the past fifty years, since Artaud at least, the two kinds of workshop-rehearsal process—transmission of whole items by direct acquisition and transmission by means of learning a generative grammar—have been linked. This linkage is, in fact, the great work of experimental theater in this century. Richard Foreman, for example, transmits to relatively passive performers a complete performance text in a method parallel to that used by Ramlila vyases. Foreman writes his plays, makes a schematic of how they are to be staged, designs the setting, and often is present as chief technician at each performance. And the "grammatical" methods of Chhou guru Sahoo and the teachers of Kathakali may be due to extensive contact with European models. Also techniques such as yoga, martial arts, mantra chanting, and the like, transmitted as whole texts in their cultures of origin, are now used in the West as training of the generative grammar kind. In 1978 at a meeting outside Warsaw convened by Grotowski, I saw Kanze Hideo of the famous Noh family put on a Noh mask, crawl on the floor, and improvise actions having nothing to do with classical Noh. And his friend Suzuki, in a production of Euripides' *Trojan Women*, combined Noh, kabuki, martial arts, modern Western experimental theater, and ancient Greek tragedy. The play was as much about post–atomic bomb Japan as Troy. Examples multiply, bearing witness to exchanges between, especially, Asian and Euro-American theater. Three kinds of workshop-rehearsal are now occurring: 1) those based on transmitting

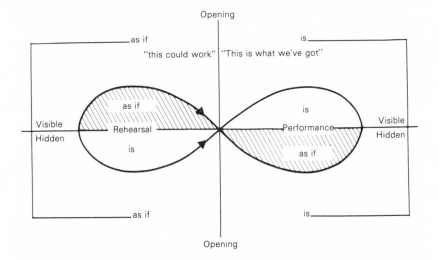

FIGURE 1–6

a total performance text; 2) those based on generative grammars result-ing in new performance texts; and 3) those combining 1 and 2. This last is not a sterile hybrid, but the most fertile of the three.

There is another way of looking at the workshop-rehearsal process in connecting Turner's ideas of subjunctivity/liminality to Stanislav-ski's "as if." Figure 1-6 shows that the deep structure of workshop-rehearsal inverts the deep structure of performance. In workshop-rehearsal, real work is being done, work that is serious and problematical. Workshop-rehearsal ironically belongs to the indicative, to the realm of the "is," but on a deep, hidden level of structure. The visible aspect of workshop-rehearsal, its processual frame, is "as if," subjunctive, tentative play: "let's try that"; "this could work"; "what would happen if?" "As if" techniques—exercises, games, improvisa-tion, therapy—bring up material from within those making the show or from the outside. The work of workshop-rehearsal is to find, reveal, express these deep things and then to integrate them into a new whole. Even while these deep things are "brought up," the workshop-rehearsal must be kept open, that is, liminal. The "as if" is a scalpel cutting deep into the actual lives of those making the work. And the most serious crises of performance—the things that can destroy a work most surely —happen during workshop-rehearsals. This is the period during which performers throw tantrums, directors fire persons who disagree, and writers phone their agents in terror. For during this time every small change can have immense consequences for the work as a whole.

The performance is the inverse of the workshop-rehearsal. The show, when it opens, becomes "real," part of history; certain public rituals such as reviewing, attendance by an audience of strangers, an opening-night party, mark the transition from rehearsal to performance. The frame and visible structure of the performance is an "is," the finished show, the more or less invariable presentation of what has been found, kept, and organized into a score. But the deep structure under this "is" is an "as if." The tears Ophelia sheds for Hamlet are real salt tears, and her grief is actual, but the cause of that grief may be something totally unrelated to Hamlet or to the actor playing Hamlet. The cause is possibly an association that the actress found during rehearsals. Or the final scene of slaughter appears to be a confusion of violence when, in fact, it is a precision of near-misses. As workshop-rehearsals move toward performance, the "as if" is intentionally sunk out of sight. If the performance is a good one, all the audience sees is the "is" of the show. Of course, there are variations of this classic scheme. The investigation of the rehearsal process by Stanislavski and Brecht made it possible to play around with the process. Brecht wanted actors to be in character ("as if") some of the time and to stand beside their characters ("is") questioning these very characters at other times. Thus Brecht introduced a part of the rehearsal process into public performance. And since Brecht, many others have staged rehearsals.

These breakings of frame occur not only in serious drama, but also in circus and Broadway musicals as well. There is a scene in *Sugar Babies* during which the star, Mickey Rooney, loses his wig. He laughs, his face turns red, he runs to the edge of the stage and shouts something at the audience; he acknowledges that underneath all the puff roles he plays there is the person, the star, Mickey Rooney. Losing the wig looks accidental, but I have confirmed that it happens in each performance in the same scene. Probably Rooney lost his wig "for real" during one rehearsal, and this nice piece of business was kept. It helps the audience feel good about paying so much money to see the star; for a brief moment they see him as himself, unmasked. Of course, this unmasking is a trick, not an unmasking at all. I do not criticize the rehearsedness of such scenes. Whenever I've tried to have "open rehearsals" and invite the public to see a work "in process," or when during finished performances I've tried to include "raw elements," such as having the green room visible during *Mother Courage,* I've noticed how quickly the processual or open nature of the workshop-rehearsal is lost. The "as if" wants to submerge when the public is present. Only while working with those they can trust, usually a few comrades who have shared a lot of working together, can performers play "as if" with "is" material. When working under the eye of a critical public, the performers present only the "is" of their "as if."

The last part of rehearsal is practice. Longer and more complicated units of restored behavior are organized into the actual performance. Music, costumes, lighting, makeup, accumulate. Each of these is blended in with the intention of making an integrated whole. During this final push gestures are edited so that they send the clearest signals and practiced until they become second nature. Pacing—the relation of the rhythm/tempo of each part to that of the whole—becomes all important. This last phase of rehearsal is comparable to the phase of reintegration in a rite of passage. Strangers to the theater often think only of this last phase when they hear the word "rehearsal," but reintegration is only the final phase of a long process.

Immediately before going on most performers engage in some ritual. The Noh actor contemplates his mask; Jatra performers in Bengal worship the gods of the performance who manifest themselves in the props assembled on the trunks set up backstage; Stanislavski advised thirty seconds of silent concentration. Warmups are universal in experimental theater. These preparations immediately preceding public performance somehow recapitulate the workshop-rehearsal process and concentrate the performer's attention on the task at hand. It's a little like the moment of prayer or the singing of an anthem before a ballgame or prize fight. But these ceremonies are not holy in the religious sense, even when they include religious ritual. I think, rather, the ritual is a way of focusing the work of workshop-rehearsal and bringing this work across a difficult threshold, limen, that separates rehearsal from public performance. Sometimes these preparatory "moments" are hours long. Tribesmen in Papua New Guinea, and performers of Yakshagana, Kathkali, and Ramlila in India spend up to four hours putting on makeup and costumes. I always met with The Performance Group two hours or more before a performance to give notes, clean up the space, and do warmups. The main function of these preparations—even the putting on of effectively transformative costumes, masks, and makeup—is not merely to make the performer "look" the role, but to set aside time immediately before the performance for the work of training, workshop, and rehearsal to be awakened and take hold.

The rehearsal process is a basic machine for the restoration of behavior. It is no accident that this process is the same in theater as it is in ritual. For the basic function of both theater and ritual is to restore behavior—to maintain performances of the $1 \rightarrow 5_a \rightarrow 5_b$ type. The meaning of individual rituals is secondary to this primary function, which is a kind of collective memory-in/of-action. The first phase breaks down the performer's resistance, makes him a *tabula rasa*. To do this most effectively the performer has to be removed from familiar surroundings. Thus the need for separation, for "sacred" or special space, and for a use of time different from that prevailing in the ordinary. The second phase is of initiation: developing new or restoring old behavior. But so-called "new behavior" is really the rearrangement of old behavior or the enactment of old behavior in new settings. In the third phase, reintegration, the restored behavior is practiced until it is second nature. The final moment of the third phase is the public performance. Public performances in Euro-American theater are repeated until there are no more customers; theater productions are treated as commodities. In most cultures performances occur according to schedules that strictly ration their availability. What we call "new behavior," as I said, are only short strips of behavior rearticulated in novel patterns. Experimental theater thrives on these rearticulations masquerading as novelties. But the ethological repertory of behaviors, even human behaviors, is limited. In rituals, relatively long strips of behavior are restored, giving the impression of continuity, stasis, tradition: for not only the details but the whole thing is recognizable. In creative arts, especially experimental performance, relatively short strips of behavior are rearranged and the whole thing looks new. Thus the sense of change we get from experiments may be real at the level of recombination but illusory at the basic structural/processual level. Real change is a very slow evolutionary process.

≫

D. W. Winnicott's ideas add an ontogenetic level and a new set of categories to my description of what the performer does. Winnicott, a British psychoanalyst (now dead), was interested in the mother-baby relationship, particularly how the baby discovers the difference between "me" and "not me." Winnicott proposed a mind/body state between "me" and "not me." This third, intermediate, state is a double negative very like Gregory Bateson's description of the "play frame" in his "Theory of Play and Fantasy" (in Bateson 1972b). It is also analogous to Turner's concept of the liminal. Winnicott (1971:3, 6):

> I am here staking a claim for an intermediate state between a baby's inability and his growing ability to recognize and accept reality. I am therefore studying the substance of *illusion,* that which is allowed to the infant, and which in adult life is inherent in art and religion. . . .
>
> I think there is use for a term for the root of symbolism in time, a term that describes the infant's journey from the purely subjective to objectivity; and it seems that the transitional object (piece of blanket, etc.) is what we see of this journey of progress toward experiencing.

Drawing from Winnicott, I believe the most dynamic formulation of what he is describing is that the baby, and later the child at play and the adult at art, recognizes some things and situations as "not me . . . not not me." So Olivier is not Hamlet but he is also not not Hamlet; the reverse is also true: in this production of the play, Hamlet is not Olivier, but he is also not not Olivier. In this field of double negativity choice and virtuality remain activated.

In children the movement from "not me" to "not not me" is seen in their relationship to security blankets, favorite toys that cannot be replaced no matter how old, dirty, or broken. Play itself uses actuality and fantasy in a "not me . . . not not me" way. The hierarchies that usually set off actuality as "real" and fantasy as "not real" are set aside for the "time being," the play-time. These same operations of dissolving hierarchies, of treasuring things beyond their ordinary worth, of setting aside certain times and places for the manipulation of these things in a world defined nonhierarchically according to ordinary standards: this is also a definition of art-making, of performance.

Restored behavior of all kinds—rituals, theatrical performances, restored villages, agnicayana—is all "transitional behavior." Elements that are "not me" become "me" without losing their "not me-ness." This is the peculiar but necessary double negativity that characterizes symbolic action. A performer experiences his own self not directly but through the medium of performance, of experiencing the Others. While performing he no longer has a "me" but a "not not me," and this double negative relationship also shows how restored behavior is simultaneously private and social. A person performing recovers his own self only by going out of himself, by entering a social field, a public field. The way in which "me" and "not me"—the performer and the thing to be performed—is transformed into "not me . . . not not me" is through the rehearsal/ritual process. This process takes place in a liminal time/space and in the subjunctive mood. The subjunctive character of the liminal time/space is reflected in the negative, antistructural frame around the whole thing. "Not me . . . not not me" could also be algebraically expressed: not (me . . . not me).

By integrating the thought of Winnicott, Bateson, and Turner with my own work as a theater person, I propose a theory that includes the ontogenesis of individuals, the social action of ritual, and the symbolic, even fictive, action of art. Clearly these overlap: their underlying process is identical. A performance "takes place" in the "not me . . . not not me" between performers; between performers and script; between performers, script, and environment; between performers, script, environment, and audience. The larger the field of "between," the stronger the performance. The antistructure that is performance swells until it threatens to burst. The trick is to take it to the brink but no further. It is the ambition of all performances to expand this field until it includes all beings, things, and relations. This can't happen. The field is precarious because it is subjunctive, liminal, transitional: it rests not on how things are but on how things are not; its existence depends on agreements kept among all participants. The field is the embodiment of potential, of the virtual, the imaginative, the fictive, the negative, the not (not). The larger it gets, the more it thrills, but the more doubt and anxiety it evokes, too. Catharsis comes when something happens to the performers and/or characters but not to the performance itself. But when doubt overcomes confidence, the field collapses like popped bubble gum. The result is a mess: stage fright, aloneness, emptiness, and terrible inadequacy when facing the bottomless appetite of the audience. When confidence—and the skills necessary for genuine confidence—prevails, there is nothing the performer can't do; a special empathy/sympathy vibrates between performers and spectators. The spectators do not "willingly suspend disbelief." They believe and disbelieve at the same time. This is theater's chief delight. The show is not real and not not real at the same time. This is true for performers as well as spectators and accounts for that special absorption the stage engenders in those who step onto it. Sacred a stage may or may not be, special it always is.

In Figure 1-7 I have tried to portray this system. It is a version of

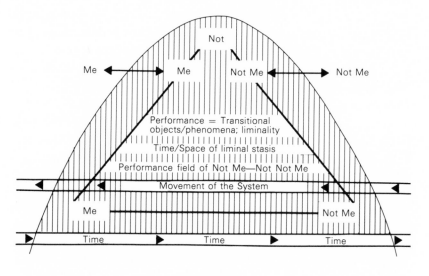

FIGURE 1–7

$1 \rightarrow 5_a \rightarrow 5_b$. Actions move in time, from the past thrown into the future, from "me" to "not me" and from "not me" to "me." As they travel they are absorbed into the special (liminal, subjunctive) time/space of "not me . . . not not me." This time/space includes both workshop-rehearsals and performances. Things thrown into the future ("keep that," says the director) are recovered and used later in rehearsals and in the performance. The system as a whole travels against the flow of ordinary time. And during the performance, if everything is working, the experience is of synchronicity as the flow of ordinary time and the flow of the performance collide and eclipse each other. This eclipse is the "present moment," the synchronic ecstasy, of liminal stasis. Those who are masters at attaining and prolonging this balance are artists, shamans, experimental scientists. Those who can keep this liminal stasis active in the presence of onlookers are performers. No one can keep it long.

≫

What about Staal and Gardner? They entered Kerala as theatrical producers-directors in the guise of anthropological researchers. Not finding a ritual worthy of being filmed, they arranged for one to be performed. They made sure there was enough lead time to get money to make the film and to import a bevy of important scholars. Their lie, if there is one, comes with the marketing of *Altar of Fire* as a document of an ancient ritual they just happened upon. In the nick of time, too. The film's audience may construe agnicayana as a "living ritual" when in fact it is a complicated kind of play-acting. But I think I have shown how play-acting itself is a living ritual, though one made reflexive through the use of rehearsals. *Altar of Fire* is not a film of Vedic ritual. The filming itself ritualizes the action of restaging/restoring the agnicayana. Too bad Staal-Gardner did not include a reflexive consciousness of this, or at least issue two films, one of the ritual "itself" and one of their making of the film about it, a kind of Truffautian film of them filming *Altar of Fire*. The same twist is at the heart of restored villages. They are not a return to earlier centuries but their own epoch's way of ritualizing our daily lives. And like all rituals, a visit to a restored village gives one a sense of tradition, of significance, of continuity and includes, of course, packing the family into the car and driving off to the village.

Maybe even today most anthropologists would agree with Turner, who said of his own stay with the Ndembu, "We never asked for a ritual to be performed solely for our own anthropological benefit; we held no brief for such artificial play-acting" (1969:10). There are two responses to Turner. First, I think the presence of the fieldworker is an invitation to play-acting. People want their pictures taken, want books written about them, want to show who they are and what they do. Second, what does he propose for traditions that are near extinction? Ought we not to recognize that in many societies patronage itself has been traditional and has guaranteed the continuation not only of aesthetic but also of ritual forms? How ought we to respond to the dooming of many varieties of ritual theater by modernization? In Karnataka, south India, not too many miles from where Staal-Gardner filmed, Martha Ashton was studying Yakshagana, a form of dance/drama hardly ever done according to the old ways. Ashton got a company together drawing on several different groups. She hired actors, singers, musicians. She assisted them in recollecting the old stories; in reconstructing the old steps, music, and training. And she filmed the results of their mutual labors. Was she wrong in doing this? Today there are three styles of Yakshagana: the popular version; a style for modern audiences developed by K. S. Karanth, a well-known writer; and the "classical Yakshagana" restored by Ashton's troupe. This last style was the one to tour America. Was it the most or the least Indian?

The position of the purists who refuse to stage the rituals they are studying and recording is not pure but ambivalent. Their position is analagous to that of Richard Foreman, who, in many of his theatrical productions, sat between his players and the audience, often running a tape recorder that broadcasts his own voice interpreting and asking questions and giving instructions. To the society the fieldworker temporarily inhabits he represents his own culture in one of its most inexplicable aspects: why send somebody to observe and record how another group lives? And to those of us who read or see the reports of the fieldworker, he is our main link with both fresh aspects of human nature and our often tested but never proven assertion that humans comprise one species, and all relate to each other culturally, "humanly," as well as biologically. The script of the fieldworker demands a pretended distance, a studied absence. He is somewhat like the aristocrat on the Restoration stage. Clearly the most visible person there, nevertheless a convention cloaks him in invisibility. Everyone watches his moves, but he is not part of the story. But those who have done fieldwork know how difficult it is to keep this aristocratic distance. Not only is the fieldworker's wealth competed for, but his presence often upsets the power balance in a small village, and a strong worker must develop strategies to stay out of power struggles.

The situation precipitated by the fieldworker's presence is a theatrical one, a showing. And the fieldworker emerges as not a performer and not a spectator. He occupies a middle ground between these two roles, just as he is in the middle between two cultures. In the field he represents —whether he wants to or not—his culture of origin; and back home he represents the culture he has studied. The fieldworker is always in a "not me . . . not not me" situation, and, it seems to me, the fieldworker goes through the three-phase process isomorphic with the ritual and rehearsal process:

1. The stripping away of his own ethnocentrism. This is often a brutal separation, which in itself is the deepest struggle of fieldwork, and is never complete. What should he eat, how? And his toilet habits. And the dozens of other things that remind the worker of the distance between his own culture and the one he wants to get inside of. But if his work is to succeed, he has to undergo some kind of transformation.

2. The revelation, often coming suddenly like inspiration, of what is "new" in the society he temporarily inhabits. This discovery is his initiation, the taking on of a new role, in his adoptive society, a role that

often includes a new identity, position, or status. The worker "goes native," even inside himself.

3. The difficult task of using his fieldnotes or other data to make an acceptable monograph, film, whatever—the way he translates what he found into items understood by the world he returns to. His promotion to full professor marks his reintegration into his own society.

As fieldwork converges on theatrical directing, the third phase of the process includes making films of performances based on what's been experienced in other cultures. It is here that confusion occurs. Clearly, monographs have been in terms of the "home culture." But films purport to show directly the "away culture." Insofar as they do, the third step of the fieldworker's progression folds back into step 1. His price of reentry and success is to authentically show his own people what the natives were like in their own terms. It may be too much to ask. Or the wrong thing.

In the past anthropologists have fancied themselves siblings of "hard scientists." But hard science works from models strictly fenced off from ordinary life; and it depends on predictive theory. The soft sciences are actually extensions of the arts and humanities: they are part of the subject they study. Theory in the social sciences is really what Geertz calls "thick description." The fieldworker is very much like the theater director. He is an evoker-observer who participates and keeps a distance at the same time, whose presence and energy make a difference, especially in the mid-phase of making a production, but who is apparently absent at its inception (scriptmaking) and conclusion (performing). The director does not author the script but guarantees its display before an audience. Sometimes, and increasingly so, the director is more than this. He helps make the script and enters into the performance. The fieldworker does not create the society he studies, but his presence gives the society an additional significance to itself and to others: a sense that someone else is interested, is listening, and, consequently, an encouragement for people within the society to be reflexive. The fieldworker is a professional link, a person not at home either in his own or in someone else's culture—an in-betweener.

Presently, theater directors are leaving the shadowy out-of-sight area offstage. The director is entering the stage, not just as another performer, but as a unique figure: the embodiment of the workshop-rehearsal process. Directors are specialists in restored behavior and so are fieldworkers. The restoration of behavior is the industry of the future. For some time now the director has been conscious of his new role; the fieldworker is just gaining this reflexivity. As he fully grasps it, he will recognize his sisters and brothers: the clowns and jugglers, the actors and acrobats, the double agents and dissimulators, the con-men and shamans.

2 DRAMATIC RITUAL/RITUAL DRAMA: PERFORMATIVE AND REFLEXIVE ANTHROPOLOGY

VICTOR TURNER

I've long thought that teaching and learning anthropology should be more fun than they often are. Perhaps we should not merely read and comment on ethnographies but actually perform them. Alienated students spend many tedious hours in library carrels struggling with accounts of alien lives and even more alien anthropological theories about the ordering of those lives. Whereas anthropology should be about, in D. H. Lawrence's phrase, "man alive" and "woman alive," this living quality frequently fails to emerge from our pedagogics, perhaps, to cite Lawrence again, because our "analysis presupposes a corpse."

It is becoming increasingly recognized that the anthropological monograph is itself a rather rigid literary genre which grew out of the notion that in the human sciences reports must be modeled rather

Originally published in *The Kenyon Review* 1 (1980):80–93.

abjectly on those of the natural sciences. But such a genre has no privileged position, especially now that we realize that in social life cognitive, affective, and volitional elements are bound up with one another and are alike primary, seldom found in their pure form, often hybridized, and only comprehensible by the investigator as lived experience, *his/hers* as well as, and in relation to, *theirs.*

Even the best of ethnographic films fails to communicate much of what it means to *be* a member of the society filmed. A selected, often slanted, series of visual images is directed at a passive audience. Discussion in the classroom then centers on the items picked out for attention by the filmmaker. Though a good teacher will plausibly relate the movie to ethnographic contexts drawn from the literature, much of the socio-cultural and psychological complexity of those contexts cannot be related to the film. Anthropological monographs and movies may describe or present the incentives to action characteristic of a given group, but only rarely will these genres catch up their readers or spectators fully into the culture's motivational web.

How, then, may this be done? One possibility may be to turn the more interesting portions of ethnographies into playscripts, then to act them out in class, and finally to turn back to ethnographies armed with the understanding that comes from "getting inside the skin" of members of other cultures, rather than merely "taking the role of the other" in one's own culture. A whole new set of problems is generated by this apparently simple process. For each of its three stages (ethnography into playscript, script into performance, performance into meta-ethnography) reveals many of the frailties of anthropology, that essentially Western traditional discipline. And the process forces us to look beyond purely anthropological accounts—to literature, history, biography, incidents of travel—for data that may contribute to convincing playscripts. Where social dramas do find their cultural "doubles" (to reverse Antonin Artaud) in aesthetic dramas and other genres of cultural performance, there may well develop, as Richard Schechner has argued, a convergence between them, so that the processual form of social dramas is implicit in aesthetic dramas (even if only by reversal or negation), while the *rhetoric* of social dramas—and hence the shape of argument—is drawn from cultural performances. There was a lot of Perry Mason in Watergate!

The "playing" of ethnography is a genuinely interdisciplinary enterprise, for if we are to satisfy ourselves of the reliability of our script and our performance of it, we will need advice from various non-anthropological sources. Professionals in the field of drama in our own culture—scriptwriters, directors, actors, even stagehands—draw on centuries of professional experience in performing plays. Ideally, we need to consult, better still, bring in as part of the cast, members of the culture being enacted. We may, sometimes, be lucky enough to enlist the aid of theatrical or folk professionals from the society we are studying. But, in any case, those who know the business from the inside can help enormously.

≫

I was given an opportunity to test these speculations in practice when, with fellow social scientists Alexander Alland and Erving Goffman, I was invited by Richard Schechner, professor of drama at New York University, to take part in what was called "an intensive workshop" to "explore the interface between ritual and the theatre . . . between social and aesthetic drama," and other limina between the social sciences and performing arts. I had often thought about the relationship between processual forms of social conflict in many societies described by anthropologists and genres of cultural performance. Several years earlier, mutual friends had made me aware of Schechner's interest in the same problem from the viewpoint of theater. The collaboration of Colin Turnbull and Peter Brook which converted Turnbull's study of the Ik of Uganda into a series of dramatic episodes alerted me to the possibility of turning suitable ethnographic data into playscripts (Turnbull 1972). That experiment persuaded me that cooperation between anthropological and theatrical people not only was possible but also could become a major teaching tool for both sets of partners in a world many of whose components are beginning to want to know one another. If it is true that we learn something about ourselves from taking the role of others, anthropologists, those cultural brokers *par excellence,* might be challenged to make this an intercultural as well as an intracultural enterprise.

Though many social scientists frown on the terms *performance* and *drama,* they seem to me central. *Performance* is derived from the Middle English *parfournen,* later *parfourmen,* which is itself from the Old French *parfournir—par* ("thoroughly") plus *fournir* ("to furnish")— hence *performance* does not necessarily have the structuralist implication of manifesting *form,* but rather the processual sense of "bringing to completion" or "accomplishing." To *perform* is thus to complete a more or less involved process rather than to do a single deed or act. To *perform* ethnography, then, is to bring the data home to us in their fullness, in the plenitude of their action-meaning. Cognitive reductionism has always struck me as a kind of dehydration of social life. Sure, the patterns can be elicited, but the wishes and emotions, the personal and collective goals and strategies, even the situational vulnerabilities, wearinesses, and mistakes are lost in the attempt to objectify and produce an aseptic theory of human behavior modeled essentially on eighteenth century "scientific" axioms of belief about mechanical causality. Feelings and desires are not a pollution of cognitive pure essence, but close to what we humanly are; if anthropology is to become a true science of human action, it must take them just as seriously as the structures which sometimes perhaps represent the exhausted husks of action bled of its motivations.

The term *drama* has been criticized (by Max Gluckman [1977] and Raymond Firth [1974], for example) as the imposition on observational data of a schema derived from *cultural* genres, hence "loaded" and not "neutral" enough for scientific use. I have to disagree, for my notebooks are filled with descriptions of day-to-day events which, added together, undeniably possess dramatic form, representing a course of action. Let me try to describe what I mean by *drama*, specifically *social drama*.[1]

I hold that the social drama form occurs on all levels of social organization from state to family. A social drama is initiated when the peaceful tenor of regular, norm-governed social life is interrupted by the *breach* of a rule controlling one of its salient relationships. This leads swiftly or slowly to a state of *crisis*, which, if not soon sealed off, may split the community into contending factions and coalitions. To prevent this, *redressive* means are taken by those who consider themselves or are considered the most legitimate or authoritative representatives of the relevant community. Redress usually involves ritualized action, whether legal (in formal or informal courts), religious (involving beliefs in the retributive action of powerful supernatural entities, and often involving an act of sacrifice), or military (for example, feuding, headhunting, or engaging in organized warfare). If the situation does not regress to *crisis* (which may remain endemic until some radical restructuring of social relationships, sometimes by revolutionary means, is undertaken), the next phase of social drama comes into play, which involves alternative solutions to the problem. The first is *reconciliation* of the conflicting

1. For a fuller account of my theory of the social drama, see Turner 1957.

parties following judicial, ritual, or military processes; the second, *consensual recognition of irremediable breach,* usually followed by the spatial separation of the parties. Since social dramas suspend normal everyday roleplaying, they interrupt the flow of social life and force a group to take cognizance of its own behavior in relation to its own values, even to question at times the value of those values. In other words, dramas induce and contain reflexive processes and generate cultural frames in which reflexivity can find a legitimate place.

≫

With this processual form as a rough guide for our work at Schechner's summer institute, I tried to involve anthropology and drama students in the joint task of writing scripts for and performing ethnographies. It seemed best to choose parts of classical ethnographies that lent themselves to dramatic treatment, such as Malinowski's *Crime and Custom,* with its young man threatening suicide from a treetop when his father's matrilineal kin urged him to leave their village on his father's death (1926:78). But time being short (we had only two weeks), I had to fall back upon my own ethnography both because I knew it best, and because I had already, to some extent, written a script for a substantial amount of field data in the form I have called *social drama.* My wife, Edie, and I tried to explain to a group of about a dozen students and teachers, almost equally divided between anthropology and drama, what cultural assumptions lay behind the first two social dramas that I described in my book *Schism and Continuity in an African Society* (1957:95, 116). It was not enough to give them a few cognitive models or structural principles. We had to try to create the illusion of what it is to live Ndembu village life. Could this possibly be done with a few bold strokes, with a gesture or two? Of course not, but there may be ways of getting people bodily as well as mentally involved in another (not physically present) culture.

The setting for all this was an upper room in the Performance Garage, a theater in Greenwich Village where Schechner's company, The Performance Group, has given some notable innovative performances, including *Dionysus in '69, Makbeth, Mother Courage,* and, more recently, the *Tooth of Crime,* and *Rumstead Road.* I knew that Schechner set great store on what he calls the "rehearsal process," which essentially consists of establishing a dynamic relationship, over whatever time it takes, among playscript, actors, director, stage, and props, with no initial presumptions about the primacy of any of these. Sessions often have no time limit; in some, exercises of various kinds, including breathing exercises to loosen up actors, may go on for an hour or so; in others, players may cast themselves rather than be cast by the director. In this complex process, Schechner sees the actor, in taking the role of another —provided by a playscript—as moving, under the intuitive and experienced eye of the director/producer, from the "not-me" (the blue-printed role) to the "not-not-me" (the realized role), and he sees the movement itself as constituting a kind of liminal phase in which all kinds of experiential experiments are possible, indeed mandatory. This is a different style of acting from that which relies on superb professional technique to imitate almost any Western role with verisimilitude. Schechner aims at *poesis,* rather than *mimesis:* making, not faking. The role grows along with the actor, it is truly "created" through the rehearsal process, which may sometimes involve painful moments of self-revelation. Such a method is particularly appropriate for anthropological teaching because the "mimetic" method will work only on familiar material (Western models of behavior), whereas the "poietic," since it recreates behavior from within, can handle unfamiliar material.

In an experimental session convoked by Schechner to rehearse Ibsen's *Doll House,* for example, we came up with four Noras, one of whom actually made a choice contrary to Ibsen's script. It happened that in her personal life she herself was being confronted with a dilemma similar to Nora's: should she separate from her husband, leave her two children with him (he wanted this), and embark upon an independent career? In reliving her own problem through enacting Nora's, she began to wring her hands in a peculiarly poignant, slow, complex way. Eventually, instead of detonating the famous door slam that some critics say ushered in modern theater, she rushed back to the group, signifying that she was not ready—at least not yet—to give up her children, thus throwing unexpected light on the ethical toughness of Ibsen's Nora. Schechner said that the hand-wringing was "the bit of reality" he would preserve from that particular rehearsal and embody in the Nora-role in subsequent rehearsals. As these succeeded one another, a bricolage of such gestures, incidents, renderings of not-self into not-not-self would be put together and molded artistically into a processual unity. Depth, reflexivity, a haunting ambiguity may thus be infused into a series of performances, each a unique event.

Particularly since I had no skill or experience in direction, the task of communicating to the actors the setting and atmosphere of daily life in a very different culture proved quite formidable. In one's own society an actor tries to realize "individual character," but takes partly for granted the culturally defined roles supposedly played by that character: father, businessman, friend, lover, fiancé, trade union leader, farmer, poet, and so on. These roles are made up of collective representations shared by actors and audience, who are usually members of the same culture. By contrast, an actor who enacts ethnography has to learn the cultural rules behind the roles played by the character he is representing. How is this to be done? Not, I think, by reading monographs in abstraction from performance, *then* performing the part. There must be a dialectic between performing and learning. One learns through performing, then performs the understandings so gained.

I decided *faute de mieux* to give a reading performance myself of the first two social dramas, interpolating explanatory comments whenever it seemed necessary. The group had already read the relevant pages from *Schism and Continuity*. The dramas were broadly about Ndembu village politics, competition for headmanship, ambition, jealousy, sorcery, the recruiting of factions, and the stigmatizing of rivals, particularly as these operated within a local group of matrilineally related kin and some of their relations by marriage and neighbors. I had collected a number of accounts of these dramas from participants in them. My family and I had lived in the village that was their "stage" or "arena" for at least fifteen months and knew it well during the whole period of my fieldwork—almost two-and-a-half years.

When I had finished reading the drama accounts, the actors in the workshop told me at once that they needed to be "put in the right mood"; to "sense the atmospherics" of Ndembu village life. One of them had brought some records of Yoruba music, and, though this is a different musical idiom from Central African music, I led them into a dancing circle, showing them to the best of my limited, arthritic ability, some of the moves of Ndembu dancing. This was fun, but off-center fun. It then occurred to us that we might recreate with the limited props available to us in the theater the key redressive ritual which was performed in the second social drama, and whose form we knew very well from having taken part in it on several occasions. This ritual, "name inheritance" *(Kuswanika ijina),* was an emotional event, for it marked the temporary end of a power struggle between the stigmatized candidate for headmanship, Sandombu, and Mukanza, the successful candidate, and his immediate matrilineal kin. Sandombu had been driven by public pressure from the village for a year, for it was alleged that he had killed by sorcery Nyamuwaha, a cousin on his mother's side whom he called "mother," a much loved old lady, sister of Mukanza. Sandombu had shed tears on being accused (even his former foes admitted this), but he had been in exile for a year. As time went by, members of the village remembered how, as a foreman, he had helped them find paid labor in the public works department road gang, and how he had always been generous with food and beer to guests. The pretext to invite him back came when a minor epidemic of illness broke out in the village, while at the same time many people dreamed frequently of Nyamuwaha. Divination found that her shade was disturbed by the troubles in the village. To appease her, a quickset sapling of *muyombu* tree, a species for memorializing the lineage dead, was to be planted for her. Sandombu was invited to do the ritual planting. He also paid the village a goat in compensation for his angry behavior the previous year. The ritual marked his reincorporation into the village, even though formally it had to do with the inheritance of Nyamuwaha's name by her oldest daughter, Manyosa (who afterwards became my wife's best friend in the village).

Stirred by the dancing and recorded drumming, I was moved to try to recreate the name-inheritance rite in Greenwich Village. For the *muyombu* tree, I found as substitute a brush handle. For ritual "white" beer as libation, a cup of water would have to do. There was no white clay to anoint people with, but I found some clear white salt, which I moistened. And to pare the top of the brush handle, as Ndembu shrine trees are pared to reveal the white wood under the bark (an operation symbolically related to the purification that is circumcision), I found a sharp kitchen knife. Afterwards, I was told by one of the group that she was terrified that I would do something "grisly" with it! But truly there is often some element of risk or danger in the atmosphere of living ritual. And something numinous.

To translate this very specific Ndembu rite into modern American terms, I took the role of the new village headman, and with my wife's help prepared the surrogate *muyombu* shrine-tree with knife and salt, and "planted" it in a crack in the floor. The next move was to persuade someone to play Manyosa's role in this situation. Someone whom we shall call Becky, a professional director of drama, volunteered.

I asked Becky to give me the name of a recently deceased close female relative of an older generation who had meant much in her life.

Considerably moved, she mentioned her mother's sister Ruth. I then prayed in Chilunda to the "village ancestors." Becky sat beside me before the "shrine," her legs extended in front of her, her head bowed in the Ndembu position of ritual modesty. I then anointed the shrine-tree with the improvised *mpemba,* white clay, symbol of unity with the ancestors and the living community, and drew three lines with the clay orbits, on the brow, and above the navel. I declared her to be "Nswana-Ruth," "successor of Ruth," in one way identified with Ruth, in another replacing her, though not totally, as a structural persona. I then repeated the anointing process with other members of the group, not naming them after deceased kin but joining them into the symbolic unity of our recently formed community of teachers and students. Finally, Edie and I tied strips of white cloth around everyone's brows, and I poured out another libation of the white beer at the base of the shrine-tree. There was clearly a double symbolism here, for I was using Western substances to represent Ndembu objects which themselves had symbolic value in ritual, making of them, as it were, situational indices of cultural symbols. Surely, at so many removes, must not the whole performance have seemed highly artificial, inauthentic? Oddly enough, according to the students, it did not.

≫

The workshop group later reported that they had gone on discussing what had occurred for several hours. They agreed that the enactment of the Ndembu ritual was the turning point which brought home to them both the affectual structure of the social drama and the tension between factionalism and scapegoatism, on the one hand, and the deep sense of village "belonging together" on the other. It also showed them how an enhanced collective and individual understanding of the conflict situation could be achieved by participating in a ritual performance with its kinesiological as well as cognitive codes.

In the following days, the group began work on the actual staging of the ritual dramas. One suggestion favored a dualistic approach: some events (for example, when Sandombu, the ambitious claimant, having killed an antelope, gave only a small portion of meat to his mother's brother, the headman) would be treated realistically, naturalistically; but the world of cultural beliefs, particularly those connected with sorcery and the ancestor cult, would be treated symbolically. For example, it was widely believed, not only by Sandombu's village opponents but also in Ndembu society at large, that Sandombu had killed the headman by paying a powerful sorcerer to summon up from a stream a familiar spirit in the shape of a human-faced serpent, owned by (and also owning) the headman, and by shooting it with his "night-gun," a musket carved from a human tibia and primed with graveyard earth. Such snake-familiars, or *malomba,* are thought to have the faces of their owners and to creep about the village at night invisibly, listening, in wiretap fashion, to derogatory remarks made about their owners by rivals. They grow by eating the shadows, or life-principles, of their owners' foes, who are usually their owners' kin. They function as a kind of Frazerian "external soul," but when they are destroyed by magical means, such as the night-gun, their owners are destroyed too. Chiefs and headmen have "strong *malomba,*" and it takes strong medicine to kill them.

Our class suggested that Sandombu's *ilomba* familiar (that is, his quasi-paranoid underself) should be presented as a kind of chorus to the play. Being privy to the political plotting in the situation, the *ilomba* could tell the audience (in the manner of Shakespeare's Richard the Third) what was going on under the surface of kinship-norm-governed relationships in the village. One suggestion was that we make a film, to be shown in the background, of an *ilomba* cynically disclosing the "real" structure of political power relationships, as known to him, while the dramatis personae of the social drama, onstage and in the foreground, behaved with formal restraint towards one another, with an occasional outburst of authentic hostile feeling.

During the discussion, a graduate student in anthropology gave the drama students in the group some cogent instruction in the nature of matrilineal kinship systems and problems, and, later, in the Ndembu system which combined matrilineal descent with virilocal marriage (residence at the husband's village), and asserted the dominance of succession of brothers to office over the succession of the sister's son—one of the causes of dispute in Mukanza village where the dramas were set. This invocation of cognitive models proved helpful, but only because the nonanthropologists had been stimulated to *want* to know them by the enactment of some Ndembu ritual and the witnessing of the dramatic narrative of political struggle in a matrilineal social context.

To give a more personal idea of the values associated by the Ndembu with matrilineal descent, my wife read to the women of the whole class a piece she had written about the girls' puberty ritual of the Ndembu. I had described this ritual somewhat dryly in the conventional anthropological mode in my book *The Drums of Affliction* (1968:chaps. 7 and 8). Her account, however, grew from participation in an intersubjective world of women involved in this complex ritual sequence, and communicated vividly the feelings and wishes of women in this *rite de passage* in a matrilineal society. Trying to capture the affective dimension the reading revealed, the women in the drama section of the workshop attempted a new technique of staging. They began a rehearsal with a ballet, in which women created a kind of frame with their bodies, positioning themselves to form a circle, in which the subsequent male political action could take place. Their idea was to show that action went on within a matrilineal sociocultural space.

Somehow this device didn't work—there was a covert contemporary political tinge in it which denatured the Ndembu sociocultural process. This feminist mode of staging ethnography assumed and enacted modern ideological notions in a situation in which those ideas are simply irrelevant. The Ndembu struggles were dominated by individual clashes of will and personal and collective emotional responses concerned with assumed or alleged breaches of entitlement. What was dominant was not the general matrilineal structures of inheritance, succession, and social placement in lineages but rather will, ambition, and political goals. The matrilineal struggles did influence the tactics used by contestants overmastered by their will to obtain temporal power, but politics was mainly in the hands of males. A script should thus focus on power-struggling rather than matrilineal assumptions if it is to stay true to the ethnography. But perhaps the ethnography itself should be put in question? This was one view some of our female class members raised. And, indeed, such a question is legitimate when one opens ethnographies out to the performative process. Does a male ethnographer, like myself, really understand or take into full analytical account the nature of matrilineal structure and its embodiment, not only in women but also in men, as a powerful factor in all their actions—political, legal, kinship, ritual, economic?

Nevertheless, the fact remained that political office, even in this matrilineal society, was largely a male affair, if not a male monopoly. Hence, the attempt to bring into the foreground the female framing of Ndembu society diverted attention from the fact that these particular dramas were essentially male political struggles—even though conducted in terms of matrilineal descent. The real tragedy of Sandombu was not that he was embedded in a matrilineal structure but that he was embedded in a kinship structure (whether matrilineal, patrilineal, or bilateral) which played down individual political gifts and played up advantages derived from positions assigned by birth. In capitalistic America, or socialistic Russia or China, a political animal like Sandombu might have thrived. In Ndembu village politics, however, a person with ambition, but procreatively sterile and without many matrilineal kin, was almost from the start a doomed man.

The trouble was that time ran out before the group had a chance to portray Sandombu's situation. But all of us, in anthropology and drama, now had a problem to think about. How could we turn ethnography into script, *then* enact that script, *then* think about, *then* go back to fuller ethnography, *then* make a new script, *then* act it again? This interpretive circulation between data, praxis, theory, and more data— a kind of hermeneutical Catherine wheel, if you like—provides a merciless critique of ethnography. There is nothing like acting the part of a member of another culture in a crisis situation characteristic of that culture to detect inauthenticity in the reporting usually made by Westerners and to raise problems undiscussed or unresolved in the ethnographic narrative. However, this very deficiency may have pedagogical merit insofar as it motivates the student/actor to read more widely in the literature on the culture.

It is hard, furthermore, to separate aesthetic and performative problems from anthropological interpretations. The most incisively or plainly reported extended case histories contained in ethnographies still have to be further distilled and abbreviated for the purposes of performance. To do this tellingly and effectively, sound knowledge of the salient sociocultural contexts must combine with presentational skills to produce an effective playscript, one which effectively portrays both individual psychology and social process articulated in terms of the models provided by a particular culture. One advantage of scripting ethnography in this way is that it draws attention to cultural subsystems, such as that constituted by witchcraft/divination/performance of redressive ritual, in a dramatic way. The workshop group's suggestion that a film or ballet should be performed in the background of the naturalistic drama portraying the *ilomba* and other creatures of witchcraft (masks and masquerading could be employed) might be an effective device for revealing the hidden, perhaps even unconscious, levels of action. It would also act as a vivid set of footnotes on the cultural assumptions of the Ndembu dramatis personae.

≫

Our experience of the theater workshop suggested a number of guide-lines for how collaboration between anthropologists and practitioners of drama and dance, at whatever stage of training, might be undertaken. First of all, anthropologists might present to their drama colleagues a series of ethnographic texts selected for their performative potential. The processed ethnotext would then be transformed into a workable preliminary playscript. Here the know-how of theater people—their sense of dialogue; understanding of setting and props; ear for a telling, revelatory phrase—could combine with the anthropologist's under-standing of cultural meanings, indigenous rhetoric, and material cul-ture. The playscript, of course, would be subject to continuous modifi-cation during the rehearsal process, which would lead up to an actual performance. At this stage, we would need an experienced director, preferably one familiar with anthropology and with non-Western thea-ter (like Schechner or Peter Brook), and certainly familiar with the social structure and the rules and themes underlying the surface struc-tures of the culture being enacted. There would be a constant back-and-forth movement from anthropological analysis of the ethnography, which provides the details for enactment, to the synthesizing and inte-grating activity of dramatic composition, which would include sequenc-ing scenes, relating the words and actions of the characters to previous and future events, and rendering actions in appropriate stage settings. For in this kind of ethnographic drama, it is not only the individual characters who have dramatic importance but also the deep processes of social life. From the anthropological viewpoint, there is drama indeed in the working out and mutual confrontation of sociocultural processes. Sometimes, even, the actors on the stage almost seem puppets on proces-sual strings.

Students of anthropology could also help drama students during rehearsal itself, if not by direct participation, at least in the role of *Dramaturg*, a position founded by Lessing in eighteenth-century Ger-many and defined by Richard Hornby as "simply a literary advisor to the [theater] director" (1977:63). Hornby and Schechner envision the *Dramaturg* as a sort of structuralist literary critic who carries on his research through a production rather than merely in his study (ibid. 197–99). But the anthropological *Dramaturg* or *Ethnodramaturg* is not so much concerned with the *structure* of the playscript (itself a definite move from ethnography to literature) as with the fidelity of that script to both the described facts and the anthropological analysis of the structures and processes of the group. Incidentally, I am not calling for a mandatory exclusion of anthropologists from the acting role! Indeed, I think that participation in this role would significantly enhance anthropologists' "scientific" understanding of the culture being studied in this dynamic fashion, for human science is concerned, as we have said, with "man alive." But I am aware of the evasiveness and voyeurism of my kind—which we rationalize as "objectivity." Perhaps we need a little more of the disciplined abandonment that theater demands! However, as second best, we can settle for the role of *Ethnodramaturg*.

The movement from ethnography to performance is a process of pragmatic reflexivity. Not the reflexivity of a narcissistic isolate moving among his or her memories and dreams, but the attempt of representatives of one generic modality of human existence, the Western historical experience, to understand "on the pulses," in Keatsian metaphor, other modes hitherto locked away from it by cognitive chauvinism or cultural snobbery.

Historically, ethnodramatics is emerging just when knowledge is being increased about other cultures, other world views, other life styles; when Westerners, endeavoring to trap non-Western philosophies, dramatics, and poetics in the corrals of their own cognitive constructions, find that they have caught sublime monsters, Eastern dragons who are lords of fructile chaos, whose wisdom makes our cognitive knowledge look somehow shrunken, shabby, and inadequate to our new apprehension of the human condition.

Cartesian dualism has insisted on separating subject from object, us from them. It has, indeed, made voyeurs of Western man, exaggerating sight by macro- and micro-instrumentation, the better to learn the structures of the world with an "eye" to its exploitation. The deep bonds between body and mentality, unconscious and conscious thinking, species and self have been treated without respect, as though irrelevant for analytical purposes.

The reflexivity of performance dissolves these bonds and so creatively democratizes: as we become on earth a single noösphere, the Platonic cleavage between an aristocracy of the spirit and the "lower or foreign orders" can no longer be maintained. To be reflexive is to be at once one's own subject and direct object. The poet, whom Plato rejected from his *Republic*, subjectivizes the object, or, better, makes intersubjectivity the characteristically postmodern human mode.

It is perhaps perfectly natural that an anthropology of performance should be moving to meet dramatic performers who are seeking some of their theoretical support from anthropology. With the renewed emphasis on society as a process punctuated by performances of various kinds, there has developed the view that such genres as ritual, ceremony, carnival, festival, game, spectacle, parade, and sports event may constitute, on various levels and in various verbal and nonverbal codes, a set of intersecting metalanguages. The group or community does not merely "flow" in unison at these performances, but, more actively, tries to understand itself in order to change itself. This dialectic between "flow" and reflexivity characterizes performative genres: a successful performance of any transcends the opposition between spontaneous and self-conscious patterns of action.

If anthropologists are ever to take ethnodramatics seriously, our discipline will have to become something more than a cognitive game played in our heads and inscribed in—let's face it—somewhat tedious journals. We will have to become performers ourselves, and bring to human, existential fulfillment what have hitherto been only mentalistic protocols. We must find ways of overcoming the boundaries of both political and cognitive structures by dramatistic empathy, sympathy, friendship, even love as we acquire ever deeper structural knowledge in reciprocity with the increasingly self-aware *ethnoi, barbaroi, goyim,* heathens, and marginals in pursuit of common tasks and rare imaginative transcendences of those tasks.

Slowly it comes out from them their beginning to their ending, slowly you can see it in them the nature and the mixtures in them, slowly everything comes out from each one in the kind of repeating each one does in the different parts and kinds of living they have in them, slowly then the history of them comes out from them, slowly then any one who looks well at any one will have the history of the whole of that one. Slowly the history of each one comes out of each one.

Gertrude Stein
Lectures in America

3 LIFE HISTORY AMONG THE ELDERLY: PERFORMANCE, VISIBILITY, AND RE-MEMBERING

BARBARA MYERHOFF

Karl Mannheim observed that "individuals who belong to the same generation, who share the same year of birth, are endowed, to that

Part of the funding for the research on which this paper is based was provided by the National Science Foundation, through the Andrus Gerontology Center of the University of Southern California, in connection with a study of "Ethnicity and Aging." The author's book *Number our days* (New York: E. P. Dutton, 1979) presents a fuller treatment of the subject. All materials quoted from the elderly subjects come from that source. All names of individuals and organizations have been changed.

Special thanks are due to Victor and Edith Turner, Richard Schechner, and Alexander Alland, whose seminar on "Performance and Anthropology" at the Drama Department of New York University in June 1979 provided information and inspiration for many of the ideas discussed here. The 1977 Wenner-Gren Foundation conference coconvened by the author and Barbara Babcock on "Cultural Frames and Reflections: Ritual, Drama and Spectacle" was a critical event in developing some of my interpretations of reflexivity. Gelya Frank provided stimulation and generously shared references and ideas. Naturally, only I am responsible for the views given here. Originally published in *Life course: Integrative theories and exemplary populations,* ed. Kurt W. Back. American Association for the Advancement of Science, Selected Symposium 41, 1980. Copyright © 1980 by the American Association for the Advancement of Science.

extent, with a common location in the historical dimension of the social process" (1969:290). Often, however, membership in a common cohort is background information, like grammatical rules, more interesting to outside analysts than members. Outsiders find and want explanations where the subjects continue unself-consciously in the habits of everyday life. Sometimes conditions conspire to make a generational cohort acutely self-conscious and then they become active participants in their own history and provide their own sharp, insistent definitions of themselves and explanations for their destiny, past and future. They are then knowing actors in a historical drama they script, rather than subjects in someone else's study. They "make" themselves, sometimes even "make themselves up," an activity which is not inevitable or automatic but reserved for special people and special circumstances. It is an artificial and exhilarating undertaking, this self-construction. As with all conspicuously made-up ventures (rituals are perhaps the best example), acute self-consciousness may become destructive, paralyzing actors in a spasm of embarrassed lack of conviction. But occasionally self-consciousness does not interfere with personal and cultural construction; rather it provides another, fuller angle of self-understanding. *Then the subjects know that their knowing is a component of their conduct. They assume responsibility for inventing themselves and yet maintain their sense of authenticity and integrity.* Such people exercise power over their images, in their own eyes and to some extent in the eyes of whoever may be observing them. Sometimes the image is the only part of their lives subject to control. But this is not a small thing to control. It may lead to a realization of personal power and serve as a source of pleasure and understanding in the workings of consciousness. Heightened self-consciousness—self-awareness—is not an essential, omnipresent attainment. It does not always come with age and is probably not critical to well-being. But when it does occur, it may bring one into a greater fullness of being; one may become a more fully realized example of the possibilities of being human. This is not small compensation in extreme old age.

The group described here is such an acutely self-conscious one, making itself up, knowing that this is going on, doing it well, and appreciating the process. This is a subtle but distinctive state of consciousness, revealed in their personal and collective concerns. Many factors enhance this self-consciousness, not the least of which is their sense of bearing what Tamara Hareven calls "generational memories."

She uses this term to refer to "the memories which individuals have of their own families' history, as well as more generational collective memories about their past" (1978). The subjects of this paper are heirs to a set of memories of a culture and society extinguished during the Holocaust. Very old and close to death, they realize that there will be no others after them with direct experience of their natal culture. And because intergenerational continuity has not been sustained, there are no clear heirs to their memories. The old peoples' sense of being memory bearers, carriers of a precious, unique cargo, heightens generational memory and intensifies cohort-consciousness, giving a mission to the group that is at once urgent and at the same time unlikely to be realized. Their machinations to accomplish their task, delivering themselves of their memories, establishing, then making visible their own identities, illuminates several matters: the nature of *performed* individual and collective definitions, the uses and kinds of witnesses needed for these performances, and the nature and uses of memory. *Life histories are seen here as giving opportunities to allow people to become visible and to enhance reflexive consciousness.* For the very old, in this population in particular, this may be construed as work essential to the last stage in the life cycle.

Ethnographic Setting

In 1972 I began an investigation of a group of elderly Jews, immigrants from Eastern Europe, who had lived on their own in an open setting for many years, often two to three decades. During this time they had developed a singularly rich and strong subculture, drawing on their common religious and ethnic past, derived from their lives as children in the *shtetls* and towns whose culture centered around the Yiddish language and the folk tradition known as *Yiddishkeit*. The childhood layer of history was augmented by that of their middle years in the New World, when they worked as unskilled laborers for the most part, toward the goal of giving their children economic advantages, education, and all that was necessary to assure their successful and swift assimilation into American society. The old people retained from this period their patriotism for America and identification with such values as freedom, democracy, and egalitarianism. Most discarded the religious orthodoxy of their parents when they immigrated at the turn of the century, but though often agnostics or atheists, they were strongly identified with cultural or ethnic Judaism. Zionism was a common bond among them, as was Yiddishkeit, and the social-political values expressed by their work as Internationalists, Bundists, Socialists, and trade unionists. These ingredients and experiences were woven together into a motley but sturdy set of practices and ideas adapted to their contemporary circumstances.

These circumstances were harsh. Most of the 4,000 individuals identified by these characteristics lived along the beach front in a transitional and dangerous neighborhood. Nearly all were poor, living on fixed incomes in small rented rooms or apartments, inadequate and overpriced. Transportation in and out of the area was also inadequate. Relatives were distant and dispersed. Children—culturally as well as geographically distant—rarely visited them. Their contacts with all outsiders were attenuated and ceremonial, not a steady part of their everyday life. Few Jewish organizations or individuals gave them much attention or aid; their isolation was extreme. Now in their eighties and nineties, most were frail, often ill but fiercely independent, determined to care for themselves and preserve their autonomy.

Paradoxically the isolation of the old people contributed to the vigor of their improvised subculture. Having been left alone, they were forced to turn to each other for company and abide the considerable ideological differences among them. And with no children around to embarrass with their "greenhorn" ways, they freely revitalized those parts of their tradition that they enjoyed and found valuable, while sloughing off those American customs that did not appeal to them.

The people were bearers of a culture that would die with them, and this was well-known to all. They were an invisible people, marginal to mainstream American society, an impotent group—economically, physically, and politically. This they fought off as well as they could, as relentlessly they struggled to maintain their place in their own community, and when possible, to find a moment's attention from the larger outside world. They knew they were irreplaceable and their consciousness of being the people who remembered a culture destroyed by the Holocaust fed their determination not to be extinguished until the last possible moment. Nevertheless, they knew they would lose in this struggle. Death, impotence, invisibility were omnipresent threats. But the atmosphere in the community was not one of defeat or despair. On the contrary, in it there was intensity and vitality, humor, irony and dignity. Always the people exuded a sense of living meaningful lives.

Despite the evidence of their insignificance offered by the outside world, they were quite clear about their own importance. It is my interpretation that their self-consciousness, promoted by collective performances and private self-narration, their recounting of stories and life histories, influenced and nourished their success as old people.

The focus of the social life of this assembly was a secular Senior Citizen Center—the Aliyah Center—funded and sponsored by a larger umbrella Jewish organization. Officially 250 to 400 people were members, but many more used the Center than joined. This use was intense, and the concept of "voluntary organization" disguises the amount of time and the importance of the Center to its constituents. The programs and services it offered made it possible for many to remain living in an open setting. Daily inexpensive hot meals were available. Social services, ceremonies—secular and religious—celebrations of life crises, classes, and recreation occurred there. Members were a genuine primary group, despite the frequent ruptures and factions among them. The boardwalk which the Center faced was an outdoor extension, almost a village plaza, in which socializing continued before the Center opened and after it closed.

I came to the Center in 1972 to examine ethnicity and aging, as part of a larger study of aging in various cultures, and remained to work there for two years on a full-time basis, and less intensively ever since.

Self-presentation and Performing: Becoming Visible

Cultures include in their work self-presentations to their members. On certain collective occasions, cultures offer interpretations. They tell stories, comment, portray, and mirror. Like all mirrors, cultures are not accurate reflectors; there are distortions, contradictions, reversals, exaggerations, and even lies. Nevertheless, self-knowledge, for the individual and collectivity, is the consequence. These portraits range from delicate and oblique allusions through fully staged dramatic productions in the course of which members embody their place in the scheme of things, their locations in the social structure, their purposes and natures, taking up the questions of who we are and why we are here, which as a species we cannot do without. Such performances are opportunities for appearing, an indispensable ingredient of being itself, for unless we exist in the eyes of others, we may come to doubt even our own existence. Being is a social, psychological construct, made, not given. Thus it is erroneous to think of performances as optional, arbitrary, or merely decorative embellishments as we in Western societies are inclined to do. In this sense, arenas for appearing are essential, and culture serves as a stage as well as mirror, providing opportunities for self- and collective proclamations of being.

Since these constructions are intentionally designed, they are not only reflections of "what is"; they are also opportunities to write history as it should be or should have been, demonstrating a culture's notion of propriety and sense. History and accident are not permitted to be imposed willy-nilly, those badly written, haphazard, incomplete recordings of occurrences that are so unsatisfactory. Rather performances are shaped and groomed justifications, more akin to myth and religion than lists of empty external events we call history or chronicle.[1]

The performative dimension of culture seen most often in rituals, ceremonies, festivals, celebrations, and the like is properly understood as both instrumental and expressive. It blurs our overstated dichotomies between art and science, myth and reality, religion and work, subjective and objective.

The central challenge to such performances is that of conviction. They must play well and persuade players and audiences that what is seen is what is. The virtual magic of "once upon a time," the "willing suspension of disbelief," "the fusion of the lived-in and dreamed-of orders"—these are some of the ways we speak about the capacity to arouse conviction through performance.[2] Because of the active dimension implicit in these forms, persuasion is achieved less by cognition than by emotion and physiology. The extreme employment of the senses in these moments convinces the body, and the mind follows. "Doing is believing" in such cases and "sensory," as opposed to what Langer calls "discursive," symbols are used, because of their extraordinary capacity to make the improbable momentarily beyond question (1960:63–83).

When such performances are successful, we receive experience rather than belief. Then the invisible world is made manifest, whether

---

1. Charlotte Linde distinguishes between "narrative" that implies an evaluative dimension and "chronicle," a list of events that does not imply evaluation (1978).

2. Clifford Geertz speaks of ritual as "the fusion of the dreamed-of and lived-in order" (1973:93–95).

Suzanne Langer uses the term "virtual power" in discussing the capacity of symbols to arouse the imagination and provide an experience of a convincing though invisible reality (1960:138–64).

this is a prosaic affair such as demonstrating the fact of a rearranged social relationship, or a grander, more mysterious presentation involving supernatural beings or principles. In all events the performed order is explicit, realized, and we are *within* it, not left merely to endlessly wonder or talk about it.[3] Any reality is capable of being made convincing if it combines art, knowledge, authentic symbols and rituals, and is validated by appropriate witnesses.

Cultural performances are reflective in the sense of showing ourselves to ourselves. They are also capable of being reflexive, arousing consciousness of ourselves as we see ourselves. As heroes in our own dramas, we are made self-aware, conscious of our consciousness. At once actor and audience, we may then come into the fullness of our human capability—and perhaps human desire—to watch ourselves and enjoy knowing that we know. All this requires skill, craft, a coherent, consensually validated set of symbols, and social arenas for appearing. It also requires an audience in addition to performers. When cultures are fragmented and in serious disarray, proper audiences may be hard to find. Natural occasions may not be offered and then they must be artificially invented. I have called such performances "Definitional Ceremonies," understanding them to be collective self-definitions specifically intended to proclaim an interpretation to an audience not otherwise available.[4] The latter must be captured by any means necessary and made to see the truth of the group's history as the members understand it. Socially marginal people, disdained, ignored groups, individuals with what Erving Goffman calls "spoiled identities," regularly seek opportunities to appear before others in the light of their own internally provided interpretation.

≫

Among the Center members, Definitional Ceremonies were a major part of their collective behavior. Again and again they attempted to show outsiders, as well as each other, who they were, why they mattered, what the nature of their past and present lives was. Many circumstances contributed to the urgency with which they engaged in this activity. Their extreme old age and sense of little time remaining intensified the desire to formulate a presentation of themselves. Added to this was their anguish due to acute neglect. The outside world had turned its eyes away. And their very bodies had abandoned them in terms of

3. For a fuller discussion of the capacity of ritual to redefine social relationships, see Myerhoff and Moore 1977.
4. This notion is derived from Victor Turner's concept of "social dramas" but is used somewhat differently; this is discussed in Myerhoff 1979.

providing evidence of their continuing clear existence. Senses and appetite had dimmed. Wakefulness often merged into dozing. Memory was quixotic and cognitive control irregular. Physical contact with others was sharply limited, because by cultural custom they rarely touched each other save for an occasional ceremonial embrace or when dancing. Sensory deprivation contributed to the blunting of a sharp sense of self and being. Others were needed to affirm not only that their lives mattered but that they were really there at all. This was made hideously plain not long ago when a bicyclist on the boardwalk struck and killed one of the old women. He said, "I didn't see her," though onlookers agreed she had been standing directly before him and he seemed to be looking directly at her. It was as though she was not a real presence.

Attention was the scarce good in the community. Everyone competed for it with astonishing fierceness. The sight of a camera or tape recorder, the mere possibility that someone would sit down and listen to them, aroused the members' appetite to have themselves documented. One of the members was heartbroken when she was not elected to the Board of Directors. "How will anyone know I am here?" she asked. If possible, the attention should come from outsiders who were more socially prestigious and therefore more capable of certifying their existence. And if possible, these should be younger people, because peers would soon be gone. Who then would be left to recall their existence? What Sir Thomas Browne said in 1658 is still true. The threat of oblivion is "the heaviest stone that melancholy can throw at a man."

Performance is not merely a vehicle for being seen. Self-definition is attained through it, and this is tantamount to being what one claims to be. "We become what we display," says Mircea Eliade in discussing the transformative power of ritual performances. The imposition of meaning occurs when we select from the myriad possibilities a particular formulation that summarizes and epitomizes. Enactments are intentional, not spontaneous, rhetorical and didactic, taming the chaos of the world, at once asserting existence and meaning.

Meaning and "Re-membering"

The necessity for meaning is probably ubiquitous. In the Center population it was elevated to a passion. The old people were inclined naturally toward self-consciousness by their tradition's emphasis on their unique status as a Chosen People. The historical facts of their lives since the Dispersion from the Holy Land exacerbated this tendency, since Jews have spent so much of their history as pariah peoples surrounded by hostile outsiders. The Holocaust further intensified their awareness of their distinctiveness and promoted among survivors a search through the events of their private and collective lives for an explanation of their destiny. Lifton has suggested that survivors of mass destruction often become "seekers after justice." They carefully examine events for evidence of something aside from chaos to account for their sufferings. Indications of a moral and sane universe become imperative to ward off despair. Sense must be resurrected by means of an explanation. Any disaster becomes more bearable once it is named and conceptualized, once support is found for the belief in the "relatively modest assertion that God is not mad," to paraphrase Bertrand Russell's minimum definition of religion. Lifton speaks of survivors of the Holocaust and of Hiroshima as restoring sanity to themselves through "the formulative effort. Any experience of survival—whether of large disaster or intimate personal loss . . . involves a journey to the edge of the world of the living. The formulative effort, the search for signs of meaning, is the survivor's means of return from that edge" (1967).

The survivors of catastrophe, like the victims of disaster, must account for their escape. Job-like, victims petition the gods to know their sins, asking for explanations as to why they deserved their fate. But we often overlook the fact that those who are not afflicted when all around them are also ask the gods, "Why me?" The sorting through collective and private histories for answers was for some Center old people nearly an obsession, and often exceedingly painful. But the members were committed to it nonetheless. "The one who studies history loses an eye," said Moshe. "The one who does not loses two eyes." More formally, Wilhelm Dilthey says, "Both our fortunes and our own nature cause us pain, and so they force us to come to terms with them through understanding. The past mysteriously invites us to know the closely-woven meaning of its moments" (Hodges 1952:274–75).

Surviving and Survivor's Guilt, then, can serve as transformative agents, taking the base materials of ordinary existence and disaster and working the alchemical miracle upon them until they result in consciousness. The consequence is a development of the capacity to lead an examined life. This includes the construction of an explicable, even moral universe despite crushing external evidence to the contrary. The

Center members had achieved this, and their use of rituals and ceremonies to enliven and interpret daily life was remarkable. Every day, even every minute, was focused in the light of all that had been extinguished and lost. "If we lose ourselves now, if we give up our traditions, if we become like everyone else, then we finish ourselves off. We finish Hitler's work for him," said one of the old women. They felt that they owed living fully to their beloved—always the "best of us"—who had perished. Thus were despair and depression held at bay. The old people also felt a certain sense of triumph at having persisted despite the attempts of so many to extinguish them. Outliving their enemies was a personal accomplishment for which they took responsibility and in which they took pride, flavored often as not by bitterness.

Overcoming physical handicaps and poverty were also moral accomplishments. The ability to remain independent and take care of themselves was closely attended and valued collectively by the elders. Senility and loss of autonomy were more feared than death. Their accomplishments were finely calibrated, nearly inconspicuous to younger, healthy outsiders. Basha succinctly stated her sense of achievement, even power, when she said:

Every morning I wake up in pain. I wiggle my toes. Good. They still obey. I open my eyes. Good. I can still see. Everything hurts but I get dressed. I walk down to the ocean. Good. It's still there. Now my day can start. About tomorrow I never know. After all, I'm eighty-nine. I can't live forever.

Center members' attitudes toward time were colored by extreme age, the closeness of death, their sense of accomplishment at outliving catastrophe, and an often righteous determination to be themselves. They were alone and angry at being alone. They were no longer willing to trouble themselves to please others or pretend to be what they were not. Decorum, grace, and courtesy were not for them. Truth was permitted to this stage of life and as someone put it, "We are just like we've always been, only more so." Time was an issue that flickered in and out of discussions often. On the one hand, the elders felt they had plenty of it, due to their enforced leisure. But on the other, every remaining day counted. This was illustrated by an exchange between some of the members discussing the existence of God.

Nathan: If we start to talk about God now we'll be here for five thousand years. These questions you could keep for posterity.

Sonya: Have you got better to do with your time than sit here and talk? Sadie interrupted and began to talk about her ailments . . . "Even the doctors don't know how I survive. I could list for you all my sicknesses." Nathan retorted: "For *this* we don't have enough time."

Yet one of the Center's leaders, a man of ninety-five, often wrote essays on the proper way to age and use time. His writings included a piece called "Ten Commandments for the Elderly." Gentle irony and a delicate sense of the preciousness of time remaining are apparent. No future exists, so time should be neither rushed nor rigidly saved—the sense is there of fully using what is left but not expecting or demanding more.

Dress neatly and don't try to save your best clothes, because after you leave this world you won't need them anymore. Keep your head up, walk straight, and don't act older than your age. Remember one thing: If you don't feel well, there are many people who are feeling worse. Walk carefully, watching for the green light when crossing. If you have to wait a minute or two, it doesn't make any difference at your age. There is no reason to rush.

Time is abolished not only by myth and dream but occasionally also by memory, for remembering the past fully and well retains it. Life experiences are not swept away as if they had never been. They are rewoven into the present. Memory was problematic very often and forgetfulness experienced as very painful. Forgetting a person, an incident, even a word was often a torment. Shmuel explained the seriousness of this. "You understand, one word is not like another. . . . So when just the word I want hides from me, when before it has always come along very politely when I called it, this is a special torture designed for old Jews."

Memory is a continuum ranging from vague, dim shadows to the most bright vivid totality. At its most extreme form, memory may offer the opportunity not merely to recall the past but to relive it, in all its original freshness, unaltered by intervening change and reflection. All the accompanying sensations, emotions, and associations of the first occurrence are recovered and the past recaptured. Marcel Proust more than anyone analyzed how this process works and how exceedingly precious such moments are. The process does not involve will, volition, or the conscious, critical mind. It cannot be forced. Such moments are gifts, numinous pinpoints of great intensity. Mendilow calls them a "kind of hermetical magic . . . when one is sealed outside of time. The sense of duration is suspended and all of life is experienced as a single moment . . . concentrations of universal awareness, antithetical to the diffuseness of life" (1952:137). Then one's self and one's memories are experienced as eternally valid. Simultaneity replaces sequence, and a sense of oneness with all that has been one's history is achieved.

These moments very often involve childhood memories, and then one may experience the self as it was originally and know beyond doubt that one is the same person as that child, still dwelling within a much-altered body. The integration with earlier states of being surely provides the sense of continuity and completeness that may be counted as an essential developmental task in old age. It may not yield wisdom, the developmental task that Erikson points to as the work of this stage of life.[5] It does give what he would consider ego integrity, the opposite of disintegration.

Freud (1965) suggests that the completion of the mourning process requires that those left behind develop a new reality which no longer includes what has been lost. But judging from the Center members' struggle to retain the past, it must be added that full recovery from mourning may restore what has been lost, maintaining it through incorporation into the present. Full recollection and retention may be as vital to recovery and well-being as forfeiting memories.

Moments of full recollection are often triggered by sensory events —taste, touch, smell. Often physical movements, gestures, and actions —singing, dancing, participation in rituals, prayers, and ceremonies rooted in the archaic past—are also triggers. Actors in the method school use these devices to re-arouse emotions, speaking of this as "kinesthetic memory." The body retains the experiences that may be yielded, eventually and indirectly, to the mind. Often among Center members it was possible to see this at work. In the midst of a song, a lullaby that had been sung to the old person as a child, a dance that seemed to dance the dancer, produced changes in posture, a fluidity of movement or sharply altered countenance in which youthfulness was mysteriously but undeniably apparent. And Center members were articulate about these experiences. One woman described her recovery of herself as a child, with her mother's hands on her unwrinkled face when she blessed the candles, as she had done with her mother decades before.

5. See especially Erikson's discussion of old age in "Reflections on Dr. Borg's life cycle" (1978).

When reciting the ancient prayer for the dead, one old man brought back the entire experience of the original context in which he first heard the prayer. Once more he felt himself a small boy standing close to his father, wrapped snugly in the father's prayer shawl, close against the cold of the bright winter morning, weeping, swaying over an open grave.

To signify this special type of recollection, the term "Re-membering" may be used, calling attention to the reaggregation of members, the figures who belong to one's life story, one's own prior selves, as well as significant others who are part of the story. Re-membering, then, is a purposive, significant unification, quite different from the passive, continuous fragmentary flickerings of images and feelings that accompany other activities in the normal flow of consciousness. The focused unification provided by Re-membering is requisite to sense and ordering. A life is given a shape that extends back in the past and forward into the future. It becomes a tidy edited tale. Completeness is sacrificed for moral and aesthetic purposes. Here history may approach art and ritual. The same impulse for order informs them all. Perhaps this is why Mnemosne, the goddess of Memory among the Greeks, is the mother of the muses. Without Re-membering we lose our histories and our selves. Time is erosion, then, rather than accumulation. Says Nabokov in his autobiography, ". . . the beginning of reflexive consciousness in the brain of our remotest ancestor must surely have coincided with the dawning of the sense of time" (1966:21).

The process is the same when done in individual lives or by a culture or a generational cohort. Private and collective lives, properly Re-membered, are interpretative. Full or "thick description" is such an analysis. This involves finding linkages between the group's shared, valued beliefs and symbols, and specific historical events. Particularities are subsumed and equated with grander themes, seen as exemplifying ultimate concerns. Then such stories may be enlarged to the level of myth as well as art—sacred and eternal justifications for how things are and what has happened. A life, then, is not envisioned as belonging only to the individual who has lived it but it is regarded as belonging to the World, to Progeny who are heirs to the embodied traditions, or to God. Such Re-membered lives are moral documents and their function is salvific, inevitably implying, "All this has not been for nothing."

The extraordinary struggle of Survivors to recount their histories is explicable in this light. Again and again concentration camp literature describes inmates' determination to come back and tell the living their stories. This is seldom with the expectation of bringing about reform or repentance. It is to forge a link with the listener, to retain one's past, to find evidence of sense—above all it is an assertion of an unextinguished presence. The redemption provided by Re-membering is well understood by the storyteller Elie Wiesel who struggled back from hell to recount the voyage. In the dedication of his book on Hasidism (1973) he says:

> My father, an enlightened spirit, believed in man.
> My grandfather, a fervent Hasid, believed in God.
> The one taught me to speak, the other to sing.
> Both loved stories.
> And when I tell mine, I hear their voices.
> Whispering from beyond the silenced storm.
> They are what links the survivor to their memory.

A young actress, Leeny Sack, working with the histories of her parents as concentration camp survivors has recently developed a theater piece. The recurrent phrase that punctuates her narrative begins, "My father told me to tell you this. . . ." The substance was unbearable, but she explained the only pain worse than recollection was the pain of considering the possibility that the stories would be untold.[6] His anguish, we may assume, was assuaged by capturing his daughter as audience and giving her the task of transmitting his account. The usual feelings aroused in the teller are gratitude and relief.

A student working with one of the Center members noted this when she completed a series of life history sessions with one of the old women. The old woman was illiterate and completely alone. She never envisioned an opportunity to find a proper listener. When the project was complete, the younger woman thanked the older profoundly, having been exceptionally moved by the older woman's strength, the range of her struggles, her determination to rise to the challenges of her life. The older woman declined the thanks saying, "No, it is I who thank you. Every night before I fall asleep here on my narrow bed, I go over my life. I memorize it, in case anyone should ask."

The prospect of death for many of these elderly was often less

---

6. Ms. Sack presented her work-in-progress (not yet titled) to a session of the seminar on "Performance and Anthropology," conducted by Richard Schechner at New York University, June 1979.

fearsome than that of dying without having had an opportunity to unburden themselves of their memories. Their stories did not have to be complete or accurate. They realized that younger listeners who could pass them on would not be capable of comprehending what they had not lived through. But the mere remembering that there had been a history, a people, a culture, a story, would suffice. Characteristically, Shmuel made this point by telling a story. He recounted a parable concerning the founder of Hasidism, the Baal Shem Tov.

When the great Hasid, Baal Shem Tov, the Master of the Good Name, had a problem, it was his custom to go to a certain part of the forest. There he would light a fire and say a certain prayer, and find wisdom. A generation later, a son of one of his disciples was in the same position. He went to that same place in the forest and lit the fire but he could not remember the prayer. But he asked for wisdom and it was sufficient. He found what he needed. A generation after that, his son had a problem like the others. He also went to the forest, but he could not even light the fire. "Lord of the Universe," he prayed, "I could not remember the prayer and I cannot get the fire started. But I am in the forest. That will have to be sufficient." And it was.
Now, Rabbi Ben Levi sits in his study with his head in his hands. "Lord of the Universe," he prays, "look at us now. We have forgotten the prayer. The fire is out. We can't find our way back to the place in the forest. We can only remember that there was a fire, a prayer, a place in the forest. So, Lord, now that must be sufficient."

Upon completing a recording of his life history, Shmuel reflected on what it meant for him to face his death knowing his recollections of an entire way of life would be lost. His town in Poland that he had loved in his childhood no longer existed; it was destroyed in the Holocaust.

. . . It is not the worst thing that can happen for a man to grow old and die. But here is the hard part. When my mind goes back there now, there are no roads going in or out. No way back remains because nothing is there, no continuation. Then life itself, what is its worth to us? Why have we bothered to live? All this is at an end. For myself, growing old would be altogether a different thing if that little town was there still. All is ended. So in my life, I carry with me everything—all those people, all those places, I carry them around until my shoulders bend.

. . . Even with all that poverty and suffering, it would be enough if the place remained, even old men like me, ending their days, would find it enough. But when I come back from these stories and remember the way they lived is gone forever, wiped out like you would erase a line of writing, then it means another thing altogether to me to accept leaving this life. If my life goes now, it means nothing. But if my life goes, with my memories, and all that is lost, that is something else to bear.

The Life History Classes

Not long after I began my work in the Center, I began to look for some appropriate means of reciprocating the members for the time they spent with me often talking about what I wanted to learn. It was soon evident that providing them with an opportunity to be heard, to recount their histories and tell stories, was ideal. This would constitute another arena in which they could appear in their own terms, and I would serve as audience, conspicuously listening and documenting what was said. I hoped also that some satisfaction would come to them from listening to each other in formal circumstances, that they would validate one another's accounts, and at the same time stimulate and encourage each other's memories. These hopes were fully realized in the form of a set of "Living History" sessions, as the members called them. Members were invited to attend "a class" that met for two hours or more each week. The series ran five months, broke for the summer and resumed for four months. Before long a rather stable group of about twenty people formed itself and attended regularly.

There were few rules. People were required to abstain from interrupting each other. Everyone would have some time to speak at each session, even briefly. Any content was acceptable. I reinforced the appropriateness of anyone's offerings, discouraging the members from challenging the speakers on matters of accuracy. The content discussed varied greatly but loosely fell into four categories: Being Old, Life in the Old Country, Being a Jew, Life in America. In time, peoples' offerings grew more emotionally varied and less guarded. They brought in dreams, recipes, questions about ultimate concerns, folk remedies, book reports, daily logs, and the like. I encouraged them to keep journals, providing notebooks and pens, and many did so with considerable pleasure.

The Life History sessions paralleled the Definitional Ceremonies in their presentational format. They were intended to persuade, and enactments were inserted as often as possible. Illustrations of points people wanted to make were taken to class in the form of objects. They brought mementos, gifts, plaques, awards, certificates, letters, publications, and photographs from all periods of their and their families' lives. One woman brought her sick husband who had grown senile and could no longer speak coherently. She spoke for him, recounting his stories, and along with them, the place he had filled in her life. Another woman brought her retarded grandson "to show you what I am talking about when I tell you about him." He was a kind of badge of honor, for she handled him with dignity and patience, an injury transcended but for which she wanted credit. Still another man brought in a yellow felt star bearing the word "Jude." It circulated throughout the room in silence. Words were not needed. The star dramatized a major facet of his existence. A number of the women regularly brought in food, demonstrating their claimed skills as cooks. Songs were sung, and from time to time there was dancing. Poems were recited frequently in many languages, demonstrations of erudition and memory. Learned quotations, of Marx and Talmud, folk and fine literature also adorned peoples' accounts. The sessions, then, were not merely verbal. Insofar as possible they were made into performances. People displayed the qualities they wanted seen as much as they could and became what they displayed.

The importance of storytelling and a strong oral tradition among the Center members were significant factors in accounting for the vitality of the Life History sessions. Though profoundly literate, the oral tradition among Jews is also highly developed, particularly in those exposed to Hasidism. The recognition that words spoken aloud to another person have particular power is a notion that weaves in and out of Jewish culture. Shmuel spoke of the esteem for the "wonder rebbes," the Hasidic teachers who traveled from one town to another in Eastern Europe.

Oh the stories they would tell us, full of wisdom, full of humor. It was immense. . . . All of us, little boys by the dozens, would follow them when they came into the town. You could always tell them by the chalk on their caftans, this they carried to mark around them a circle of chalk that would keep out the spirits. My father did not approve of me listening to them, but I would sneak out whenever I could, because what they brought you was absolutely magic. This experience was developing in me a great respect for telling stories. This is why it is important to get just the right attitude and just the right words for a story. You should get everything just right because no matter how pleasant, it is a serious thing you are doing.

The sessions were not cosmetic. Catharsis occurred but often more than that. Re-evaluations were clearly being undertaken, too. Having witnesses to this work proved essential. The elders found it hard to convince themselves of the validity of their interpretations without some consensus from the listeners. In time, they became better listeners. Though they knew their audience of peers was going to die out with them, members of the same generational cohorts have advantages as witnesses. They knew the reality being discussed through direct experience. Less had to be explained and described to them, but the work of persuasion was often all the more difficult because deception was less likely to be successful. When Jake quoted his father to demonstrate the latter's wisdom, one of the members promptly corrected him. "This you are getting not from your father. It comes from Sholom Aleichem." "And don't you think Sholom Aleichem learned anything from ordinary people?" he persisted. But no one was impressed.

>

A story told aloud to progeny or peers is, of course, more than a text. It is an event. When it is done properly, presentationally, its effect on the listener is profound, and the latter is more than a mere passive receiver or validator. The listener is changed. This was recognized implicitly by Rabbi Nachman of Bratzlav who ordered that all written records of his teachings be destroyed. His words must be passed from mouth to ear, learned by and in heart. "My words have no clothes," he said. "When one speaks to one's fellows there arises a simple light and a returning light." The impact of the stories told by the old people to outsiders who would stop to listen was consistently striking. Among those old people embarked in the deep and serious work of Re-membering, struggling toward self-knowledge and integration, it was especially clear that something important was going on. Sensitive young people, students, and grandchildren, often found themselves fascinated by the old people's life histories. The sociological shibboleth that claims in a rapidly changing society the elderly have nothing more to teach must be reconsidered. Anyone in our times struggling toward wholeness, self-knowledge based on examined experience, and clarity about the worth of the enterprise exerts a great attraction on those searching for clarity. In the company of elders such as these, listeners perform an essential service. But they get more than they give, and invariably grow from the contact.

When the sessions were at their best, the old people were conscious of the importance of their integration work, not only for themselves but for posterity, however modestly represented. Then they felt the high satisfaction of being able to fulfill themselves as individuals as Exemplars of a tradition at once. Then they were embodiments of the shared meanings—true Ancestors—as well as individuals in full possession of their past. Rachel described such a moment most eloquently when she talked about what the sessions had meant to her.

All these speeches we are making reminded me of a picture I have from many years ago, when we were still in Russia. My brother had been gone already two years in America. I can see my mother like it is before me, engraved in my head. A small house she goes out of in wintertime, going every morning in the snow to the post office, wrapped up in a shawl. Every morning there was nothing. Finally, she found a letter. In that letter was written, "Mamalch, I didn't write to you before because I didn't have nothing to write about." "So," she says, "why didn't you write and tell me?"

You know this group of ours reminds me of that letter. When I first heard about this group, I thought to myself, "What can I learn? What can I hear that I don't know, about life in the Old Country, of the struggles, the life in the poor towns, in the bigger towns, of the rich people and the poor people? What is there to learn, I'm eighty-eight, that I haven't seen myself?" Then I think, "What can I give to anybody else? I'm not an educated woman. It's a waste of time."

That was my impression. But then I came here and heard all those stories. I knew them, but you know it was laid down deep, deep in your mind, with all those troubles mixed. You know it's there but you don't think of it, because sometimes you don't want to live in your past. Who needs all these foolish stories?

But finally, this group brought out such beautiful memories, not always so beautiful, but still all the pictures came up. It touched the layers of the kind that it was on those dead people already. It was laying on them like layers, separate layers of earth, and all of a sudden in this class I feel it coming up like lava. It just melted away the earth from all those people. It melted away, and they became alive. And then to me it looked like they were never dead.

Then I felt like the time my mother got that letter. "Why don't you come and tell me?" "Well, I have nothing to say," I think. But I start to say it and I find something. The memories come up in me like lava. So I felt I enriched myself. And I am hoping maybe I enriched somebody else. All this, it's not only for us. It's for the generations.

Part Two

Visualizing Experience

My new conception of the film is based upon the idea that the intellectual and emotional processes which so far have been conceived of as existing independently of each other—art versus science—and forming an antithesis heretofore never united, can be brought together to form a synthesis on the basis of CINEDIALECTIC, a process that only the cinema can achieve. A spectator can be made to feel-and-think what he sees on the screen. The scientific formula can be given the emotional quality of a poem. And whether my ideas on this matter are right or wrong, I am at present working in this direction (from a speech given by Sergei Eisenstein at the Sorbonne —quoted by Brody 1930).

4 ETHNOGRAPHY AS TROMPE L'OEIL: FILM AND ANTHROPOLOGY[1]

JAY RUBY

The sentiment expressed in this quotation exemplifies the issue I wish to explore in this essay. Eisenstein wanted to develop a cinematic form that would imbue content with a Marxist ideology. He was not the first or last Marxist to hypothesize that the medium had this potential. From Dziga Vertov to Jean-Luc Godard, many filmmakers have tried to create a revolutionary cinema.[2] In an analogous manner, anthropologists since 1896 (e.g., Regnault) have advocated a visual anthropology (cf. Ruby 1975 for a more detailed discussion of the relationship between a revolutionary and an anthropological cinema). Neither has met with much success.

1. Some of the ideas presented in this paper have appeared in a more extended form in earlier publications. See Ruby 1976, 1977, 1980.
2. Cinema is used here to stand for all the socio-cultural processes and events surrounding the production and consumption of film.

In this essay I would like to convert Eisenstein's conception from one of unwieldy magnitude to a manageable problem. I will therefore seek to explore the following seemingly paradoxical question: Why is it that anthropologists were among the first social scientists to examine the potential of the motion picture and yet a visual anthropology has played only a minor role in the development of anthropological thinking?

It seems to me that there are two possible explanations for the paradox: (1) There is something "inherently" unscientific about pictorial media, that is, film is, by its very nature, an art form; or (2) Our culturally conditioned assumptions have prevented us from exploring the potential of these media.

While it may be commonplace to talk about the "art" of the film, to restrict film to being exclusively an art form, that is, to insist that audiences pay primary attention to the syntactics of a film as a sign event, is premature because there is no evidence to support the position. To make an analogy, it is equivalent to restricting writing to poetry. On the other hand, most people do have aesthetic expectations when they view a film—regardless of its stated intent—and these expectations do pose a problem for the anthropological filmmaker.

Furthermore, our cultural assumptions create additional problems. These assumptions are situated within the folk models of art and science that pervade our culture and serve as the basis for the two most common film theories—Realist and Formative (cf. Andrews 1976 for a more detailed discussion of film theory). Given the alternatives of regarding film either as an expression of emotion, feeling, and art (The Formative) or as a surrogate for reality and the most accurate means for data collection (The Realist), most anthropologists have chosen to use the printed word to communicate their ideas. Hence the lack of an anthropological cinema and the virtual absence of professional filmmakers who are also professional anthropologists.

These culturally conditioned interpretive strategies for making sense out of a film—one strategy leading us to make inferences about film as art, as aesthetic object, and as fictionalized fantasy designed to amuse us, and a second causing us to deal with film as a document of reality that should be unbiased, objective and truthful—are at odds with what might be called a fundamental purpose of an anthropological communication, namely, to make scientific/humanistic statements about culture.

The strategies have their origins in the basic Western idea of the dichotomy. This dichotomy is formulated in pairs like art and science; mind and body; thought and feeling; cognition and emotion; and objectivity and subjectivity. It produced the opposition of realist versus formative in film theory and leads most people to assess films as being understandable either as fiction, that is, made-up fantasy, or as documentary, that is, real and truthful.

Stated in the terminology suggested by Worth and Gross (1974), films are interpreted either as natural sign events[3] that are assumed to exist with meanings assigned on the basis of attribution, or as symbolic articulations created so that meaning can be inferred from them.

To make an attribution, one makes an assumption that a particular sign-event is natural and existential, that is, the sign-event just happened to be there. Meaning is then assigned to such a sign-event by attributing to it characteristics associated with similar sign-events or with socio-cultural or psychological stereotypes of such events. For example, one is shown a photograph of an oak tree and responds to it by saying, "That's a beautiful tree." If asked why, and the response is, "It's beautiful because it's an oak tree, and oak trees are beautiful," then the viewer is attributing to the photograph what he or she knows and feels about oak trees. The interpreter, in this case, is interpreting not a photograph but a tree.

To make an inference about a sign-event, one begins by making an assumption of intention. One assumes that someone created the sign-event; that it was organized, structured, put together on purpose. One can discuss the purpose but only after the assumption of intention is granted. Meaning is assigned on the basis of a variety of socio-cultural conventions assumed to apply to the particular structure one recognizes. Not only does one infer from existing conventions of structure about persons, places, and events in general, but one uses the particular structures that apply to particular media and modes of communication. To return to the photograph of the oak tree, if one says that the photograph is beautiful because the photographer back-lit the tree, and back-lit trees are supposed to be beautiful or "art," then one is making an inference. Note that the viewer making the inference from a photograph doesn't have to guess whether or not the photographer thought backlighting

3. Sign-event is used here to mean an organized group of signs—signs that are syntactically related and clearly delineated or framed in a way that sets them apart from other sign-events.

was beautiful. He knows the convention and assumes an intentional backlighting.

It should be emphasized that this model attributes no intrinsic meaning to the signs themselves. They are polysemic. The perceiver assigns meaning either by assuming existence and therefore attributing meaning to the sign-event, or by assuming intention and inferring meaning from the sign-event.

For our purposes, this suggests that films are interpreted either as natural sign-events that are assumed to exist and have meaning assigned on the basis of attribution, or as symbolic articulations created so that meaning can be inferred from them.

The range of inferential and attributional paradigms currently employed in our culture to assign meaning to films appears to be limited. I have suggested elsewhere (Ruby 1976) that when we infer from a film, we employ the conventions of art and deal with a film as an aesthetic object, that is, the sign-events are regarded as having primarily a syntactical significance. When we attribute to films, we assume they are "documents of reality" interpreted in the same way we would interpret the reality the films are thought to mirror.

The film as an aesthetic object need not be discussed at length. It should be obvious that the canons of science and not art are assumed to govern an anthropological communication. Therefore, if the most prevalent inferential system available for the construction of meaning for film is based on aesthetic criteria, we must look elsewhere, since a paradigm of science is more appropriate for an anthropological film.

If we dismiss an inferential strategy that causes us to regard film as art, we are led to an attributional strategy that causes us to see film as a record of the real world. In this schema a viewer attributes to the film what he or she knows about the events, objects, and persons depicted. The film as document becomes transparent—a mere conveyer of the content. Many documentary and ethnographic filmmakers thus assume that meaning resides in the world, that events and people can speak for themselves (that is, communicate meaning through the film without the interpretive aid of the filmmaker), and that the role of the filmmaker is to unobtrusively record this reality.

Employing attributions to understand an anthropological film leads viewers to meanings antithetical to anthropology for two basic reasons: (1) the use of attributional systems is based on a theory of perception counter to the idea that culture organizes experience; and (2) the folk models underlying attributions are ethnocentric.

The belief that film can be an unmediated record of the real world is based on the idea that cameras, not people, take pictures and the naive empiricist notion that the world is as it appears to be.

The former concept, already examined by Byers (1966), reflects a profound navieté about the physio-chemical process of picture taking. The latter and more fundamental supposition presupposes a theory of visual perception called phenomenal absolutism that has been discredited at least since the work by Segall, Campbell and Herskovits (1966) on the effect of culture on visual perception. It is not feasible to present a detailed refutation of these positions here. I will simply assert that the camera creates a photographic realism reflecting the culturally constructed reality of the picture-taker and is not a device that can somehow transcend the photographer's cultural limitations. We cannot capture reality on film, but we can construct a set of images consistent with our view of it.

The argument against making attributions has a second thrust, namely, that the folk models available for the construction of these attributions are ethnocentric. Most anthropological studies deal with cultures foreign to the experience of the viewer. The characteristics commonly attributed to exotic people are based on either the folk model of the Noble Savage—the Rousseauian, invincible, ignorant, natural man—or the Primitive—underdeveloped, culturally deprived, illiterate beast who is sorely in need of the benefits of civilization. Both models are obviously inappropriate.

Is the logical conclusion, then, that it is impossible to generate anthropological meaning from a film? Are anthropologists wasting their time taking pictures? If that were my conclusion, I would have not written this essay. One solution to the quest for an anthropological cinema may be found in the general shift in cultural attitudes toward being publicly self-aware or reflexive; the recognition of the social construction of reality; and the associated changes in science, anthropology, film, and communication.

I have suggested elsewhere (Ruby 1980) that being reflexive in public has now become respectable. I believe there is a growing realization that the world is not what it appears to be, and that what you don't know will and often does hurt you. People now want to know who made it and what's in it before they buy anything—aspirin, cars, television news, or education. We no longer trust the people who make things to be of good will. Ralph Nader, the consumer protection movement, laws requiring financial disclosures by political figures, truth in lending and truth in advertising laws are all part of this felt need. The naive empiricism that pervaded our society and dominated nineteenth-century social science is being eroded. We are moving away from the positivist notion that meaning resides in the world, and that human beings should strive to discover the inherent, immutable, and objectively true reality (Stent 1975). We are beginning to realize that human beings construct and impose meaning on the world. We create order. We don't discover it.

The consequences of these changes are far reaching and interrelated and can be seen in science in general and anthropology in particular. They are reflected in the public acknowledgment of the scientist's role in the process of scientific investigation; the limitations of science as an epistemology; and the need to explicate clearly the methods employed in any scientific inquiry and to see them as a process integral to the products of science.

A convenient marker for this change is the 1962 publication of Kuhn's *The Structure of Scientific Revolutions*. Kuhn recognized that scientific knowledge is the product of a particular paradigm, and that science changes through the process of discovery of the inadequacy of the old paradigm and the subsequent construction of a new one. Labrot has said (1977:7):

Science is not static. Its development is determined to a great extent by the body of science as it stands at any given moment. This determinism is not one of a natural progression to a greater and greater number of known facts built on those previously discovered. It is rather one in which the fundamental principles, the structures in a broad sense, determine the nature of search for the facts and finally, to some extent, the facts themselves. So science which describes the world, also determined the world which it describes.

My position in this essay is that the paradigm of Positivism is insufficient to deal with questions now being asked. We need a new paradigm—in science in general and in anthropology in particular—one that will allow us to examine the symbolic environments (culture) people have constructed and the symbolic system (anthropology) we have constructed.

Within anthropology the foundations for this new paradigm already exist. I will mention only two of the sources: Clifford Geertz and Margaret Mead. From Geertz (1973a) comes the notion of anthropology as an interpretive science and ethnography as "thick description" in which data and theory cannot be separated; theory instead is regarded as the origin of data generation. (In other words, one regards data not as a property of entities but rather as an artifact of the questions one is researching.) From Mead (1976:908) we obtain a resolution of the science versus humanities conflict through the development of human science capable of accommodating both quantitative and qualitative knowledge:

It is in the sciences of living things that we find the greatest confusion but also the clearest demonstrations of the ways in which the two kinds of observation —human beings by human beings and physical nature by human beings—meet. One group of students of living beings have attempted to adopt as far as possible the methods of the physical sciences through the use of controlled experiments, the deliberate limitation of the number of variables to be considered, and the construction of theories based on the findings arrived at by these means. The other group, taking their cues from our human capacity to understand through the observation of natural situations, have developed their methods from a natural history approach in which the principal reliance is on the integrative powers of the observer of a complex, nonreplicable event and on the experiments that are provided by history and by animals living in a particular ecological setting. . . . I would argue that it is not by rejecting one or the other but by appropriately combining the several methods evolved from these different types of search for knowledge that we are most likely in the long run to achieve a kind of scientific activity that is dominated neither by the arrogance of physical scientists nor by the arrogance of humanists who claim that the activities which concerned them cannot meaningfully be subjected to scientific inquiry.

These ideas are the foundation of an anthropology that is a humanistic and interpretive science of humankind, a science that accepts the inherently reflexive relationship between the producer, process, and product, a science founded on the idea that

Facts do not organize themselves into concepts and theories just by being looked at; indeed, except within the framework of concepts and theories, there are no scientific facts but only chaos. There is an inescapable *a priori* element in all scientific work. Questions must be asked before answers can be given. The questions are an expression of our interest in the world; they are at bottom valuations. Valuations are thus necessarily already involved at the stage when we observe facts and carry on theoretical analysis, and not only at the stage when we draw political inferences from facts and valuations (Myrdal 1969:ix–xvi).

Logically this point of view causes one to regard anthropology as "not only a general set of general statements about mankind, it is also the product of a particular culture with its history of ideas proper to itself; its formulations are culturally committed and in major part determined" (Krader 1968:885). When it is recognized that anthropologists ask research questions based on their overt theoretical positions and their less conscious cultural assumptions, and that when the questions are asked in a particular way, there is a logical way to generate data and an equally logical way to present the analytic descriptions called ethnographies, then the necessity of publicly disclosing the entire process becomes inescapable, and the phrase "reflexive anthropology" becomes redundant.

The implications of this general shift in consciousness for communication have already been partially discussed in terms of Worth and Gross's ideas about inference and attribution. They suggest that communication is "a social process, within a context in which signs are produced and transmitted, perceived and treated as messages from which meaning can be inferred" (1974:30). The implication is that all forms of human communication are motivated and ideologically based within the culturally conditioned expectations of what messages can occur in which contexts.

An application of this model to film produces some interesting results. If one regards film as communication, or more precisely, as an articulatory medium used for communicative purposes, it is possible to posit a range of filmic discourses—some of which are intentionally constructed to be regarded as art and others to be regarded as science. Given this perspective, the "film as art" model becomes transformed and contextualized as the aesthetic component of the communicative process, or, to put it in a semiotic framework, the syntactic elements of the sign-event.

If it is acknowledged that film has the potential for a variety of discourses, that it can have a variety of voices, the concepts of "film as art" and "film as documentary truth"—the foundations of Realist and Formative theory—can be seen not as a dichotomy but as having a dialectical relationship and, therefore, as a stage in the historical development of film. This false dichotomy of film as aesthetically satisfying experience versus film as the objective revelation of truth should be recognized as the product of a particular ideological structure called positivism.

Seeing these two approaches to film in a dialectical relationship makes it possible to construct the synthesis: a theory of film and the accompanying interpretive strategy that reflects the general change in self-awareness and the new paradigm of science discussed earlier.

The origin of the synthesis can be found in the re-emergence of the idea of film as a language. First proposed by Eisenstein in the 1930s, there has been a recent swell of interest in linguistic paradigms for interpreting film, probably the result of the growing popularity of structural linguistics and semiotics. In spite of the cine-structuralists' initial enthusiasm, semiotics is not producing the breakthroughs we had hoped for. If film is a language, it is unlike any other language known, since it does not respond to linguistic analysis.

Whether it is possible to construct a science of signs that is not so heavily dependent upon linguistic models—a semiotic that deals with all sign systems without making the automatic assumption of the primacy of language—remains unclear at this time. In any case, it is necessary to separate the idea of film as a communication system from the idea of film as a language. Language is only one variety of communication.

Film semiotics and cine-structuralism with all of their limitations do represent an attempt to break from the Realist/Formative dichotomy. Because this approach deals with film as a construction of culturally coded signs, it provides a basis for the development of the synthesis of Realist and Formative into a theory of film as communication, in which sign-events (films) can be organized to emphasize the syntactic (aesthetic), the semantic (informational), or the pragmatic (the call to action) elements.

Such a theoretical structure would allow for the construction of an ethnographic *trompe l'oeil* for film: the development of filmic codes and conventions to "frame" or contextualize the apparent realism of the cinema and cause audiences to "read" the images as anthropological articulations. Once constructed, it will be possible to explore the consequences of transforming abstract thoughts, such as theories or models, into images. The exploration can shed light on both the nature of anthropological thinking and the potential for images to communicate ideas.

I am obviously using the term *trompe l'oeil* metaphorically. According to Webster's *Third International Dictionary, trompe l'oeil* is the "deception of the eye, especially by a painting as (a) the intensification of the reality of component objects in an unnaturally arranged still life through the use of minute detail and the careful rendition of tactile and tonal values . . ." (quoted in Mastai 1975:8–9). In a still life the painter attempts to create a tension between the aesthetic, or, as Webster puts it, "unnatural" arrangements of the parts of the painting—that is, the spatial relationships among the fruit and between the fruit and the bowl —and the painter's ability to realistically portray the fruit and the bowl. The painter strives to produce a temporary illusion that the apples are so real we could pick one up and eat it, while at the same time displaying his compositional skills. Bateson said it well, "Conjurers and painters of the *trompe l'oeil* school concentrate upon acquiring a virtuosity whose only reward is reached after the viewer detects that he has been deceived and is forced to smile or marvel at the skill of the deceiver. Hollywood filmmakers spend millions of dollars to increase the realism of a shadow" (1972:182).

The parallel with the anthropological filmmaker is striking. If we grant Susan Sontag's (1977) notion that the apparent realism of photo-graphic reproduction is its greatest achievement and gravest danger, it can be argued that the anthropological filmmaker has to contextualize the realistic effect of film as merely an illusion by making overt the theoretical basis of the construction of the image. The tension between the indexical resemblance of the film sign-event to its referents, which causes people to attribute meaning to the film, and the ideological con-struction of the film, which causes people to infer meaning from the film, must be made overt, explicit, and unavoidable. It is essential that audiences understand the differences between the images we make of what people do and what people say they do, and what we interpret both to mean.

Audiences can have the pleasure of the illusion that they are par-ticipating in something they are actually watching so long as we make it very clear to them that they are seeing a representation we have constructed because we were motivated to present them with our view of the world. In an anthropological film we never see the world through the eyes of the native, but if we are lucky we can see the native through the eyes of the anthropologist. The beginnings of such a cinema can already be found in the films of the French anthropological filmmaker Jean Rouch, particularly in his African films—*Jaguar, Petit a Petit,* and *Cocorico, Monsieur Poulet*—in which anthropological interpretation is blended with folk explanations and fantasies in a way that defies the labels of fiction and documentary.

I have tried to suggest in this essay that the conditions are ripe for the development of a cinema of anthropology. It has become increasingly more common and acceptable to be self-aware and to be publicly concerned with integrating one's personal and social selves. We seem ready to accept the idea that science is a limited epistemology and not a religion. There is a growing interest in the implications of reflexivity within anthropology. The boundaries between a positivist-based anthropology and humanistic and artistic expressive forms are being regarded as temporary historical stages rather than rigid barriers. We seem amenable to the idea that anthropology is at its best when we are telling the stories of our experiences to others. Since film allows us to tell stories with pictures, its potential becomes enhanced within a reflexive and narrative anthropology.

5 HOW TO LOOK AT US LOOKING AT THE YANOMAMI LOOKING AT US

ERIC MICHAELS

When ethnography moves off the printed page, it becomes unmoored from its literary origins and biases. We begin to ask questions about the nature of ethnographic investigation, its scientific and ethical basis. Film and video ethnographies are recordings of people and events by audio-visual hardware that bypass the particular complex encoding of observation into print and language. Because science has been associated with literate, articulate analysis, we raise the question: are these visual documents scientific? Because we export the images from their place of origin and package them for consumption by Western audiences, we ask, "Do we have a right to steal these people's images?" At the root of the dilemma is the still undefined term "ethnographic" as applied to nonprint media. The question we raise by rethinking ethnography in this new visual context may ultimately apply to literary ethnography as well.

The ethical question, whether we can justify the appropriation of images, is not necessarily limited to visual images. There is no reason why the appropriation of literary images is more ethical than the appropriation of visuals. Solutions that have been suggested for the ethical problems of literary image appropriation are equally applicable to film and video.

Margaret Mead proposed that we treat the interview, indeed, all fieldwork, as a cooperative venture. In film and video, such cooperation requires restructuring the standard commercial production system. It may also imply a more complex restructuring of the ways in which we distribute and display visual media. The following account of my collaboration with independent video producers is intended to suggest specific ways film and video production and display can be accomplished as a cooperative cross-cultural exchange. The anthropologist's role in this exchange is also altered. Stripped of our notebooks and portable tape recorders, we become dependent on visual media specialists. It is important that we develop models for working relationships with these new image makers.

But are these films and videotapes "scientific?" Can they enter into the ethnographic tradition? Can they be used for comparative analysis? The answer to these questions hinges on the scientific status of ethnography itself, and the answer is beyond the scope of this discussion. A proposed solution would be to make the analytic categories of the visual documentation equivalent to the ethnographic categories developed in literary formats and thereby beg the epistemological question. There are dangers in making film or video into illustrations of textual descriptions; these dangers will be considered and alternative solutions proposed.

While the scholarly community seems no closer to resolving these issues than it was ten years ago, the broadcast and film industries are rapidly advancing into our territory whether we sanction their products or not. An inherent fascination with exotic societies represents a potential market for programs of ethnographic content, which television and film producers currently are cultivating. As tourists invade more and more remote areas, they equip themselves with increasingly sophisticated recording devices. Television series about tribal and small-scale societies proliferate. Whatever images are selected to be broadcast on television will undoubtedly influence the popular imagination, and notions about traditional society will be revised. It is impossible to overstate the effect this will have on the anthropological profession or on the societies that are packaged for the consumption of television viewers.

≫

I became involved in the study of visual imagery as practiced by a particular tribe of New York-based "video artists." My choice of tribe was partly fortuitous (the result of associations made at the 1978 Conference on Visual Anthropology) and partly intuitive. The videotapes Juan Downey, a Chilean artist, showed at that conference were provocative, intelligent, and visually unlike most of what I had previously seen of the documentary genre. Moreover, they were of the Yanomami Indians, a group for whom the Chagnon/Asch films (Chagnon and Asch 1970, 1973) provided a point of comparison. I was particularly impressed by the pervasive differences between the films and the tapes. The fierce people whom Asch recorded in a manner that made my students recoil became transformed into attractive human figures in the Downey tapes. Since I believe a fundamental objective of ethnographic film must be to capture evidence of human diversity without ethnocentric bias, I was determined to discover the source of the difference between these two records. When Downey suggested a collaboration, I began a year of research from which the observations in this essay are drawn.

Mr. Downey spent his first four months in the rain forest much as an anthropologist would, developing word lists from informants, learning interpersonal skills. He was not sure it would be appropriate to tape in this context. When he did bring out his equipment, it was first used in nonrecording capacities: games based on feedback and monitoring distances. His sensitivity may, in part, be traced to a concern with process, as opposed to product, current in certain contemporary art circles. He was interested in involving himself and the Yanomami in a communication process, not in retrieving a product. When he began to tape, the Yanomami acted as directors, suggesting taping events, and forbidding others. Through this interaction, Downey came to appreciate certain features of Yanomami sense of time, event, color, and appropriate subjects for representation. His discoveries in these areas provided a basis for decisions to be made in the editing room, as he directed these tapes toward a further interactive process with a viewing audience.

For twelve months I worked with videotape and transmission in nearly all aspects of production: camerawork, recording, editing and display, scripting, narration, and fundraising. I kept a running record of observations and procedures, since I was both defining the communication process and feeling out a role for the visual anthropologist in these kinds of collaboration. Worth's and Adair's (1972) model of film communication provided an initial theoretical framework, allowing me to separate the process into three describable stages: recording, editing, and display.

Following a brief discussion of portable television, these stages will provide the organizing framework for what follows. However, it should be noted that the application of this model to video may be limited. Film is a product-oriented communication, but video is a transmission event requiring no creation of product/artifact. The video tape recorder is an afterthought in television hardware. The tape is an artifact of a communication, not the communication itself. This means that the potential of the medium can be explored in many ways without even producing a videotape. Video artists, unlike commercial film and television producers, are at least as interested in this essential communication property of video.

A Brief History of Portable Television: Distortion of Information Through One-Way Flow

In the late 1960s, several manufacturers developed a portable video apparatus: the portapack. A handful of artists, communication, and aesthetic theorists immediately saw applications for this technology. Television had been developed in an almost wholly commercial framework. Programs were designed as contexts in which to sell products and therefore catered to certain assumptions about the tastes of mass Western audiences. As the hardware diffused from urban industrial centers to rural areas and nonindustrial countries, the urban programming accompanied it, so that soon, not only was technology, but cultural content imported to the third world.

The dream of the "global village" was actually realized as a global amphitheater, and it was the Western technological societies that were mostly onstage. Corporate manufacturing policies, not limitations of the technology itself, kept nonindustrial and small-scale societies from gaining access to this monopolized theater.

Some artists and theorists, however, recognized that the portapack could be used to retrieve images of nonindustrial society for the Western world and to provide access to the technology to non-Western peoples for purposes the people themselves might determine. It was a curious assortment of artists and philosophers who took their portapacks into the field in the early 1970s, a kind of McLuhan Missionary Society. But unlike missionaries, their intention was not to civilize or school the savages. A very pragmatic attitude prevailed. In the face of inevitable cultural homogenization, perhaps the video camera could help represent and preserve tradition, providing a less obtrusive voice for non-Western peoples than any other cultural borrowing (even print) might entail.

For the most part, these associations between artists and societies became ongoing commitments. Much time was spent in the field, and expeditions produced a kind of delayed feedback loop, in that tapes could be shown from community to community in a given area, providing an electronic newspaper, as well as a record of traditional life.

It has not been possible to open up the airways controlled by Western broadcast monopolies, so the exportation of American culture has not been matched by an importation of these tapes to mass American audiences. But tapes such as these still serve valuable purposes for the communities that participate in their production.

One outcome of this work has been the collection of hundreds of hours of raw videotape of traditional cultures, a catalog of daily life, ritual activity, ceremonial, and mundane events. Access to this material is limited; distribution is almost nonexistent. One of the great rewards of this study for me has been the viewing of this raw tape from several private collections. The raw tape provides an excellent entry point for a description of the work and its distinguishing characteristics.

Raw Tape (Field Recording)

For those trained to look at social content, unedited tape and unedited film look superficially alike. The subjects of Downey's raw tapes are mostly the same as those in the Chagnon/Asch films: shaman activity, hunting, feasting, and manufacture. But there are two important differences: the spatial relation of cameraman to subject and the temporal scope of the taping event.

These differences may be a function either of differences in technology or differences between artists and ethnographers/filmmakers. I believe they primarily are due to differences in the hardware and only secondarily to the practitioner's understanding of his tool. And contrary to current opinion, I see little evidence in raw footage itself that distinguishes between images retrieved in collaboration with anthropologists and those shot by the anthropologically untrained producer.

Video is best recorded in intimate to social distances, which means closeup or medium shots. Video is a low-resolution medium. Electronic impulses do not translate detail as successfully as film. It is better to cover events and activities from a few meters distance at most, giving particular attention to facial expression, small-scale groups, and interactions. The portapack, as its name implies, is compact and easily handled by a single person who can approach an event without needing too many physical or mechanical extensions.

Contrast this to the bulky 16mm film camera, which often must be physically tied to the sound equipment, and which usually requires two or more persons to operate, making movement in personal or intimate spaces particularly obtrusive. But film is a high resolution medium, so it can be used effectively from public or spectator distances (long or telephoto shots). Such distances have the advantage of providing spatial contexts for events. But consider what the communicative value, the metamessage, of these different perspectives might be.

The image of the primitive as exotic is that he is the other; he is out there; he is far away, and only peripherally a member of the human family. I submit that the longer focal length lens associated with film cameras reinforces this notion and provides a voyeuristic perspective. The tendency of video to get up close collapses these communicative distances. If we also consider typical viewing contexts, we realize that television is seen on relatively small screens in private spaces, while film is usually projected in relatively large public auditoriums. Notice that popular television shows use close-up and medium shots when they want to encourage viewer empathy. (In movies, close-ups are monumental and are the signature of the Hollywood star, a shining body at a great distance.)

If we intend to collapse cross-cultural distances to develop empathetic relationships with unfamiliar societies, it seems reasonable to recommend video for this purpose. The least successful solution is, in fact, the one most frequently resorted to: televising film. This places high resolution information, best viewed at public and spectator distances, in a low resolution format intended for intimate and personal spaces.

What the video camera loses in spatial detail is compensated for in the temporal. Video is cheap to make. Tape can be erased and used again. The relative economies of the different media imply significant differences in the retrieval procedures. It is very rare to run movie film continuously. One tries to determine when an event will begin, hope that one can start filming just prior to it, and finish filming soon after the event is determined to be over. This interjects the filmmaker's bias in his expectations of what constitutes a temporal boundary for an event and causes him to miss events he had not anticipated, or start late filming those he had misjudged.

It is quite common, on the other hand, to videotape continuously, even when events are not anticipated. For this reason, I have been able to watch on unedited tape, events as they are organized and framed and then observe the transformation of an event into another or less focused activity. My own (sociolinguistic) understanding of the contexts of events, as well as a reasonable consideration of what occurs during periods of analytically insignificant activity has clarified many questions the film record has not answered. Remarkably, the eerie immediacy of an unanticipated event recorded on video leads filmic-biased viewers to regard certain scenes as staged, since they realize film could not capture, for example, the onset of aggression directed at the cameraman, as in Mr. Downey's tape, "The Singing Mute."

Finally, the simplicity of the portapack from an operator's viewpoint allows the subjects to become involved in taping with relatively little difficulty. The instantaneous feedback of the monitor permits the image to be comprehensible and self-rewarding. Nonrecording feedback loops and games apparently appeal to the Yanomami, who used these systems to monitor visitors to the Shabono. So video becomes more than a recording device and can act as a research tool itself in a variety of experiments in communication. The taping event can easily become a collaboration between subject and object, collapsing dichotomies that plague our work in general, and continually raise ethical and moral questions about ethnographic film in particular.

Editing

Video editing is radically different from film editing. These differences are a result of both the greater flexibility of the video editing system and the express intention of video artists to manipulate images by exploiting the characteristics of electronic technology.

The technical processes are easily distinguished. Film is a photo-chemical process which impresses on the film stock a graphic representation of what the cameraperson sees through his lens. Film editing is a mechanical process, whereby a series of graphic images are juxtaposed into a linear series. The artfulness of film editing is mostly limited to the serial manipulation of already retrieved images.

Videotape, on the other hand, is not a series of graphic impressions, but an electronic coding of information retrieved by the camera. You can't hold videotape to the light and read the image. This electronic quality of video information allows for an astonishing array of operations to be performed in the editing room, since signals can be manipulated electronically for an almost limitless variety of purposes.

Video artists are highly conscious of the unrealized potential of the electronic editing process and are using it to develop video styles that look like video, not an electronic imitation of film.

To experiment with original, video-based techniques is permissable if one is handling nonrepresentational patterns of the sort popularly associated with avant-garde video art. But if one extends these video-based experiments to representational forms, one treads on filmic conventions for documentary which television has borrowed.

Documentary film in general and ethnographic film in particular are highly literal forms of visual representation. Documentary appears to be an evolutionary adaptation of the lecture format to an increasingly visual environment. The lecturer, for example, to late nineteenth-century audiences at the Royal Society might include slides of his travels to accompany his talk. When these travelogues became filmic, the lecturer became a narrator, and with sound movies, he became the sound track. This narrative monologue is considered to be a minimum requirement for informational documentaries. The narrator is an omnipresent, conventionalized figure standing between the audiences and the images. He acts like a priest, mediating meanings and reducing the potential richness, complexity and provocative ambiguity of the images to a linear, doctrinaire message. (An alternative developed by direct cinema, cinema verité, and the like, is the interview as substitute for narrator. But notice that the interview is a byproduct of print journalism involving problems comparable to the narrator format.)

Video artists seem to agree on the inappropriateness of the omnipresent narrator for video nonfiction as do some documentary filmmakers. They explore alternative ways to cause visual materials to yield information. In the case of the Yanomami tapes, Downey explored a complex array of techniques to communicate essentially nonlexical information. Tests performed in the field with both color and black-and-white film, as well as with colored writing implements and native pigments, led him to develop a system of native color categories for the Yanomami. For example, interviews and tests determined that the visual distortion accompanying shamanic hallucinogenic states consistently include a particular purple coloration to the visual periphery. Since coloration is easily manipulated in the editing room, Downey often colors trance scenes with a purple tone informants produced for him with colored pens. Similarly, the Yanomami seem to regard differences between color and black-and-white video as insignificant, so Downey feels justified in cross-editing one to the other. Culturally significant numerical systems can also be manipulated for temporal effect. For example, a particular Amazonian group uses the number six extensively in weaving, architecture, myth, and chant, so the tapes of these groups were edited at six pulse beat intervals to subliminally convey an emic quality of temporal organization.

The term "format" emerges as the most appropriate for describing different approaches to the organization of raw material. Formats are based on sets of conventions loosely correlated with the intended audience and transmission context. Formats include documentary, narrative fiction, Public Broadcast System-style ethnography, and Soho gallery installation, for example. The same raw tape can be packaged in many different formats, and video artists in general want to find out how different formats affect the same raw information. In Downey's completed programs, you will often see the same sequence of images in different contexts. This investigation into the effect of format is not conducted in the manner of a reduplicatable scientific inquiry. Instead of testing audience response, the audience is confronted with its own conventions as format shifts recontextualize information, much as Monty Python plays on frames for its humor. In fact, satirical and parodic frames seem the most accessible to the artist. A problem arises when these frame shifts are not adequately cued, and audiences confuse the serious and the ludic. Anthropological critics of Mr. Downey's work have fallen into the same trap, and perhaps it is the trap, not the observer, that is at fault.

The criteria most appealing to the artist—"aesthetic criteria"—are not easily defined. When Downey (or any other artist trained in formal aesthetic tradition) looks through the lens of a camera or at an editing monitor, he considers aspects of images that anthropologists are not trained to see and cannot easily describe. Aesthetic criteria are based on particular balances of information, formal, spatial and color organization, and visual coherence. Skill in this area allows video artists to deemphasize narrative explanation by loading visual and auditory channels with the weight of information. There is an attempt to conventionalize video styles that can transcend linguistic constraints, exploiting more universal qualities of the medium, as music is claimed to do.

The exercise of aesthetic criteria is rightly the province of artists. Art is itself a discipline, a tradition, and an ongoing investigation. It is distinguished from analytic scholarship in that it does not reduce its findings to linguistic discourse, but engages in a nonlexical discourse of forms. Any explanation of art is less accurate than the art itself.

There should be no confusion of traditions here. Anthropologists interested in modes of communication can provide much needed services to artists or media craftsmen in exchange for the opportunity to investigate the communication processes which they (the producers) use. While this has traditionally been limited to the anthropologist providing literate skills—scripts, research and narrations—more sophisticated critical input is possible. Collaborations in which the anthropologist assists in analyzing and articulating the complex problem of translation across cultural boundaries through the agency of a particular communication channel can be most productive. This kind of collaboration frees the scholar from a subservience to the producer/director that has sometimes meant the reprocessing of scholarly research into unrecognizable forms in the final product. The reason scholars feel exploited and misrepresented in media collaborations stems in part from the scholars' failure to recognize how fragile and manipulatable written scripts are in the production of visual programs. By extending the range of involvement beyond any single state of production—recording, editing (including script/research), or display—and taking critical responsibility for the entire process, collaboration becomes possible in a larger sense.

Display

A basic problem in displaying video is to reorganize the expectations of audiences trained to look at television as if it were cinema. Another is to break out of the constraints placed on video by commercial formats and engage audiences in temporal segments more varied than their attention spans are used to (Antin 1975:64–70). For ethnographic and nonfiction programs, it is additionally important to create a kind of critical, Brechtian distance that will provoke an audience to view images as something other than entertainment. In short, the characteristics of commercial television as a mesmeric medium in which programming functions primarily as a setting for commercials need to be attacked. How best to go about this is uncertain, given the present condition of broadcast television, but other displays are currently available that can be manipulated toward these ends. Video artists, for whom access to broadcast channels is still problematic, have explored alternative displays and have developed a particular fondness for their possibilities. "When I sit down with friends at home to view a segment of the sixty hours of African culture which I have in my tape vault or sit in a museum around a glowing tube, the effect is similar to sitting by a campfire" (Ramos 1979:13).

The possibilities for single- and multiple-channel displays in which the artist is able to control contextual and spatial information have become highly developed in the last five years. Certain kinds of displays, those most closely approximating cinema, are avoided. The simple addition of a second monitor, even in a classroom, assists in disturbing viewers' conventions for proscenium theater viewing, which was borrowed by film and subsequently television. It is this proscenium effect of an audience attending across a spatial division to a single source of information which was the origin of the "willing suspension of disbelief" (which made the artifice of the "realistic" theater possible). The collapse of critical distance renders performance entertainment. It is accomplished, curiously, by the maintenance of a spatial distance. In the case of creating humanistic images of unfamiliar peoples, this combination has uncomfortable implications. It is difficult to justify appropriating images of native peoples for the entertainment of Western audiences. It is dangerous to imply that the manipulated reality represented by any medium is the same as the actual events, as theatrical documentaries presume.

Funding agencies, broadcasters, networks—public or commercial —are not particularly receptive to these questions or to the work of either artists or scientists who would like to experiment with alternative possibilities to contemporary television. It is perhaps not the essential qualities of the broadcast medium and its hardware that have earned television a reputation as a "boob tube" but the uses to which it has been put. As a commercial industry, television succeeds in selling sponsors' products and making sizable profits. It has not proved particularly receptive to criticism based on ethical or scientific criteria. A year spent in applications to funders and broadcasters has impressed me with the byzantine structure of these interlocking interests that perpetuates the present style and content of television. The system appears to be relatively stable and unlikely to change from within. This might be a source of frustration and worse except that external changes, occurring in the public and private sectors involving cable, satellite, and other transmission alternatives, appear to have the immanent capability of transforming television programming by external alterations on the system.

Observers believe that the number of channels and program sources available to a home television viewer will dramatically increase in the next ten years. The appeal to the mass audience that characterizes network television will become less significant. The kinds of filmic-based packages audiences have been conditioned to expect will be offset by programming for specialized audiences and innovative video-based techniques.

In such a climate, it may be possible to reverse the unidirectional flow of information and begin a reciprocal exchange more suited to the nature of electronic media. In this context, the roles of both anthropologist and video artist are altered. Indigenous peoples become more responsible for the information transmitted, and it becomes possible for us to limit our roles. The confusion about who we are with respect to media and with respect to audiences may, in fact, be an unavoidable outcome of the present structure of the broadcast and film industry.

We are faced with a disparity between the potential for mass media to convey important humanistic lessons and the existing structures and values of the media industry, which has trained audiences to a narrow, conventionalized set of expectations and responses. Artists and scientists are in a similar bind selling products (although we both have a right to expect our work to be valued and rewarded). Art museums have serious limitations as display spaces. Audiences there tend to postures not particularly pertinent to the work displayed. But within the severe limitations imposed by commercial circumstances, video artists have done remarkably well in keeping alive their experimental approach to video and developing audience sophistication in their work. In a more limited fashion, academics have made some use of media, especially film, in classroom settings where they can control audience attention to the end of creating intelligent viewing. Commercial mass media *appeals* to audiences. Artists and scholars, in contrast, *develop* theirs. It may be impossible to develop satisfactory media of high artistic and informational quality until the combination of software, hardware, and access constraints are matched to an active, rather than passive audience. Given these situations, we may find we have more in common with nonbroadcast, noncommercial media artists than with commercial craftsmen at the present time.

Conclusion

When anthropologists ask what is wrong with ethnographic film, we offer naive solutions based on our own limited sophistication in visual media and our concern for accuracy of data in literary terms. We presume that if a cameraperson collaborates with an anthropologist in the field, or if we anthropologists participate in script research or writing, some kind of democratic collusion will create a good, accurate program. We do not tend to address more formal questions of concern to experimental artists, such as presentational styles, formats, aesthetic appeal, and continuity, and their effect on information and audience. But the problems of visual ethnography are not necessarily literary, and anthropology lacks a vocabulary for assessing the effectiveness of visual images. As professionals who often make our living lecturing, we may be unlikely to appreciate popular audiences' tolerance for being lectured to outside the classroom. Yet commercial television's solution—to turn all educational programming into "entertainment"—is at odds with academic purpose and implies a further exploitation of small-scale societies whenever they are media subjects.

A solution is to address the entire process of visual media as a problem in communication, more specifically in cross-cultural translation. To accomplish this, research is necessary at all levels of the production process. Scholars who intercept media at only one stage are not adequately meeting their responsibilities.

While commercial broadcast media, by their very nature, cannot be receptive to our goals, independent, noncommercial producers, such as video artists, can provide a source of collaborative projects in which anthropologists can develop an understanding of the potential of certain media. In the case of video and television, I suggest that such collaboration might not only be productive, but also may generate an audience able to benefit by its outcomes. Television has additional appeal for anthropology in that it is the most processual of media. We can envision a kind of information flow from small-scale cultures to large, technological ones through direct broadcast, in which our interference as the exporters of media products is reduced.

We should not be surprised to find ourselves confused and dissatisfied with the present products of ethnographic documentary, since they are generated in a confusing and dissatisfying context of venture capital in the entertainment industry. Instead, we can develop collaborations with media practitioners outside this limited area. The artistic tradition and the sciences historically and logically share a more productive relationship than either does with the business world.

Part Three

Writing about Experience

"I am the Alpha and the Omega," says the Lord God.

—Revelation 1:8

Let S stand for Scientist.

—Noam Chomsky

6 ANTHROPOLOGICAL HERMENEUTICS AND THE PROBLEM OF ALPHABETIC LITERACY

DENNIS TEDLOCK

When discourse finally reaches your eyes in printed form, dear reader, it has been shaped by many forces beyond the control of an author. In the case of my pages in the volume now before you, those forces included a book designer's choice of type face, a choice that is even now affecting you in ways analogous to the impact of tone and timbre of voice, ways that are explicitly set forth in handbooks of type styles. A less subtle force was the admonition of the editors (and of the readers who evaluated the manuscript for publication) that the talk printed below "needed more context." Without their intervention, you would already be reading the talk itself. But perhaps they were right: after all, speakers often preface their prepared speeches with remarks that address themselves to the immediate occasion. As you will see, I did just that in the present talk, whose first paragraph (except for the last two sentences) reached its final form only as it was being spoken in a ballroom in Los Angeles. The publication of this book is a new and separate occasion and provides the opportunity to precede the original opening remarks with new opening remarks.

I mention all these normally hidden or implicit matters here because it seems to me that if the concerns expressed in the symposium from which this book arises are to have a radical dimension, our mood of reflection must begin at the moment we come before a microphone or typewriter rather than taking its means of expression for granted. If we may speak of degrees of implicitness, then perhaps *the* most implicit feature of our mental landscape as anthropologists is the assumption that nearly everything we might want to say in words can be said adequately —and in fact *should* be said—in the alphabetically written prose of journal articles and other scholarly forms (unless we happen to be writing one of those confessional books). Increasingly even the oral genre called "giving a paper" might just as well be what its name already suggests: the passing out of copies of a paper, a paper in no way composed with *hearers* in mind. I know of at least one anthropologist who even reads his parenthetical citations aloud, complete with year and page numbers, and adds the name and volume number of the journal as an aside if the article happens to be one of his own.

The gray masses of what we might call "journalese" are, of course, sometimes relieved by graphic devices, the most common of these being lists, tables, and perhaps geometric diagrams, variously constructed from isolated nouns, isolated letters of the roman alphabet, arabic numerals, and mechanically drawn lines. The packing of alphabetically written words into the dense rectangular blocks now identified with prose goes back to the dawn of alphabetic writing itself, and also of great antiquity, as Jack Goody has been pointing out (1977), is the use of lists, tables, diagrams, and other devices much like the ones favored (for example) in *Science* today, though some of these devices made their early appearances in texts now considered occult. Some of the finer details of journalese have a much shallower time depth. Punctuation, for example, served as a guide to oral delivery during the Middle Ages; it was only during the last two centuries or so that it came to mark the boundaries of grammatical units more than it marked the drama of the speaking voice, which often counterpoints grammar rather than marching in unison with it.

We could go on enumerating graphic and other features of journal prose, but the main point here is that even in its purest form it is heavy with historical sediments. One of those sediments is the deliberate contribution of our own anthropological forebears, though by this time it may seem a "natural" feature of our landscape. I am thinking of the style of citation prescribed by the *American Anthropologist,* which interposes such monstrosities as "(Friedländer 1969:185–86, 271–72, 370, 482n)" directly in the path of our prose rather than making use of tiny superscript numbers referring to footnotes. Our citations are so gross, graphically speaking, that they can be spotted from a reading distance of six feet. This form of citation was not an invention of our forebears, nor did they choose it merely because of a distaste for authors who abuse "op. cit." or for editors who lazily postpone footnotes to the very end rather than placing them at the foot of each page. Rather, they made an *ideological* decision for a species of citation that unmistakably belonged to one of two established genera of scholarly citation. It has recently been claimed that anthropology is the most humanistic of the sciences and the most scientific of the humanities, but when the original citational decision was made (and it has been echoed many times), it came down clearly (and graphically) on the side of scientific appearances.

The burdens of journalese do not end with its immediately visible graphic features. There are the subtler sediments of rules of diction that have been taught in Western grammar schools since they began in Athens; these rules in their present form call for extreme restraint in the use of underlining (or italics), exclamation points, imperatives, rhetorical questions, ironic question marks, and first- and second-person pronouns. What all these restraints have in common is that they make prose less and less like something a person might say to other persons and more and more like the voice of a disembodied "it," standing nowhere except on the authority of the printed word and speaking to no one in particular. Most of what passes for scientific objectivity in anthropology consists of nothing more than adopting a form of discourse in which surprises, differences of intensity, irony, urgency, and "you" and "I" have all been removed—or not so much removed as hidden by various disguises, like repressed desires.[1] By some magic, the result should not only stand outside individual experience, but escape ethnocentrism as well. But just this once let us allow ourselves to think of journal prose as a highly culture-specific artifact, inherently limited in its power to

---

1. For some reflections on the educational issues raised by such rules of discourse, see Hymes 1978.

transmit the features of cultures whose internal communications are shaped by quite different pathways and whose direct communications with anthropology are not limited to typewritten messages composed solely of declarative sentences in the third person.

The text that follows includes bracketed notes and other indications of gestures (including the display of props), tones of voice, selective emphasis, and pauses that are every bit as much a part of the talk as its words. The conventions of alphabetic literacy, and of a linguistics that was spawned within and remains utterly dependent upon that particular form of literacy, misled us into believing that the properly linguistic features of a verbal performance belong to the domain of cognition, while the paralinguistic and kinesic features belong to a separate domain called emotion. Yet each of the paralinguistic and kinesic details noted below was a *calculated* act. Conversely, some of the properly linguistic details were doubtless shaped by hidden emotional forces. Even in the flattest prose, the goal of a purified cognitive objectivity is an illusory one—unless, of course, someone invents a type that has no face.

The Talk

I didn't have an epigram—or, better, an *outer word*—for this paper until yesterday morning about this time. I had just entered an elevator, and an old friend called to me from out in the lobby: "Dennis!" "Oh!" [reach out with both arms, then bring them together like the closing doors of an elevator]. The doors closed, and the elevator took off before I could find the right button. Then I saw that someone was standing there with me in the elevator, and he said [voice of authority],

> The moving
> finger
> writes.

Just now I found a second epigram, a written one this time [hold up scrap of paper] and judging by the evidence with which it was associated, right here on this table, it must have been left by someone in that ESP session yesterday. It is written all in capitals, in block letters [reading]:

The other day I was reading a book—[aside, in self-mocking tone] "The other day, I was reading a book"?—How to begin? That is our

Bauman

As an anthropological linguist who lived with the Cheyenne Indians of Montana for 4 years, I find myself philosophically and theoretically at odds with my more orthodox colleagues. My paper would be unacceptable at linguistics conferences — So... Here I am.

problem in anthropology right now, isn't it, how to begin. Anyway, the other day, I was reading a book about how narrative is put together. The author of this book argues strenuously that the important thing in narrative is the combination of incidents, while character is entirely secondary to the action and can even be dispensed with. But it wasn't Vladimir Propp's *Morphology of the Folktale* I was reading. It was Aristotle's *Poetics* (1450a).[2]

Then I read further that in drama, the composition of speech and melody is secondary to the composition of plot. I thought I'd seen that somewhere before, too, and I found a passage in another book where a different author, writing about myth, says that "its substance does not lie in its style, its original music, or in its syntax, but in the *story* which it tells." That, of course, is Lévi-Strauss (1963:206), who goes on, in that same place, to use a linguistic model for myth, arguing that what myth does on the high level of plot is analogous to what language does, on a lower level, in phonology. The more was my surprise when I returned to Aristotle's *Poetics* and ran smack into linguistics again. Discussing the composition of speech, or *lexis*, Aristotle says, "The letter [or *gramma* in Greek] is an indivisible sound of a particular kind, one that may become a factor in an intelligible sound" (1456b). If we substitute "phoneme" for "letter," it sounds like the doctrine of the arbitrariness of signs, but remember, it's not Saussure, it's Aristotle again. Just three pages later we find him—Aristotle, I mean—detaching letters from their places in words and using them as signs in higher-level relationships. I quote again: "A cup (B) is in relation to Dionysus (A) what a shield (D)

2. Citations from Aristotle follow the convention of referring to numbered sections of the Greek text and thus serve to locate the proper passage in any edition or translation of the *Poetics*. All quotations of Aristotle are from the translation of Bywater (1954), except for the quotation from 1462a, which is from Else (1967).

is to Ares (C)," and, on that same page, "As old age (D) is to life (C), so is evening (B) to day (A)" (1457b). When I read this, I could not help but think that, as Aristotle (A) is to Greek tragedy (B), so is Lévi-Strauss (C) to South American mythology (D). It is tempting to go on and line up Aristotle and Lévi-Strauss as the day and the evening of a whole line of Western thought, but if we kept on this way much longer, we might get swallowed up in old age and have to turn in our shield for a cup.

Back to Aristotle. In his closing arguments, he is concerned to separate the high art of the dramatist, which is called *poiēsis*, poesis, from the low art of the actor, which is called (get this) *hypokrisis*. This reminded me that the view of Lévi-Strauss, and indeed of anthropologists in general, has been that the "authors" of myths have names, like Bororo, Sherente, and Nambikwara—[aside] just imagine o senhor Nambi Kwara flying to Stockholm to receive the Prize—while the individuals who *tell* the myths, the mere "performers," have no names at all, though they are sometimes assigned letters of the alphabet: Informant A, Informant B, Informant C, Informant D.

Aristotle's central argument for the clear separation between the competence of the dramatist and the performance of the actor—this is Aristotle again, not Chomsky—is that "tragedy does its work even without performance, . . . for it can convey its qualities through reading" (1462a). *Reading?* That reminded me that Greek theater was nearly dead by the time of Aristotle, and that Aristotle participated in a network of Athenians who passed manuscripts around. Turning back to Lévi-Strauss, I found him declaring (1963:206) that "a myth is still felt as a myth by any reader anywhere in the world." *Reader?* Here I remembered that Lévi-Strauss's entire mythological magnum opus was based on written documents, and that not a single one of the myths transcribed and translated in those documents was collected, from some lowly performer, by himself.

At a "high" level, Aristotle and Lévi-Strauss begin to sound rather bookish. To say the least. At a lower level, their *alphabet* keeps showing, not only in their A and B, C and D, but in the primacy of plot over characters and composer over performers, which seems analogous to the primacy of relations over things in the doctrine of signs. I say it's ultimately the *alphabet* showing through here, not just a recent borrowing from the phonologically-based science that Saussure is supposed to have founded, simply because Aristotle is already making low-level Saussurian and high-level Lévi-Straussian arguments, and some of these arguments directly involve reading and the letters of the alphabet. The picture becomes even clearer when we look at Aristotle's immediate predecessors, who lived at precisely the time when alphabetic literacy first became commonplace among the citizens of Athens. One of the ideas very much in the air at that time (and finding its way onto paper) was the particular variety of atomism first argued by Antithese—Antisthenes—that found its way into several of the Platonic dialogues (Friedländer 1969:185–86, 271–72, 370, 482n). The argument uses alphabetic writing as a model, and it runs something like this: just as the sounds of words are composed of irreducible letters, so the world of objects is composed of irreducible elements. And just as letters are in themselves unintelligible—that is, meaningless—so the elements are in themselves haphazard—that is, arbitrary—in their forms. Now, this makes me think of C. S. Peirce [pronounce like "purse"], patron saint of semiotics, who said that "the entire universe . . . is perfused with signs, if it is not composed exclusively of signs" (as quoted in Sebeok 1977:epigram and ix). It also makes me think of the cover of Terence Hawkes's new book, *Structuralism and Semiotics* (1977) [here, hold up the book, whose cover art consists of a huge, three-dimensional letter *N*]. The blurb on the back cover begins, "We live in a world of signs."

At this point we can certainly say that the universe described by Antisthenes, Plato, and Aristotle—and by linguists, structuralists, and semioticians—is perfused with signs all right, but that universe begins to look suspiciously like a projection of the experiences of the grammar school, starting in Athens—and remember, *gramma* means "letter" in Greek—onto the rest of the world. The generative gramma of Chomsky won't help us here, either: it generates correctly spelled and correctly constructed sentences, all right—all you have to do is hook it up to a piece of chalk—but [here, begin moving left and right forearms around each other, as if winding yarn] it doesn't tell us anything whatever about diction, that is, about how to *speak*. [3]

Now as anthropologists whose duty it is to attempt to experience and describe the worlds of others, we must at least hold open the possibility that the world of South American Indians may not be perfused by, or constructed from, letters of the alphabet, and we must face up to the fact that the alphabet has a peculiar culture history of its own.

---

3. See Hymes 1971 for a sociolinguistic critique of Chomsky. The gesture I use here is in imitation of Chomsky, who continuously moves his arms in this way whenever he is simply lecturing rather than applying chalk to the blackboard.

This is not just a matter of dividing the peoples of the world into nonliterate and literate: as Leroi-Gourhan points out (1964:chap. 6), writing, in the sense of markings that are not intelligible solely from their resemblances to the world of objects, is a human universal that goes all the way back to the paleolithic.[4] Rather, it is the nature of the alphabet in particular that should give us pause before we analyze and discuss the experiences we store in tapes, films, and—above all—in so-called native texts.

The first thing we will want to notice about our alphabet in our roles as cultural anthropologists is that it is properly called the roman alphabet, although we use it with certain English adaptations and eccentricities. Yes, there are the "phonemic" alphabets devised for individual unwritten languages by Euro-American academic linguists and Christian missionaries, but, as Dwight Bolinger remarks (1968:158), phonemic writing can "be characterized as simply a clean-up job on alphabetic writing." We can realize just how alphabecentric our own linguistics is when we reflect that classical Arabic linguistics flung itself headlong at the problem of vowels, whereas our linguistics relegates its own unwritten phenomena—such as syllables, suprasegmentals, and, yes, *para*linguistic features—to its farthest fringes, as if it were more concerned with proper alphabetical appearances than with spoken sounds.

The time has come to realize when we examine, say, a Zuni Bible that if its signs seem arbitrary, relative to the meanings of the Zuni words they spell out, it may be because Zuni has been written as if it sounded somewhat like English (but with Romance vowels), just as English was once written as if it were Latin, Latin as if it were Greek, Greek as if it were Phoenician, and Phoenician as if it were Egyptian.[5] By the time we get back to the Phoenician, and even more so when we get to Egyptian, we begin to recognize A as the head of an ox, B as the ground plan of a house, C as the hump of a camel, and D as a doorway. But allowing ourselves to be carried away into Egypt does not mean a loss of the tie between writing and sound. What is most remarkable

4. In *Of grammatology* (Derrida 1976), part 1 of which began as a review of Leroi-Gourhan's *Le geste et la parole* (1964), Derrida raises questions that require the reexamination of alphabetic writing and of lines of thought that may be modeled upon it.
5. Gelb (1952) remains the major modern treatment of the history of writing in general, though it is distorted by an almost unbelievable alphabetic chauvinism. But at least this is an explicit chauvinism, as opposed to the implicit chauvinism of a linguistics that ignores the cultural historicity of its major tool.

about Egyptian, as contrasted with an idealized or perfectly phonemic alphabet, is that it plays off sound and meaning, syllable and word, rather than being governed by [hold up forefinger] one single principle. Like Chinese and Mayan, it contains a great many logograms, or characters that stand for entire words. These are symbols rather than pure signs, in the sense that they do imitate the qualities of the things their words denote, and each character has a measure of intelligibility, even when read all by itself. At the same time, and especially when uncommon or foreign words are written, logographic symbols are pressed into service as signs for the sounds of syllables.[6] In effect, a word or passage written in syllabic *signs* is read according to its symbolic *resonances*.

At this point we should observe that if we tried to decipher one of these heterogeneous scripts in the same way that Lévi-Strauss reads myths, using an alphabetic model that begins by reducing characters to mere signs in a plot, we would be doing violence to the symbolic values or weights of the characters, and the full depth of the text would escape us. This is exactly what happened when Russian formalism, in the person of Yurii Knorozov, confronted the task of deciphering Mayan. Overreacting to the symbolic and logographic prejudices of Sir J. Eric S. Thompson, he ran up against the particular limits of a totally syllabic approach, but he did succeed in reading some previously opaque passages as strings of signs. In the hands of Thompson, on the other hand, some texts tended to fall apart, as if unable to support the weight assigned to each symbol. If Knorozov makes us think of Lévi-Strauss, Thompson makes us think of [pause] Jung. The twin dangers here—and they are twins, specifically enantiodromic twins—are what Paul Ricoeur calls allegory and gnosis (1962:203–4). On the one hand [hold out right hand] Lévi-Strauss reduces all myths to the status of allegories of a grammar lesson, while on the other [hold out left hand and lower it at each stress], Jung seeks the knowledge that dwells in the depths of each separate character. A hermeneutical approach seeks to retain its ambidexterity long enough to discover what some of the symmetries and asymmetries of the text itself may be, seen both within its own historical (or cultural) horizon and within that of its present interpreter. Nothing less is required for the interpretation of Mayan texts.

But, you may say, isn't the approach of Lévi-Strauss two-sided in

---

6. In this discussion of nonalphabetic scripts, I rely heavily on the carefully balanced work of David Humiston Kelley (1976:chap. 9) and on Samuel E. Martin (1972).

its own way? Doesn't he display for us the synchronic, as well as the diachronic, dimensions of myth? The answer is that with the alphabetic model, the text is treated as if its synchronic dimensions arose solely from the recurrence of the elements in its diachronic sequence; properly speaking, synchrony is not allowed to extend outside the text and take root in the world of objects. Linguistics and structuralism stand within the mainstream of Western metaphysics, which ultimately reads *everything* as a syntagmatic chain, a monologue that claims to have no roots anywhere unless——unless—unless it is read backward, or traced upward, to the First Principle.[7] While missionaries were in the field substituting alphabetic Bibles for the enactments of savage myths, Lévi-Strauss was in Paris, discovering that those myths were really allegories of the Logos [hold up forefinger], that ultimate monologue, a story written, and written without characters, by our old friend Aristotle (in the *Metaphysics*), a story that was later fleshed out in the Gospel According to John—which is, incidentally, the first book that an S.I.L.-trained missionary translates (from the Greek) into a native tongue.

What the book called *Jesus Christ An Penan' Qok'shi John Tsinan Yaakyakowa* (Yff et al. 1941) has in common with Lévi-Strauss's *The Male Nude* (1971)—pardon my French—is that they both claim to tell us a story that transcends all historical, cultural, and personal particularities. The syntagmatic chain preserves its transcendent purity by finding meaning only within itself, synchronicity only within itself. If American Indian myths have a different story to tell, then something has been lost in the translation.

Back to the texts—or back to the ears, back to the eyes that do more than read type. When we find a Zuni performer, or rather the composer-performer Walter Sanchez, saying something like, "It was a morning just like this one," we will have to at least suspect that it is not only Lévi-Strauss who seeks to transcend the diachrony of narrative. When Andrew Peynetsa, on an evening when we have forgotten our tape recorder, names the characters in his story after people in the audience and looks each of them in the eye as he does this, and when they squirm at the tight places in the story, we may have to——hypothesize?——

7. The phrase "Western metaphysics" is from Derrida, but he ultimately lays this metaphysics at the door of the voice, as if alphabetic writing told the full story of the voice, whereas I would contend that the voice (1) is multidimensional rather than limited to carrying the syntagmatic chain; and (2) is rooted in the gross physicality of the body. In Aristotelian terms, the alphabet writes only what is truly human in the voice and leaves out the animal part, and this is the departure point of his (and Western) metaphysics.

that stories have characters *in* them, and that the characters in the audience may have stories *about* them. When Andrew Peynetsa, on finishing an episode in which the people who first emerged from the earth are destroyed, remarks that "their ruins are all around the land, as you can see," or when he tells us how the Ahayuuta twins emerged from the foam of a waterfall and remarks, "Well, you know how water can make suds," we may suspect that though the world be perfused with signs, it may be equally true that texts are perfused with the world.[8] When Andrew Peynetsa tells about how the present human beings, we survivors, emerged from the earth, and when he has the Ahayuuta tell us,

> Even though it will be hard
> you must do your best
> to look at your Sun Father
> for you will hardly be able to *see.*
> There in the room full of darkness, when we entered upon
>   your roads, we could hardly *see.*
> This is the way it will be with you, *certainly,*

then we are no longer in a position to say that it will take a structuralist to discover that the twins (who are the sons of the Sun) and the people (who are the children of the underworld) are in symmetrically inverted positions when it comes to the inability to see in darkness or in light. And when we *hear* that the elder twin speaks in a normal voice and the younger one in a high and breaking voice, we will know that the twins stand just on either side [hold up fore and middle fingers together] of the rift of adolescence, something that printed texts had not told us.

Thank you.

Postscript

The moment we listen to the dimensions of speech sound removed by the filter of alphabetic transcription, as when we take note of a narrator's imitation of the voice of a character he is quoting, we also exceed the limits of strict and tidy codification of the kind that is aesthetically and

8. See Tedlock 1980 for a more thorough discussion of this narrative. All Andrew Peynetsa quotations are from Tedlock 1978, "The Beginning, Part I." Each change of line in the longer quotation indicates a pause.

morally pleasing to a linguist. At a higher level, the moment we attend to the dimensions of meaning that are removed by the filter of formalist or structuralist perception, as when we take note of narrator's self-conscious asides or commentaries, we exceed the limits of thinking of texts as the products of unreflective "performers" who obey (or fail to obey) hidden "competencies" that are exclusively ours to discover.[9] Spoken discourse is always already in the world, implicitly and explicitly breaking the bonds of a code whose metaphysical character is only thinly disguised by attempts to assign its ultimate source to unseen structures located in the upper layers of the vault of the head rather than of the sky. The linguist begins to do serious work only after the worldliness of speech has been reduced to alphabetic textualization, and the semioticist who capitulates to linguistic hegemony longs for the discovery of an analogous elegance at the semantic level of these same reduced texts. In both cases, the original event is reduced to terms that will in no way disturb or exceed the canons of journal prose and its accompanying graphic devices.

If there is to be an alternative, hermeneutical anthropology that will interpret the discourse heard in the field in a way that respects its full complexity, its grounds will be different from those of the hermeneutics encountered in philosophy. Hermeneutical phenomenologists do not cross the boundaries of the world defined by alphabetically written texts: they write alphabetical texts that embody interpretations of previous alphabetical texts. When they sit down to write a *general* statement of the hermeneutical project, the peculiar features of the spoken word are a mere inconvenience, most easily set aside by the claim that *behind* a formal speech event lies a sort of nonvisual equivalent of a written text.[10] From the perspective of an anthropological hermeneutics, such a position ought to appear ethnocentric, to say the least. When we sit down to interpret the transcript of an interview or formal performance, we must be wary of the effects of our own alphabetic literacy, both as

9. Michael Silverstein reminds us (1979) that "natives" are capable of reflection even at the properly linguistic level, producing what he calls "linguistic ideology." Noting that linguists are trained to ignore such ideology, which they call "secondary explanation," he argues for a direct link between this studied ignorance and the inability to adequately account for changes in language structure, which are at least partly caused by native ideology. An analogous critique could obviously be made of structuralism at the semantic level.

10. This is the argument Paul Ricoeur made when I raised the problem of speech at the Boston University Institute for the Philosophy of Religion in 1977.

medium and as model for interpretation. Secondly, we must remember that the transcribed words were once embedded in a dialog to which an anthropologist was one of the parties.[11] A dialogical anthropology would recognize that there is no such thing as an absolutely "native" text or "ethno" science. Plato may be pristine in the sense that he has never been "contacted" by contemporary philosophers, but there is no such thing as "pre-contact" ethnography. Contact has always already happened, and in writing about or quoting from that contact, we move back from the dialog and into the cozy but dangerous world of alphabetic literacy, where we sit and write in solitude.

11. For a development of this subject along lines that are very much a continuation of the present talk, see Tedlock 1979.

7 RHETORIC AND THE ETHNOGRAPHIC GENRE IN ANTHROPOLOGICAL RESEARCH

GEORGE E. MARCUS

Northrop Frye concluded his essay "Rhetorical Criticism: Theory of Genres" (1957) with a discussion of rhetoric in nonliterary prose and a claim that, although assertive, descriptive, or factual writing attempts to eliminate its purely expressive and persuasive dimensions, it cannot hope to succeed. As he wrote (p. 331): "Anything which makes a functional use of words will always be involved in all the technical problems of words, including rhetorical problems. The only road from

This paper is inspired in part by the teaching of a course for advanced undergraduates and graduate students at Rice University, "Classics in Ethnography," which was designed to combine the aims of standard social science method and theory courses in a format specific to anthropology. Selection of representative ethnographies led directly to a consideration of their genre context. For useful discussions, I am indebted to Harold Burris; to Richard Cushman, who originally conceived the course and with whom I taught it; and to Stephen A. Tyler, whose hermeneutic perspective on discourse analysis has been a particularly important stimulus for me. Originally published in *Current anthropology* 21(1980):507–10. Copyright © 1980 by the University of Chicago Press.

grammar to logic, then, runs through the intermediate territory of rhetoric." This brief essay examines some implications of Frye's claim for an understanding of the prose form that anthropology has evolved both to report the results of fieldwork and to develop theory—the ethnography. At the same time, it makes a point about the emphases of past epistemological discussions in anthropology.

While these discussions have paid attention to the experience of doing fieldwork and to theorizing at an abstract, paradigmatic level, they have virtually ignored the activity through which anthropologists determine and represent what they know in the writing of ethnographies. This inattention is not surprising, since, consistent with anthropology's past development within a positivist tradition of science, ethnography has been an unproblematic middle ground—a form for reportage and exposition—between the substantive categories of method and theory. In fact, anthropologists as writers of ethnographies have always been aware that what is learned in fieldwork finds primary expression within the bounds of a genre, with certain kinds of constraints and rules of construction. As readers of ethnographies, they have developed a body of theoretical and topical issues on the basis of the implicit, but primary, evaluation of ethnographic texts. The point, however, is that the awareness of the independent importance of ethnographic writing as a genre with its own evolution has been largely tacit, masked instead by discussions cast in the categories of a positivist tradition, for which anthropology's semiliterary presentation of its data and findings is unique, if not peculiar.

Malinowski (1922) came close to discussing explicitly the standards for a successful ethnography even though he couched his remarks primarily as a description of the fieldwork method. Firmly within the functionalist tradition, Kaberry (1957) provided a brief evaluation of Malinowski's effect on the writing of ethnographies. Cursory and limited as it was, she has provided one of the few explicit discussions of ethnography as a genre. Interestingly, in his critical review of the social sciences, Louch (1966:160) recognized clearly that a genre form, which he caricatured as "travelers' tales," and the kind of moral explanation structuring it, were anthropology's (specifically, functionalist anthropology's) major contribution to human knowledge. For him, anthropology is distinguished by its rhetoric as "a moral realm of discourse" (ibid.:162) rather than by its self-selected focus upon conventional scientific concerns with theory and method.

With the decline of functionalism as anthropology's major paradigm, and the failure of structuralism to replace it as completely, fieldwork and ethnography stand in relief even more clearly as the two modalities unifying a discipline that has become thoroughly eclectic in searching for theoretical stimuli beyond its traditionally permeable boundaries. Largely as a reaction to the positivist assumptions in orthodox functionalism and structuralism, there has been strong interest in hermeneutic and phenomenological perspectives that were well established philosophically long before anthropology sought a new source of inspiration in them. With this searching has come a substantial literature on fieldwork, a research activity that might be seen as always having been more compatible with the interests of phenomenology and hermeneutics. What is remarkable about this literature is how generally similar reported fieldwork experiences have been, regardless of the diverse sorts of theoretical and analytic approaches motivating these projects.[1] In contrast, variations in ethnographic writing reflect perfectly differences in theoretical viewpoints. Yet an understanding of the ethnographic genre rather than of fieldwork as personal experience and method remains a blindspot.

The recent sensitive and insightful works by Rabinow (1977) and Dumont (1978) go considerably beyond the confessional quality of much of the fieldwork literature. In unprecedented depth, they show not only how the fieldworker's personal relationships constitute the primary data of anthropological research, but also how, in the process of self-reflection, they are the epistemological base from which interpretations and claims, presented in objective language and formal conceptualizations, originate. Both of these works were preceded by what each writer would acknowledge as more conventional ethnographies (Rabinow 1975; Dumont 1976), which were more about "the comprehension of the other" than "the comprehension of self" (after Rabinow—and Ricoeur—1977:5), and more about "their thing" than "an anthropology

1. I readily admit that the limited, introspective concerns of this literature may have missed substantive differences among anthropologists in what phenomena they focus upon as sources of data in the field, according to how they are respectively taught to "see" in their theoretical training. However, I do not think that theory in anthropology has this degree of cognitive power over fieldworkers. Rather, theoretical differences are most clearly and uniformly established as different ways of viewing and emphasizing aspects of similar kinds of primary field data, collected through the apparently widely shared experiences of fieldworkers with differing theoretical orientations. Theory has most bearing on the secondary selection and determination of ethnographic facts in the course of working out the quite discrete problems of constructing ethnographic texts.

of the subject" (after Dumont 1978:3). As such, their fieldwork books implicitly raise an important issue about ethnographic writing, which they in no way address. While both authors have clearly set a different focus for their latter works than their former ones, their claims for the epistemological importance of reflexivity in fieldwork relationships, nonetheless, lead immediately to the question of how in their own ethnographic writing, their two sets of texts are, or should be, related —more generally, how ethnographic accounts of subjectivity in the field might be related to the objective aims of conventional ethnographic accounts. Also, by the mere fact that the works were written in the order that they were, one might wonder whether the latter, reflective works, given their epistemological significance, should not have been a distinct, but earlier step on the way to, or even an integral part of, accounts concerned with "the other" or "their thing." It is not a question of breaking the hermeneutic circle, but of how this circle is to be represented in a genre of writing, which continues to have a priority concern with knowledge of "the other" rather than "the self."

Explicitly addressing themselves to past fieldwork literature and also going beyond it, Dumont and Rabinow are actually experimenting with the form of ethnographic texts. From their philosophical interest in phenomenology and hermeneutics, the issue that they implicitly suggest, and that is in fact being addressed in the diversity of current ethnographic styles, is how the established ethnographic genre can accommodate reflexivity while still retaining the traditional authority of its texts, that is, the rhetorical usage of language and format by which ethnographers have constructed their accounts as certain and objective knowledge about others.[2] What is unsatisfactory about the most recent works of Rabinow and Dumont is that they fail to deal directly with or develop this aspect of their work. Instead, reflexivity for them seems to be "a thing in itself," either with an endpoint at the ethnographer's self-knowledge, or at least, with its relationship to the representation of objective knowledge in conventional ethnographic writing unexamined.

2. Jane Bachnik's dissertation (1978) about Japanese household structure and her long-term association with a particular household is an integrated text that skillfully merges a subjective, experiential account of her gaining knowledge with an objective representation and expansion of that knowledge. It is the most successful ethnography I have read that deals with the problem implicitly raised for ethnographic writing by the works of Rabinow and Dumont.

Especially now that fieldworkers gain attention and are critically rewarded for personal innovation in ethnographic writing, a general perspective on post-Malinowskian genre styles is needed in order to assess fully how particular strategies of text construction affect the credibility of ethnographic claims. The ethnographic form is, in turn, anthropology's way of both applying and adapting to its own concerns the theoretical stimuli it borrows. With Frye, I argue that a genre can only be understood in terms of its rhetoric, a dimension of their research activity about which anthropologists have been silent. The fundamental question concerning rhetoric as the basis of genre is the characteristic manner by which a text's language and organization convince its readers of the truth, or at least of the credibility, of its claims. With ethnography as its main product, anthropology's development of knowledge has proceeded more by changes in its rhetoric than by close conformity to a rhetoric-denying scientific model, concerned with rules of evidence and verification. The task of providing this general perspective on the past and present development of the ethnographic genre awaits a more ambitious work, including a study of representative texts, and is beyond my scope here.[3]

As an alternative or complement to a comparative study of ethnographic texts themselves, one of the most easily accessible ways to grasp the genre dimension of ethnographic writing in anthropological research would be to gauge readers' tacit expectations concerning what ethnographies should do by surveying past and current reviews in periodicals such as the *American Anthropologist* and the *American Ethnologist*. While reviews reflect the varied personal tastes, motivations, and critical reactions to specific ethnographic arguments among reviewers, on one level, at least, they have been keyed to broad expectations about the appropriate coverage, focus, and language of ethnographic writing. Such expectations are most often revealed in critical comments touching on the trade-off between specific argumentation and descriptive cover-

3. Refusal to undertake this task now makes this paper a programmatic note rather than a treatise. Here, I would only direct the reader to an important work by White (1973), who performs the sort of analysis for historical writing that I am suggesting for ethnographic writing. Although historians have long been conscious of the significance of writing in their research, and there is a richer and more varied tradition of historical than ethnographic writing, much of White's elaborate framework would be relevant for a genre analysis of ethnography. While the work of Michel Foucault is one obvious source of inspiration for thinking systematically about genres, White prefers the perspectives of Northrop Frye and Kenneth Burke.

age in contemporary ethnographies. Whatever the particular arguments or topic of an ethnographic text, readers expect an ethnography to give a sense of the conditions of fieldwork; of everyday life (Malinowski's "imponderabilia"); of micro-process (an implicit validation of participant observation); of holism (a form of portraiture integrated with the pursuit of particular claims); and of translation across cultural and linguistic boundaries (the broad, contextual exegesis of indigenous terms and concepts). There are no standard ways—particularly now—in which an ethnographer accomplishes these tasks, but however interesting or strongly argued a text's claims may be, a work fails as an ethnography if it does not realize these traditional genre characteristics in some recognizable way for the reader. These tasks depend importantly on the literary ability of the author as well as on strategies of organizing material.

Contemporary ethnographies are rarely catalogs or encyclopedias that exhaustively describe a culture, but there is a general sense in anthropology that they should provide a holistic view in which the reader is confident—perhaps an illusion—that the blanks can be filled in. If the reader as reviewer does not have such confidence, this is frequently cause for criticizing an ethnography for its omissions. This criticism may not in fact concern data which have been omitted so much as the ethnographer's failure to sketch vividly enough the boundaries of a cultural unit.

While a reader may isolate and evaluate the focal arguments of an ethnography independently of how well the author has accomplished the general task of placing a text within the ethnographic genre, these two levels of text construction, although analytically distinguished here, are fully integrated both in the activity of writing and in the reader's general assessment of any particular text. The important point, then, is that while the accomplishment of the rhetorical task of setting a work within the ethnographic genre does not wholly determine the reaction to its specific, focused claims, it does subtly and importantly affect this reaction. By the manner of conforming to ethnographic rhetoric, an author establishes a generalized authority and knowledge as an integral dimension, pervading the text, against which specific reactions to arguments are formed by readers. The expression of this general knowledge, which is not the same as exhaustively reproducing it, is the ethnographer's way of insuring a basic persuasiveness and credibility, reflecting in turn the broad scope of what one is expected to know from fieldwork.

To establish this generalized persuasiveness and authority, while pursuing a specific organizing argument, data focus, or mode of analysis, is perhaps the major problem of rhetoric confronted more or less consciously in the writing of ethnographic texts.

One text that deserves special consideration in light of the foregoing discussion is Gregory Bateson's *Naven* (1936). It is perhaps the only ethnography that expresses a sense of its own emergence as a text while still undertaking the tasks of explaining and describing another culture. Bateson's rhetorical problem is clearly not the conventional one of representing the ethnographer's knowledge gained from fieldwork in such a way as to provide authoritative, generalized data that convinces the reader of the text's arguments and descriptions. He has little concern for discussing methods of collecting or defining data; he is markedly inexplicit about his field experience, personal relationships, linguistic competence, or length of stay; nor does he differentiate clearly second-hand data from firsthand observations. Rather, he is primarily concerned with the form of explanation and description as they develop in the writing of a text. He convinces the reader as he goes along that choices he is making in text organization are the appropriate ones for pursuing, however diffusely, an original set of arguments. *Naven* grows from a composite description of a puzzling, complex ritual to a selective, rambling investigation of Iatmul culture, through discussions of diverse, but related topics. This textual movement is punctuated by Bateson's commentaries on his changing terms of analysis, which he introduces in the course of making his transitions.[4] As such, *Naven* is an unruly, but coherent book, which has never been quite satisfying as an ethnography, especially within the genre context of functionalist ethnography at the time of its writing, but which nonetheless has always been stimulating to anthropologists in other senses. In one sense, at least, its enduring appeal has lain precisely in its explicit "playing" with the interrelationship between forms of writing and explanation, a problem which ethnographers have always faced, but which they have treated tacitly and without much novelty.

Although widely respected, *Naven* long remained an oddity with minimal substantive influence on established ethnographic styles. In the present period of experimentation with ethnographic writing, *Naven*'s

---

4. In a later paper (1972 [1940]), Bateson discusses explicitly his handling of certain conceptual problems in the writing of *Naven*.

relevance is more apparent, not so much for its point about the close relationship between ethnographic writing and explanation, as for its particular style of textual organization and analysis, which has served as an inspiration or model for particular contemporary ethnographies (e.g., see Schieffelin 1976).

Aside from the present diversity of ethnographic texts, it is interesting to consider kinds of research involving fieldwork for which the writing of ethnographies may not be the appropriate product. Any investigation entailing a more rigorous research design of fieldwork than common in anthropology may lead to alternative forms for reportage and theorizing. One of the clearest past examples of this was the so-called new ethnography (Harris 1968), which provided rigorous procedures of data elicitation, and produced a series of programmatic papers and demonstrations, but ironically, very few ethnographic texts. More recently, sociobiologists have tried to find the necessary evidence in existing ethnographies to establish credibility for applying a perspective from evolutionary biology to human societies (Chagnon and Irons 1979:509). While suggestive, relevant ethnographic descriptions, shaped by the traditional rhetoric of the accounts in which they appear, do not seem to be adequate as evidence for sociobiological claims. Thus, in designing more focused and methodologically self-conscious fieldwork, sociobiologists may write accounts that either remain within positivist styles of constructing ethnographies or eschew ethnography for a more general style of scientific writing, which has remained perhaps more insensitive than ethnography to its own conceptual rhetoric.

Also, experimentation firmly within the tradition of ethnographic writing may lead to other kinds of texts in which the distillation of the diffuse, encyclopedic knowledge from fieldwork into a structure of facts and interpretations is no longer the main rhetorical task in constructing a text. Rather, field experience may serve merely as a stimulus and background to thought for broadly synthetic, philosophical, or reflective works, the rhetoric of which is suggestive of the ethnographic genre, but outside it (for example, Lévi-Strauss's rhetoric of a classical essayist in *Tristes Tropiques*). Whether such works are to be considered ethnographies is partly a matter of convention and arbitrary categorization, but most importantly, depends on an understanding of their relation to the ethnographic genre as it has developed.

In conclusion, I wish to anticipate two objections to the suggestion that the study of ethnographic writing *sui generis* merits the analytical importance I claim for it. First, it cannot be denied that there are closely interdependent relationships between the development of fieldwork, ethnography, and theory, and that these should not be artificially isolated. Yet, a separate treatment of ethnographic writing is justified, not only because it is in fact a temporally and intellectually separate activity —deskwork as opposed to fieldwork—but also precisely because its substantive identity has been so thoroughly submerged in discussions focused on the other two terms. Far from being epiphenomenal, ethnographic writing is the actual context through which anthropologists learn of each other's fieldwork and theoretical claims. Thus of the three terms, it is *only* ethnographic writing which is perhaps completely deserving of a separate treatment, since it embodies the process by which anthropologists synthesize fieldwork and theory.

Second, providing a perspective for understanding ethnographic writing should not be construed as suggesting a method or set of standards for writing ethnographies. Although such a perspective might have quite different ultimate aims and interests from those of literary criticism in relation to prose, it nonetheless has a similar relation to its object— attention to the language and form of a text as an integral expression of the author's intentions and claims. A discussion of variations in ethnography's rhetorical style is just as important for assessing the strengths and limitations of any particular work as is an evaluation of its logic and evidence. In fact, the two kinds of assessment are entwined, complementary, and only analytically distinguishable. Taking for granted the option of examining rhetoric impoverishes any overall assessment of a work's arguments and descriptions.

8 MASKED I GO FORWARD: REFLECTIONS ON THE MODERN SUBJECT

PAUL RABINOW

The search for an epistemological subject who would be the locus of unbiased certitude is usually traced to the seventeenth century. The *locus classicus* of this position is, of course, Descartes. His *Discourse on Method* lays out the program of certitude for the knower through analytic progression against which philosophy for the last three hundred and fifty years has measured itself.

The search for a nonmystified, nonreified subject has taken many turns in modern times. It has also generated strong counter-reactions. Perhaps the most basic of these, or at least the most relevant in anthropology, consists in criticizing without pity the illusions which surround the supposed autonomy and substantial firmness of the subject. This task consists in demonstrating the illusions and interests embedded in the

Originally published in *Philosophy and social criticism* 2(1979).

view of the anthropologist as a value-free, decontextualized, passionless, and objective spokesman of science. The theoretical underpinnings of such a neutral, unsituated subject have been thoroughly undermined for a long time. The attempts to ground such a subject epistemologically —whether in Cartesianism, positivism, or Husserlian phenomenology —have all floundered. Whether one looks to the mockery of Classical essayists, or to recent arguments of Habermas and critical theory or to those of hermeneutical philosophers or to the tidal wave of structuralism in France, the bankruptcy of the mere observer position is today manifest.

Perhaps the most subtle refutation of them all, however, is that despite the vast array of theoretical arguments brought into play against it, the scientistic paradigm still holds sway in the everyday practices of the discipline. Surely if reason were the yardstick, then the form in which ethnographies are written, the way research is conceived and judged, would look drastically different than they do today. The sustained hold which the model of science for anthropology maintains is a tribute to the deep embeddedness of these assumptions in our culture and how much interest there is in protecting them.

Several alternate modes of discourse, more reasonable models of anthropology, are currently available. Roland Barthes points to one strategy for overcoming the illusions of either the scientific and anonymous subject or its mirror image; the Romantic, creative, individual subject. This strategy is one which generalizes the subject. Barthes traces this position to Nietzsche, but for anthropology, Rousseau also springs to mind. Barthes says that in this position the subject "is interpretation itself, as a form of will to power which exists not as a 'being' but as a process, a becoming, in the form of a passion" (Barthes 1975:98). This style is not well represented in anthropology. Perhaps Stanley Diamond would be the most renowned of its champions in his attempts to re-appropriate the sources of anthropology not as a personal quest but as a trailing dialectic in which civilization is forced to negate itself when it weighs its own image of progress against its actions in the world. This is certainly a promising path which deserves more attention (Diamond 1974).

Another strategy is to annihilate the subject altogether. Particularly in France, in the last twenty years, it has become almost *de rigueur* to celebrate the obliteration of the illusions of the substantial and creative subject. In its place one talks in the name of structures, texts, intertexts, objective fields of discourse, epistemes, and so forth. Within this tradition there is no subject, transcendental or otherwise; there is only the play of signifiers, the play of difference. Systems generate systems across and through the crumbling remains of the humanistic (or in France the Cartesian) subject. The aim of anthropology, Lévi-Strauss tells us, is to dissolve man. Whatever their other intramural animosities, Foucault, Derrida, and Bourdieu would gladly participate in splashing the corrosive acid of deconstruction on the traditional subject.

But it is not easy to live with or be totally persuaded by a world which is merely the endless play of arbitrary signifiers, in which mysterious archaeological shifts in the epistemological foundation occur abruptly and determine our perceptions, in which consciousness is seen as the most dangerous of snares. Perhaps most distressingly, since *conscience* means both consciousness and conscience, in such a world an ethics in a strict sense is unthinkable.

Roland Barthes, himself formerly a champion of structuralism, in his delightfully unorthodox *Le Plaisir du Texte*, suggests that now that the subject has been destroyed: "Then perhaps the subject returns, not as illusion, but as fiction. A certain pleasure is derived from a way of imagining oneself as individual, of inventing a final rarest fiction: the fictive identity. This fiction is no longer the illusion of a unity; on the contrary, it is the theater of society in which we stage our plural: our pleasure is individual—but not personal" (Barthes 1975:62).

Fiction, pleasure, social theater, plural unity, impersonal identity: a set of terms most anthropologists would certainly refuse to entertain as central either for the discipline or for themselves. One can easily conjure up the moralizing snort of outrage or the perhaps slightly too raucous laughter of dismissal which such a set of terms would occasion.

Let me be direct and state that I believe they offer a promising path for anthropology to follow. To embellish my pronouncement of faith, let me turn for aid to a recent book on North Africa in which a similar road is traveled. The author of this book is Jean Duvignaud, a French sociologist, playwright, novelist, critic.

Duvignaud's book is entitled *Change at Shebika* (1977). Over a period of several years, while he was a visiting professor of sociology at the University of Tunis, Duvignaud directed a team of young Tunisian students in the study of a small, isolated, poor village named Shebika in the southwest corner of the country. His book is a subtle and complexly studied recounting of the processes of change which oc-

curred during the research. Duvignaud himself, the villagers, *and* the
Tunisian students, the fledgling sociologists, were all changed in vital
and interconnected ways. The power of the book lies in the artful
presentation of this transformation. Duvignaud shows us that it is only
when all of these themes are kept together that the story is worth telling.

Change at Shebika can be likened to a modern Platonic dialogue in
which memory, knowledge, and ironic dialectic are interwoven in an
artfully constructed theatrical form. The form is modern and not Platonic, however, in the fact that the central term of the story is becoming
and not being.

Duvignaud and his team of researchers came to this typically out-of-
the-way village to conduct what was to be an essentially standard study
of underdevelopment. As the study progressed, however, it became
clear to Duvignaud that the process of inquiry, the presence of the
young Tunisian investigators, was having an important effect both on
the researchers themselves (originally one of anxiety acted out by contemptuous distancing or sentimental denial) *and* on the villagers, who
began to develop (or to continue the Platonic imagery—rediscover)
their identity, not, it should be added, their selves.

Duvignaud centers his construction of this re-memorization and
revalorization of existence around the image of the saint's tomb in the
village. The modern Tunisian researchers were initially sure of their
cultural and emotional distance from and contempt for the shabby
remnants of the past represented by the neglected marabout's tomb.
Their complacency was reinforced by the extreme reluctance of the
villagers to discuss their saint. Their reluctance stemmed from the fact
(the story emerges over time) that although the saint was the locus of
identity for the village, the villagers knew nothing about him. In a
stunning moment of collective self-realization the villagers were forced
to admit to themselves and to Duvignaud's equip that the saint's tomb
was empty. But it was precisely at that moment of self-realization that
the dialectic process of investigation and re-telling is most forcefully
brought to the fore by Duvignaud. The anxiety, contempt, and distance
—the jealously guarded identities of the urban students and the peasants
—began to change, were put radically in question. The destruction
wrought by colonialism and an inner enervation of tradition were
brought to consciousness. A cathartic process of rage, reflection, and
active seeking of retribution began.

Duvignaud chronicled the social theater of renewal which took place. The contemptuous distances, masking fear, began to fade and the silent routine and obsessive repetition of everyday forms began to alter. Active social self-definition and valorization replaced them. The villagers, with the help of the sociologists, and the sociologists, with the help of the villagers, began to form a sense of their own identity and worth —of their connectedness to a larger Tunisian world. This led, in a complex dialectic operating on the emotional, reflective, and political levels, all beautifully chronicled by Duvignaud, to a demand by the villagers for government aid and recognition. The refusal of such aid led to a strike—a stunning public self-dramatization of collective worth— which would have been unthinkable in such a village only months previously.

But Duvignaud's modernity and honesty are displayed in his portrayal of events. The strike fails. There is no soap opera ending. In a postscript to the book written several years later, Duvignaud (1973) tells us with a good deal of wistfulness that the village had been turned into a kind of tourist trap partly because of a minor notoriety his book had given it.

The limits of consciousness and self-awareness to achieve revolutionary change are today starkly apparent. The immense destructive potential of neo-colonial forms of domination is honestly set forth. The myths of self-mobilization through consciousness-raising under whose banners the project had been undertaken and which Duvignaud obviously shared, are presented. To see all of this as a failure, however, is to miss at least half the point.

To blame Duvignaud for not having a happy ending is obviously absurd. The happy endings we were promised in the sixties must be seen as a collective delusion under which too many of us labored. But abandoning hope or counting calories is not the point either. If we can no longer rise to the timeless Platonic forms of the Good, then we had better face the dissociation and partial victories available to the unhappy consciousness. Duvignaud's fiction is one of hope, ethically cast, offering the image of wholeness, social action, and understanding, even in defeat. Winning is not the only thing.

If, as Stanley Diamond argues, the task of anthropology is the unending critique of civilization, then Duvignaud is the anthropologist's anthropologist. Our collective plight is presented as social theater: men in dark times representing to themselves images of their own worth. A fiction, to be sure. We are shown the possibility of collective identity beyond that of late capitalism: the tomb is empty, the tomb is full. A plural fiction of the subject. We see clearly that social science arrives with modernization but so too does an expanded horizon of possibility. Small consolation to be sure. As Duvignaud shows, the moment of messianism is past. However, in this complex anthropological fiction the good and the beautiful once again rejoin the true.

Had Duvignaud's dialectic of theory and practice played itself out, the logical result would have been that the Western social scientist would have ceased to exist. Certain methods, certain insights, a self-reflective and critical stance would have been passed along to his students. The success of the French anthropologist would have been total if he could have suppressed himself (perhaps to reappear in another guise). Then the synthesizing analysis and creative social action could have been carried forward by the Tunisians themselves. As I suggested, this is not quite what happened. Duvignaud did in fact leave. However, his presence, or more precisely, French presence, did not disappear so easily. In place of Duvignaud's dialectic wisdom came tourism: the commoditization of tradition, space, and, one fears, ultimately of identity. As Duvignaud has given us only a limited account of this sad path now opening to these villagers, let us leave them be.

To follow out this chronicle of modernity and the subject, let us leave Duvignaud's account and shift to another; a startlingly powerful but depressing book entitled *La Plus Haute des Solitudes* (1977). Its author is Tahar ben Jelloun, a Moroccan poet, novelist, and columnist for *Le Monde*. Jelloun lives and works in Paris. Interestingly enough, Jelloun has moved, for the moment at least, from the mode of professed fiction (poems, novels) to social science. He decided to work for a doctorate in social psychiatry in Paris. His subject matter would be the sexual and emotional problems of North African workers in France.

So here we have a reversal of the preceding situation. Duvignaud was an outsider whose role was to start a process of reappropriation of tradition. Jelloun was an outsider whose role was to unmask the deepest meanings of modernity. Duvignaud's role (as he gradually found out) was to facilitate and understand the plural unity which was being acted out in the social theater of the village. Jelloun's will be, as we shall see, to look reflectively on *pleasure*—or more precisely its suppression—as being terribly relevant to the modernity in which the North African emigré workers find themselves (1977:8):

The theme is a profound one: "from these men who have been ripped from their homelands, their families, their culture, only their labor power is asked. For the rest, no one is interested. The rest is a lot. Go measure the need to be accepted, loved, recognized, the need to live among one's own, in the love of the earth, the friendship of the sun . . . these men, coming from another culture, are denied the right to emotion and desire.

There is no professional subject/object split here. He says: "My account *(témoignage)* is not that of a neutral and innocent observer. My presence, my work, engaged me in the private lives of others; I can't say exactly how much I moved into this space and consequently I no longer know who was observing whom" (ibid.:10).

This is not to say in the least that Jelloun's concerns or intent were personalistic or rampantly subjectivistic (as the tag usually goes); he in fact is too deep a thinker, too complicated an author to accept such shallow positivistic distinctions. Rather, he is telling us that it is only by refusing such alienating splits that he could form an image of his own identity as a socially mediated character. He understood that both he and the workers were caught in a nexus of modern industrial civilization in Paris, although he never loses sight of the fact that he is situated in a very different part of the social field than they are. He thereby avoids the false romanticism or mysteriously narratorless chronicles common in anthropology. Jelloun is constantly in the narrative because that is what constitutes it after all. But its structure is one which moves away from his personal situation toward a social field.

These are men in extreme distress. He aids them with the critical tools at his disposal—his psychoanalytic understanding, his keen awareness of the wounds of colonialism and the destructiveness of their situation—but he sees and feels, all too often, the obvious limits of his insights, the societal constraints on his help, the limited ability he has to alter the larger conditions which have brought these men to the clinic in the first place.

Jelloun writes beautifully. His prose is analytic and lyric at the same time. It is his deep sensibility and his openness to the reality of suffering that feeds his writing and brought him to undertake this project. But these talents, these sensibilities are deepened and broadened by his studies of cross-cultural social psychiatry. They in no way work at cross purposes here. Theory and practice enhance each other. The deeper the one, the deeper the other. The old categories no longer hold.

Jelloun situates the problematic of the book as the crossing of two cultures, two worlds at war with each other. Two societies: on the French side, these men have been brought to France to work. "Capitalism desires anonymous men, emptied of their desires, but full of labor power. The dominant classes in France as in North Africa institutionalize immigration" (ibid.:9). The racism so rampant in France is evoked, the miserable conditions of life which these men must endure are present throughout, the brutality of the whole context is never absent. But, these infrastructural conditions have been described many times now; there is a minor industry in French sociology concerned with them. Well and good. Jelloun's real task and his contribution is to begin where these other studies leave off.

The heart of the book is a series of cases in which these men express their problems, fears, experiences, lives. The voice from the Other—the reflection back of the callousness, brutality, and indifference of modern industrial society—is not easy to listen to (ibid.:117–18):

> Let's listen to a Moroccan, 45-years-old, father of two children. In 1971 he lost a finger on his right hand in a work related accident. Since, his left testicle has swollen up and his sexuality weakened. The following year he had pulmonary problems and spent six months in a sanitarium. He has seen several urologists for his sexual problems. Weak erections. Low morale. He speaks slowly:
> Before, I had erections all the time, night and day. But since I have been sick, for three years now, I have done nothing; no sex. I go to the whores but that is worthless. I lose my money that's all.
> Why speak of my life, of my past? I don't see the relationship. Before, I wasn't sick. It's now that things are bad.
> Why aren't there drugs in France for my illness? Perhaps they don't want to cure me? Maybe because I am a Berber. So, what are you going to give me which will help me get an erection.
> Since I've been ill things are getting worse and worse. Here, people don't have anytime to live. I can't live with these people. Our religion, our language have no place here. So, I must return to my homeland, my family. But there is no work for me there. In my region the earth is barren.

For the North African the cause of these sexual and emotional problems (which are often associated with an accident at work) must be physical. The idea that the anxiety they are feeling is caused by their psychic dilemmas or, more importantly, could be cured by working on their psyches simply is not a possibility. Therefore, the worker begins to search for the physical causes of his illness. He is convinced that a physical illness is a curable one and that it is Western medicine, which he has invested with enormous mythical power, which must be able to achieve this cure. This attitude is reinforced by the fact that in North Africa it is only the bourgeoisie who can afford the fancy new hospitals or the trips to France to be cured by Western medicine.

"When something is upset in the body or in the psyche, the North African goes first to consult a medical doctor" (ibid.:41). In popular Moroccon beliefs the sexual act is dependent on physical force. When there are sexual problems, it must be that the body's force has been damaged; the doctor must restore the man's force; the magic of science is invoked. This being the case, the therapeutic situation is made even more complicated by the fact that the worker believes that he has been deceived and failed by the doctors he has already seen. There must be a cure; if they have not found it, it is because they don't want to have him cured or because they are incompetent. He will try another doctor, another clinic. This is the fundamental demand: cure me. As Jelloun remarks, it is fundamentally a magical view. The doctor has the secrets of health if he will only reveal them.

The stakes are high. Almost all the expressions the workers use to describe their sexual problems bring in their death. "My sex is cold, like death. . . . My breath is finished, Dead. . . . Life is nothing if I can't make love, like a cemetery" (ibid.:45). The worker has suggestions as to what to do, which he pushes on the doctor: X-rays, surgery, drugs (particularly injections). In a word, there is an urgent appeal to Western technology, that supreme magic, to save him. An Algerian told Jelloun: "I am like a car, a Mercedes, but without a motor" (ibid.:47).

This appeal to modern technology as a magical cure is the first step, which can entail many many visits and demands in various clinics around Paris. When the worker seems to feel that this recourse is not going to work, he turns to a second level—the demand for retribution. He demands a pension or a cash settlement. He knows that the soldiers who fought for the French and were wounded received recompense. The connection between the wounds of the old colonial empire and those of the new, modern, neo-colonial one are assimilated.

Jelloun is chronicaling for us the fate of the attempt to create an objective self—stripped of its passions, freed of its subjectivity, its needs quantifiable and known: the dream of modernity. What he shows us is one end point of such a project; the counterimage of modernity, that state beyond all desire, beyond death, which many of these men reach, however unwillingly. For the North African workers in France are put into a condition closely resembling a black parody of economic man.

Just as in an earlier stage of anthropology we searched for the "primitive," now that we have come of age, we go to find economic man, calculating man, laboring man around the world, lurking under the veil of strange customs and costumes.

These workers are brought to Paris for their labor power. Their needs are defined in the most radically minimal of ways. This is not to say that they are totally ignored. There are quarters of the city where shabby and substandard workers' dormitories are maintained. Jelloun calls these rooms "suitcases" in one of his novels. There are by now substantial areas of Paris with largely North African cafes, restaurants, even Arabic-language movies (from Egypt and Algeria). There are, of course, the clinics which service the workers. And, of course, there are a larger number of prostitutes reserved for these men.

It is perhaps in the great cities of Europe that the commerce of illusion is the most ruthless. It embodies a misery suited to the highest of solitudes; those of the prostitutes who are used, tired, bitter; those who work the immigrants, emptied of the last illusion, destined to that beaten category of man who comes from time to time to empty his testicles in a burst of uneasy heat, of shame and of despair. They come and line up in the hallway, silently. No words are exchanged. Certain lower their heads, especially on leaving while crossing the corridors and passing by those who wait their turn (ibid.:83).

So pleasure is taken into account in late capitalism: as a commodity and an alienated passion reduced to the physical. There is a social theater (work place, boarding houses, cafes, clinics, whores of Barbès), but the stage is rather shabby. Impersonal identity, one of ontological degradation, is achieved.

Jelloun chronicles all this beautifully, if that word is tolerable for such a grim panorama. Jelloun does not stop there. Rather he traces the fantasy images of revenge, the faint and desperate attempts to seek retribution from this social theater of late capitalism; he paints or brings to discourse the archaic and suppressed images of wholeness which appear in the narratives of the therapeutic interviews. The fantasy revenge on these institutions, their deconstruction through dream and regression revealing earlier, deeper images of a particular cultural self before its distortions by the modern, objective conditions of labor. Through the reports of the therapy sessions in which these men are at least given the power to speak, we see fragments, moments, symbols of what is missing in this terrifying reduction.

Again, there is not much hope here. There is no easy sense on

Jelloun's part that talking or even therapeutic discourse can offer a
solution. What it can do is affirm the resistance and humanity of these
men in face of what they are submitted to. Perhaps, it helps some to keep
going, or to return to North Africa. Perhaps, for some, to fight for better
conditions. But the limits of discourse are always clear to Jelloun. For
the wounds are real, and it is not in books that they will be healed. For
that to happen, the Maghreb would have to change drastically and so
would France. But again the fictive image of hope, the collective power
of an articulated resistance to Object man, the fantasy of more fully
meaningful community—not now found on either side of the Mediter-
ranean—is held forth as necessary.

One feels all too strongly that these contradictions—these plural
unities—both tear Jelloun apart and in a subtle sense sustain his own
sense of self-worth. His naiveté (meant as a positive virtue of character
and imagination) is both greater and smaller than Duvignaud's. Duvignaud saw the possibility of collective action in the world. The transformation of social passivity into another form. Jelloun explicitly operates
on the fictive level of derealization from the start (although we should
remember that Duvignaud is also a playwright and novelist). But as
Duvignaud went to Tunisia in search of Otherness, Jelloun finds himself in France seeking brotherhood with the most downtrodden. This
is simultaneously a political act, one of social science and one of poetry,
of fiction. As Jelloun says elsewhere, "Listen: I am not trying to make
you ashamed. Moralising raised no one from the common grave. Only,
realize that we share the same shroud" (1976:55).

I began by alluding to Descartes as the *locus classicus* of modern
meditations on the subject. I then sketched some of the alternatives
which developed in opposition to what is usually taken as the Cartesian
position. I then gave two accounts of recent attempts to formulate new
conceptions of the subject, object, and method of the human sciences.

In concluding, let me return briefly to Descartes. Descartes, too,
was an outsider, living most of his life in exile (if not in penury) in
Holland and Sweden. He probably never married; he certainly lived
without family. He was the object of severe attacks, both personal and
philosophical, although, of course, he also had many followers. He was
a Catholic, trained by the Jesuits, who spent the majority of his life in
Protestant countries.

One of the chief metaphors that Descartes uses in his *Discourse* is
that of the traveler. The implications of a subject journeying through

the different experiences of life is evoked. But it is qualified by an awareness that one should beware of spending too much time in transit; the traveler is best advised to pretend that he knows where he is going, even if he does not.

Descartes traveled a great deal in his life, as he tells us. From his travels he concluded that they were beneficial in that they showed the variability of customs, and this produces a certain respect for difference in the traveler, a tolerance, if you will. Descartes counsels the traveler that he is well advised to obey the customs and usages of the people he is visiting, as attacking them can be personally dangerous. Further, he cautions that "if one spends too much time traveling, one becomes a stranger in one's own country" (1968:3). He prudently takes the stance that in the world of custom and historical accident there is not the same kind of certainty as there is in mathematics.

Let me be clear here. Descartes certainly thought that it was possible to discover a clear ethical order, which God had laid out. But this order was not his chief concern, and he never quite got around (as the current saying has it) to telling us about it. This order would not lie on the level of the customary, the accidental, the quixotic, the level of habit and passional exchange which we call the social. It would lie in a God-given order.

Consequently, those moderns who point to Descartes as the founder of modernity are guilty of some quick redefinitions. For Descartes, there is a divine order in the world, and ultimately it can be known with appropriate scientific tools. An ethics comes along in the package. The frenzied world of everyday life, would, for Descartes, be outside the scope of his sure and distinct procedures. Although, again, for him this is not a problem. For the modern social scientist, however, there no longer is a God-given plan of nature or ethics. There is a new object of study—society—which lies in precisely that realm of history and petty interests and passions which Descartes had put aside. So, claiming Descartes as the founder of their enterprise is an absurdity.

Descartes's motto was *larvatus pro deo* "Masked I go forward." He says in *Les Preambules:* "In order that the blush on their faces does not show, actors on the stage put on a mask. Like them, when I go out into this theatre of a world, where hither I have been but a spectator, masked I go forward.[1] Obviously this is not the place to explore the complexity

1. For further reflections on this subject, see Nancy 1977:15.

of Baroque aesthetics or the philosophical, theological, and sexual (re-member the blush) implications of what Descartes was saying. Perhaps it will be sufficiently tantalizing to remember that Descartes was himself an actor and a dancer and wrote at least three plays and a ballet, which have been lost to us. Modern interpreters have stripped away all of these masks in the name of revealing the true Descartes, the precursor of their modernity, Descartes the scientist. But they want to ignore the blush-ing, God-ordained actor they find shivering there.

I certainly am not claiming that Descartes's position is the same as those of Barthes or Duvignaud or Jelloun or my own.[2] To take just one example, clearly his view of the subject as having a "true" self hidden behind the deceitful masks of social life is not one which is tenable any longer. I raise the example of Descartes only to indicate that from the very beginning of what is known as modernity the situation was a great deal more complicated than is usually allowed.

If we can agree with Stanley Diamond that "anthropology is the study of men in crisis by men in crisis" (1974:53), as I think we can; and if we can agree with Jean-Paul Sartre when he says that a new anthropology will have arisen when we realize that "the questioner, the question and the questioned are one" (1968), then I would argue that the way forward for anthropology—away from and beyond positivism —begins by looking backwards to the multivocal traditions in which we are inevitably embedded and forward to possible new modes of relating to the social world, in which, for better or worse, we find ourselves.

2. For a more extended version of my position, see Rabinow 1977 and 1979.

9 RITUAL UNDRESS AND THE COMEDY OF SELF AND OTHER: BANDELIER'S *THE DELIGHT MAKERS*

BARBARA A. BABCOCK

I do not believe that the process of interpretation really can or should be separated from the product. Neither do I believe that we can or should separate the understanding and interpretation of Others and their texts from an understanding of our Selves. I would like to begin, therefore, with something of a personal foreword and to conclude with an equally personal afterword. In between, I would like to talk about that *picarón* of southwestern anthropology Adolph Bandelier and the uncommon tale he told of Pueblo ritual clowning.

This essay was begun in 1978 at the School of American Research. I am greatly indebted to Douglas Schwartz and members of his staff for creating an atmosphere conducive to reflection and writing. I am also indebted to Alfonso Ortiz, Joseph Jorgensen, and Charles Gallenkamp for comments and conversations that clarified and encouraged. My greatest debts are to Helen Cordero and Keith Basso who, in very different ways, made it "all come together."

Pretext

In 1969 I began studying folklore and anthropology, and in the ten years since, I have been fascinated and frustrated by one form or another of trickster tale, ritual inversion, or literary deconstruction. After chasing clowns through many dusty tomes, I finally reached Santa Fe in the fall of 1977 and began following them around even dustier Pueblo plazas. If anything, the fascination and the frustration were compounded. One can observe and try to interpret, but one cannot easily, if ever, interrogate these sacred makers of disorder and delight. So, in the days and nights between dances I returned to the libraries and archives to study portraits made of clowns in an earlier day under very different constraints.

Since the Spanish Conquest, Pueblo clowns have been persecuted in person and in print by priests, missionaries, and the Bureau of Indian Affairs. This persecution as well as an emphasis on the normal and serious aspects of culture and society in the anthropological literature have meant that the subject of clowns has been and generally is avoided. But, in this as in other respects, Bandelier was unorthodox and iconoclastic. Page after page of his *Southwestern Journals* and archaeological reports are given over to description of these "disgusting creatures" in "full ritual undress," and the Koshare—one type of Keresan clown—are the protagonists, or rather the antagonists, of his 500-page ethnographic fiction. Published in 1890 in both German and English, *Die Koshäre* or *The Delight Makers* was the first novel written about Pueblo Indians and is still one of the best—and the only full-length—published accounts of ritual clowning. The novel is rarely read and then only for its ethnographic content, and is generally regarded as a quaint, if informative, document in the history of Keresan anthropology.

As I watched the clowns myself, reread his "romance" and compared it with his journals and scientific reports, questions of style and form and intention became as interesting as the Koshare themselves. I cannot separate the literary critic in me from the ethnographer, nor could I separate the whys and hows and the verbal world of Bandelier's text from a concern with the world from which and about which it speaks. It taunted me, as did a remark by the noted German archaeologist C. W. Ceram (1971:67): "The book is unique and remains outside the categories of literary criticism. Not that the literary critics have taken the slightest notice of it up to the present day." I began to wonder if this "unique hybrid's" resistance to definition by literary canons might not be a clue to its purpose, and if the uneasiness it created in the reader by confounding his expectations might not be a key to its meaning.[1]

Text

Adolph Francis Bandelier was born in Berne, Switzerland, on 6 August 1840, the son of a Swiss army officer and a Russian aristocrat. When he was eight, his family emigrated to the German-Swiss community of Highland, Illinois. After a spotty formal education, Bandelier worked in various failing enterprises of his father's, including a bank, a foundry, and the Confidence Coal Mine. He hated these "dreary and annoying" businesses and survived their "life of mental slavery" by escaping on evenings and Sundays into the Indian cultures of Mexico and Latin America described by early Spanish explorers and historians. In 1873 he met Lewis Henry Morgan and thereupon began a vigorous correspondence and a series of publications on the prehistoric cultures of Mexico that changed his life. Bandelier's strenuous double life led to a nervous breakdown early in 1880, after which he appealed to Morgan to help him find work suitable to his temperament and scholarly interests and get out of Highland and "that infernal hole" of a coal mine. Morgan was successful, and under the auspices of the newly founded American Institute of Archaeology, Bandelier went to New Mexico later that year "to study prehistoric and living Indian cultures."

While waiting in Highland for the completion of official arrangements, he wrote to Morgan: "How long this drudging day and night will last till it carries me to the grave or the insane asylum, I cannot tell" (L. A. White 1940[II]:194). Three months later while exploring the Pueblo ruins in Pecos, New Mexico, he wrote: "I am dirty, ragged, and sunburnt, but of best cheer. My life's work has at last begun" (ibid.:212–13). Bandelier spent the better part of twelve years in the Southwest, traveled thousands of miles unarmed and poorly clad on foot and on horseback, and under the most severe and unfavorable conditions—he was reported dead several times and read his own obituaries—laid the foundations for future research in the archaeology, early history, and

---

1. Cf. Froma Zeitlin's argument (1971) regarding Petronius' *Satyricon*.

ethnology of the Southwest. Beyond the much-repeated words insatiable, indefatigable, and encyclopedic, it is difficult to characterize either the man or his work. His was a complex and contradictory personality: at once condescending toward the poor benighted savages, while living with and loving them "as a brother," enthralled with the complexities of their culture; at once aristocratic, aloof, and confident, yet extremely sensitive to and desirous of the friendship and respect of others, and so on. Even his good friend and co-explorer Charles Lummis was to write when he died: "I have known many scholars and some heroes—but they seldom come in the same original package. As I remember Bandelier with smallpox alone in the two-foot snows of the Manzanos, I deeply wonder at the dual quality of his intellect. . . . I have never known such student and such explorer lodged in one tenement" (Bandelier 1971:xxvi).

It is equally difficult to categorize and evaluate his work within disciplinary boundaries. His unique contribution was his determined attempt to combine several disciplines—notably documentary history, archaeology, and ethnography—with rare linguistic gifts (he spoke four European languages and easily mastered dialects and Indian tongues) in an effort to reconstruct a significant phase in southwestern cultural history *and* to deconstruct stereotypes of the savage, past and present. Whatever its faults, all of his work is distinguished by an overriding concern with cultural relationships.

After leaving New Mexico in 1892, he continued the same sort of work in Peru, taught "his favorite subject" (Spanish-American literature in its connection with ethnology and archaeology) at Columbia University, and died in Seville, Spain, in 1914 while deciphering documents of the conquest.

The first pueblo in which Bandelier lived was the Keres village of Santo Domingo. After being quite literally "starved out" (Bandelier 1933:171), he went across the Rio Grande to Cochiti where he was received "with open arms" (L. A. White 1940[II]:214), and where he remained for three months on that first visit. His attitude toward and relationship with the people of Cochiti, he summed up as follows: "My relations with the Indians of this Pueblo are very friendly. Sharing their food, their hardships, and their pleasures simple as they are, a mutual attachment has formed itself, which grows into sincere affection. They begin to treat me as one of their own, and to exhibit toward me that spirit of fraternity which prevails among them in their communism. Of course, they have squabbles among themselves, which often reveal to me some new features of their organization; but on the whole they are the best people the sun shines upon (Bandelier and Hewett 1937:248).

The Cochiteños also shared their stories, myths, and legends with him and took him to the ruins north of Cochiti from whence they had come. On 23 October 1880, he entered Frijoles Canyon and the ruins of the pueblo Tyuonyi, which he described as "the grandest thing I ever saw" (Bandelier 1966:165). He returned again and again, lived in the caves of "this Stone Age of the past," made detailed drawings and archaeological reports, and three years later, when again trapped in Highland, Illinois, began a novel recreating prehistoric Keresan life in this setting.[2] The Tewa dimension of the novel was added later after he returned to Santa Fe in 1885 and lived and worked in the pueblo of San Juan.

Less than a month after discovering El Rito de los Frijoles, Bandelier first encountered Cochiti clowns, whom he referred to as Koshare or *entremeseros*—the latter a Spanish term denoting those who perform farces between the acts of a play. Among the Keres themselves, these sacred clowns associated with the Turquoise Kiva are called *Ku-sha'li*. Their equivalent appears throughout the Rio Grande Pueblos. Among the Tewa they are called *Kossa;* among the Tiwa, Black Eyes or *chifunane.* His reaction to these nearly naked black and white apparitions with corn husk horns, creating a pandemonium of disorder and delight, was one of disgust, fascination, and characteristically detailed description (1966:199–200):

During [the dancing] the skirmishers kept acting around them. One of them, who was particularly fond of rolling in the dust, was at last dragged about and through the lines [of dancers] by his companions till he was completely naked. There an exhibition of obscenity hard to describe took place. Sodomy, coitus, masturbation, etc. were performed to greatest perfection, men accoupling with each other on the ground or standing, and to the greatest delight of the spectators . . . looking on with greatest ingenuity and innocence, not the slightest indecent look on the part of the women, and applauding the vilest motions. I was terribly ashamed, but nobody seemed to take any concern about it . . . [When the dancers departed] the clowns followed them with their abominable gestures, and actually carried back one girl, threw her down, and while one was performing coitus from behind, another was doing it against her

2. In his preface, Bandelier (1970:146) says the first chapters were written at Cochiti. However, in his journal entry of 24 August 1883 from Highland, Illinois, he says, "Began to write my novel."

head. Of course, all was simulated, and not the real act, as the women were dressed. The naked fellow performed masturbation in the center of the plaza, alternately with a black rug and with his hand. Everybody laughed. I went home.

Bandelier was neither the first nor the last Anglo observer to be unsettled by the Koshare, but he was perhaps the most accurate and the most honest. These powerful beings are unsettling to insiders as well as outsiders because of their ability to violate all boundaries, to upend and ridicule routine cultural reality, and to transform clear-cut and customary precepts into ambiguous, confused, and problematic ones. They are particularly disturbing to us, because they confound our time-honored (at least since the Reformation) distinctions between the sacred and the secular, the serious and the ludic, and so on. Like the critic of Sterne's *The Sermons of Mr. Yorick,* we are inclined to question "if the solemn dictates of religion are fit to be conveyed from the mouths of Buffoons and ludicrous Romancers?" (quoted in Swearingen 1977:38). The cross-cultural dilemma is best summed up by a Hopi clown responding to an observer not unlike Bandelier: "Well, white man . . . you think business is vulgar, but it means something sacred to us. This old katcina is impersonating the Corn maiden; therefore we must have intercourse with her so that our corn will increase and our people will live in plenty. If this were evil we would not be doing it. You are supposed to be an educated man, but you had better go back to school and learn something more about Pueblo life" (Simmons 1942:190).

As the preceding suggests, clowns are a great deal more than delight makers, and Bandelier's English title is something of a misnomer, probably derived from his friend Cushing who spoke of the Zuñi Koyemci as "makers of delight for the people" (Hobbs 1942b:165). Pueblo clowns are among the most powerful of ritual personages, mediating between the worlds of the spirits and the living; controlling weather and fertility; associated both with curing and with warfare; given punitive and policing functions, particularly against witches; and in fact managing and supervising many of the ceremonies they appear to disrupt. As the novel makes evident, the Koshare inspire fear and awe as well as delight. In this respect, as in others, the novel is unique, for no other study is so concerned with how clowns are regarded from the native point of view.

Given Bandelier's initial reaction to these "disgusting creatures," which was reiterated year after year with every clown performance, one wonders why he gave the Koshare the title role in his novel, or why, given his interest in a scientific rather than a romantic portrait of the Indian, he wrote a novel at all. What he never says, but what I would like to suggest, is that *Die Koshäre* was a seven-year imaginative effort to come to terms with that which was most alien, most other. In contrast to his "scientific" writing, fiction gave him the license to indulge in wish fulfillment, to recreate a very different cultural world that all the research in the world could not put back together or enable him to enter, and to talk about himself in relation to that Otherness. Perhaps, too, his derogatory remarks notwithstanding, Bandelier recognized with characteristic perspicacity that

Burlesque and caricature best permit insights into Pueblo modes of conception since they reveal what the Pueblos find serious or absurd, baffling or wrong, fearful or comical about life and about other people. When these center about the lives of other people, they can be particularly instructive. . . . Much of what the Pueblos are and are *not,* as well as how they perceive alien groups can be deduced from the dramatic performances of clowns, those permanently equivocal and liminal characters who present a fundamental challenge in studying Pueblo world view. . . . The wonder is that this has gone almost completely unrecognized by ethnographers (Ortiz 1972:147, 155).

But what *did* this ethnographer who recognized the challenge really say about his motivations and intentions? In the preface to the first edition (Bandelier 1971:xxi), he explained: "I was prompted to perform the work by a conviction that however scientific works may tell the truth about the Indian, they exercise always a limited influence upon the general public; and to that public, in our country as well as abroad, the Indian has remained as good as unknown. By clothing sober facts in the garb of romance I have hoped to make the 'Truth about the Pueblo Indians' more accessible and perhaps more acceptable to the public in general." In a letter written to Thomas Janvier in 1888 while he was translating and revising *Die Koshäre,* he defended his delay in writing up his Mexican research by saying that he regarded his "novel" of much greater importance, that "it remains to unsettle the Romantic school in literature on the American aborigine and to show that Fenimore Cooper's Indian is a fraud" (Radin 1942:3). What better way to upend the idealized noble savage than presenting the Koshare in "full ritual undress"; what better demystification than writing about "the enemy, the Indians, as if they were real (that is, white) people struggling in a muddled social world rather than mythical creatures or savage beasts grazing in a long-extinct forest" (Jovanovich, in Bandelier 1971:xvii). To see Indian life on its own terms is always hard work; it was especially so in the 1880s, given the "long and popular tradition of ignorance concerning the Native American" (Bandelier 1971:vi).

Despite his commitment to the task, Bandelier was frequently discouraged both in writing and in trying to publish his tale. In a letter written in January 1889, he described his "so-called novel" as "a laborious attempt to represent the Indian as he really WAS" (Radin 1942:6). After the manuscript had been rejected by Scribner's, Harper, and Henry Holt, he wrote to Janvier in November of the same year: "The *Koshare* I have almost given up. They were a dream and that dream has vanished. As soon as I hear from Mr. Parkham again and it turns out to be impossible to use them, I shall call the manuscript back. Whether I will destroy it or keep it as a warning, I cannot tell as yet" (ibid.:15). Happily for the starving Bandelier and for us, it did turn out to be possible "to use them." The novel appeared serially between January and May of 1890 in German in the *Belletristisches Journal* and in English later the same year with Dodd, Mead.[3] The first reviews were favorable, but *The Delight Makers* was never the popular or financial success Bandelier had hoped for.

As to the content of his "romance," which he also referred to as his "novel" or "so-called novel" in quotation marks, he goes on in the preface (Bandelier 1971:xxi–xxii) to remark:

The sober facts which I desire to convey may be divided into three classes,—geographical, ethnological, and archaeological. The descriptions of the country and of its nature are real. The descriptions of manners and customs, of creed and rites are from actual observations by myself and other ethnologists, from the statements of trustworthy Indians, and from a great number of Spanish sources of old date . . . The descriptions of architecture are based upon investigations of ruins still in existence on the sites where they are placed in the story . . . The plot is my own. *But* most of the scenes described I have witnessed; and there is a basis for it in a dim tradition preserved by the Queres of Cochiti that their ancestors dwelt on the Rito de los Frijoles a number of centuries ago, and in a similar tradition among the Tehuas of the Pueblo of Santa Clara in regard to the cave-dwellings of the Puye . . . The dialect spoken by the actors is that of Cochiti for the Queres, that of San Juan for the Tehuas.

3. After writing the last twenty chapters in four-and-a-half months, Bandelier finished the German draft of the novel in May 1886. Three months later he began to translate *Die Koshäre* into English, which he finished with considerable help from his friends in January 1889. The translation involved a good bit of expansion and elaboration, for the English version is appreciably longer.

Despite the fictive frame and invented plot, Bandelier was obsessed with portraying the reality of Keresan life. The novel ranks with the best of late nineteenth-century naturalism without the latter's heavy dogmatism. As C. W. Ceram has remarked (1971:66), "The material that Bandelier gathered in his 490 pages, each scientific detail embedded in a well-constructed story, is absolutely enormous. There is scarcely a book in which the modern reader can find so much lore presented so readably." Nor, I should add, so accurately. Once Bandelier started writing the novel, he repeatedly rechecked details and revised accordingly (see, for example, journal entry of 8/1/85 in 1975:77). And, the larger portion of his "sober facts" have been confirmed by subsequent research.

Before I talk about that lore and the very unusual style or rather styles in which it is presented, let me summarize the plot and its complicated intrigues that resemble the historical romances of Sir Walter Scott. The story opens on a June day in Tyuonyi with a taunting conversation between an adolescent boy, Okoya, and his younger brother, Shyuote, the latter chiding his brother about his hunting prowess and his less than favorable attitude toward the Koshare. Okoya is afraid and suspicious since he has talked with no one but his mother, who shares his feelings about the Koshare, since his father, Zashue, is a Koshare and his younger brother pledged to be one, and since "those people were in possession of knowledge of a higher order, and practised arts of an occult nature" (1971:11).

The scene then shifts to their home where their grandfather, Topanashka, the Maseua or war chief, tells his daughter Say Koitza of the Koshare's accusations of witchcraft and asks her if indeed she has listened to the "black corn" and used owl feathers. In response to her antagonism toward the Koshare, he tells her the origin myth about the role and importance of the Koshare and warns her to be careful. Say Koitza has been ill for several years, and all remedies have failed, even shamanistic fire-eating. Shotaye, the ex-wife of Tyope, a Koshare, and a supposed witch (who, in fact, deals in herbal medicines and is the pueblo prostitute), befriends Say Koitza, convinces her to inquire into the cause of her illness with the black corn, and then persuades her that her illness, which coincides with the rainy season, is the doing of the Koshare. They bury owl feathers near the Koshare chamber to eliminate the disease and punish them; there is no rain and Say's illness does not recur. In the meantime, Tyope is scheming with the Navajo both to spy on Shotaye to support his witchcraft accusations and to kill Topanashka.

The plot is further complicated when Okoya becomes involved with Mitsha, Tyope's daughter. During the summer solstice corn dance, the Koshare, who routinely plunder houses, attempt to find evidence of black magic in Say's house, which she removes just in time, again forewarned by her father. Hayoue, Zashue's younger brother and Okoya's friend and a Kuirana, the clowns of the Squash kiva, predicts there will be trouble in the tribe if Tyope and the leader of the Koshare are not soon restrained. His suspicions are borne out, for in fact they are plotting a schism among clans in order to expel part of the people for the benefit of the remainder and to assume power themselves. The murder of Topanashka is part of the plan. Through their doing a council meeting is called in which the clan with the most Koshare demands that another smaller clan share its fields with it. When the Water Clan refuses, the Koshare blame it, through the actions of its member Sho-taye, for crop failure. Meanwhile Shotaye encounters Cayamo, a Tewa warrior from Puye, and makes plans to flee there, already planning revenge on Tyope and other Koshare. Topanashka witnesses this meeting and follows Cayamo. He is later found dead, scalped in the Tehua manner, a circular Tehua war sandal near his body. The Queres assume a Tehua killed their war chief and demand immediate revenge. In fact, it was the Navajos with whom Tyope plotted. While the tribe is in mourning, Shotaye flees to the Tehua and tells them of the impending attack. Tyope leads a war party and is defeated. Meanwhile, the Navajo devastate Tyuonyi, but thanks to Hayoue all is not lost and many flee to safety. Hayoue and Zashue leave the Rito in search of the latter's wife and children, and go first to the Tehua pueblo at the present site of Santa Fe.

The scene then shifts to the Tewa pueblo of Hishi, thirty miles south of Santa Fe, where a Harvest dance is in progress, the Koshare again performing, and Say Koitza dying. Zashue and Hayoue arrive in the midst of it all, moments after her death. The story ends the following May on the Potrero de las Vacas, the site of the stone lions, where these fugitives from the Rito are building a new village, Pueblo Quemado.

So much for the tale. The telling is, if anything, a more complicated matter. *The Delight Makers* is something of a monstrous jumble held together by an authorial presence, which epitomizes what Bakhtin called "the hybrid construction of authorial speech and the 'multi-speechedness' of novelistic discourse" (Bakhtin 1975:149ff). Bandelier's basic narrative technique is one of complete omniscience, revealing the thoughts of one character after another, being several places at the same time, and moving forward and backward in time and space. Much of the narrative is composed of third-person description and dramatic dialogue, but the author is not at all averse to intruding in the first-person plural to shift the scene, comment on the characters, their thoughts and actions, ask a rhetorical question, or make reflexive remarks about his own narrative. For example, after setting the scene in chapter 1, he begins his story "On the day of which we are now speaking, a voice arose from the thicket . . ." (1971:5). After introducing Shotaye, he remarks, "Now that we have seen her home and her person, let us proceed with the tale of her doings on the afternoon to which the close of the preceding chapter has been devoted . . ." (ibid.:108). And, when he first describes the Koshare at a corn dance, he remarks, "The association whose name has been selected as the title of our story is now before us fully represented, arrayed in its appropriate dress and engaged in the discharge of some of its official duties" (ibid.:134–35).

Another type of intrusion is his frequent comparisons and contrasts between the past and the present and the facts and the fictions, whether it be the dwellings (now ruins), customs, and beliefs, or the relationship between a scene he has just described and a legend he has recently heard. Bandelier also interrupts his story with impersonal commentary in the form of both brief and lengthy generalizations about Nature, Human Nature, or "the Indian." While sometimes condescending—"The Indian is a child"—these remarks are invariably very telling. One of the best, given our stereotypes of the Indian, and the most ironic, given Bandelier's own position as inquisitive ethnographer, occurs in the opening scene after Shyuote has refused to answer Okoya's question about the Koshare (ibid.:8, 12–13):

Whenever the Indian does not wish to speak on any subject, whatever it be, no power on earth can compel him to break silence. . . . The boy was old enough to enjoy that great and often disagreeable quality of the American Indian, reticence. Furthermore, he might have been forbidden to speak. If the Indian is not an ideal being, he is still less a stolid mentally squalid brute. He is not reticent out of imbecility or mental weakness. He fails properly to understand much of what takes place around him, especially what happens within the circle of our modern civilization, but withal he is far from indifferent toward his surroundings. He observes, compares, thinks, reasons, upon whatever he sees or hears, and forms opinions from the basis of his own peculiar culture . . . There is no difference between him and the Caucasian in original faculties, and the reticence peculiar to him under certain circumstances is not due to lack of mental aptitude. He does not practice that reticence alike toward all. A great number of examples seems to establish the fact that the Indian has developed a system of casuistry, based upon a remarkably thorough knowledge of human nature. Certain matters are kept concealed from some people, whereas they are freely discussed with others, and *vice versa.*

And sometimes, particularly when it involves a linguistic or ethnographic explanation, Bandelier's commentary takes the form of a footnote. Had editorial friends not prevailed, there would have been a good deal more of these, as well as illustrations and a glossary. A typical example occurs in the first chapter when, in conjunction with a description of the kiva and activities therein, such as the teaching of myths, songs, and prayers, Bandelier glosses the Spanish term *estufa* in one footnote and in a second remarks (ibid.:19): "The preservation of traditions is much systematized among the Pueblo Indians. Certain societies know hardly any other but the folk-tales relating to their own particular origins. To obtain correct tradition it is necessary to gain the confidence of men high in degree. That is mostly very difficult." Another occurs in chapter 2 when Topanshka recounts the story of the emergence and the Koshare to his daughter (ibid.:34): "This tradition was told me by Tehua Indians, and some friends among the Queres subsequently confirmed it."

The preceding is one of two stories within the story and one of the author's rare appearances in the first-person *singular.* The latter occur in those instances when he shifts from being the narrator of a novel to the ethnographer talking about himself and the material he had collected or tried to collect. The other notable example of both an embedded narrative and a first-person appearance occurs in chapter 19 (ibid.:420) when the war party returns to the Rito:

The reader will forgive a digression. We will leave Tyope and his companions on the brink of the Rito, and abandon them for a while to their sombre thoughts; nay, we will leave the Rito even, and transport ourselves to our own day. *I* desire to relate a story, an Indian folklore tale of modern origin, which is authentic in so far that it was told me by an Indian friend years ago at the village of Cochiti, where the descendents of those who once upon a time inhabited the caves on the Rito de los Frijoles now live. My object in rehearsing this tale is to explain something I have neglected; namely, the real conception underlying the custom of taking the scalp of an enemy.

The way in which he presents this tale is particularly interesting given the recent emphasis in folk narrative scholarship on the role of the collector, the importance of context, and on storytelling as a communicative event. What Bandelier gives us is neither the tale itself nor the narrative monologue of a Cochiti Indian, but the storytelling dialogue that occurred between himself and Juan José Montoya, replete with setting. Here, as elsewhere, Bandelier repeats with little embellishment material recorded years before in his journal (1966:165–66) but with a significant change in setting. He heard the story, at least the first time, not in Cochiti, but by a campfire his first night in Frijoles Canyon!

In addition to shifting his position and his role vis-à-vis his narrative, Bandelier also shifts styles. Obviously, his comments to the reader and his reflective digressions are stylistically very different from his dramatic and descriptive prose, but they still fall within the canon of styles that we label novelistic. When Bandelier is describing scenes and scenery, however, he frequently shifts from a novelistic mode to the style appropriate to one of his three orders of facts. In addition to lengthy and detailed descriptions of the terrain and a great deal of archaeological reconstruction, there are long and very ethnographic discussions of social and ceremonial organization, religious practices, and beliefs and customs. There is also considerable discourse concerning the sobering social fictions of witchcraft that are so central to the plot, much of this verbatim from his journals. But for the occasional authorial intrusion, these descriptions are indistinguishable in style and content from his "scientific" reports to the American Institute of Archaeology. Nor does he hesitate in the novel to use the technical and native terms suitable to the former modes of discourse.

If there are style shifts, there are also code switches. Throughout there is an immense amount of Keresan and Spanish vocabulary, sometimes glossed but more infrequently not. And polyglot that he was, Bandelier interlards his narrative prose with other foreign language phrases and quotations. For example, he describes Tyope eating his breakfast *"à la mode du pays"*; he quotes Goethe's *Faust* in relation to Shotaye's ambivalently good and evil behavior (ibid.:119); Tacitus about the designs on Cayamo's shield; and Schliermacher on primitive religion in his description of the corn dance (ibid.:149). He is also quite fond of English proverbial expressions. All this linguistic dialogism and intertextuality is further complicated by the fact that the entire narrative was written first in German and then translated and retranslated over a period of three years into English.

The Delight Makers' melange of past and present, them and us, author and audience, art and science in assorted styles and codes culminates in the last chapter in something of a grand finale of frame-breaking. It begins as follows: "After 21 long and it may be tedious chapters, no apology is required for a short one in conclusion. I cannot take leave of the reader, however, without having made in his company a brief excursion through a portion of New Mexico in the direction of the Rito de los Frijoles, though not quite so far" (ibid.:485). In the manner of a tour guide, he takes the reader from Santa Fe to Cochiti, where "I could introduce you to Hayoue, to Zashue, to Okoya, and the rest." We then take a guide, "possibly Hayoue" and proceed northward in the direction of the Rito. Following several pages of scenic description, we end up at the enclosure of the stone pumas on the Potrero de las Vacas: "We are on sacred ground in this crumbling enclosure. But who knows that we are not on magic ground also? We might make an experiment; and though our Indian guide is not one of the great shamans, he might help us in an attempt at innocent jugglery" (ibid.:488). He then proposes that we be blindfolded and turned around three times from left to right. When the blindfold is removed the ruins have disappeared and we are back among the fugitives from the Rito, building the foundations of a new pueblo. Just as easily the magic is undone and we are returned to the present with the ruins where Cochiteños still pray back in place. An eagle flies overhead and the real Hayoue, Juan de Jesus Pancho, points and has the last word: "Look! see! the Siuana are good!" (ibid.:490).

Fortunately for us, nobody told Bandelier about scientific and novelistic conventions or that his audience wasn't supposed to see backstage. If they did, he ignored them, as he wrote in 1888: "I am getting tired of these many conflicting corrections. In the end, I shall go my own way without consulting anybody at all" (1975:288). As a result of his naiveté or his iconoclasm or both, we are privileged to experience a rare experiment in anthropological modes of presentation. In contrast to the majority of folkloristic and anthropological studies, here self and work, representation and reflection, fact and fiction, product and process, knowing and being are not separated, but engaged in a continuous dialogue. They always are, in any interpretive act, but given the screens of positivism and objectivism that have been thrown up in the years since *The Delight*

Makers, we are rarely privy to the real process of understanding an Other.

What is even rarer, given the fact that most interpretations of clowning end up negating their subjects, is that without knowing or intending, but as a consequence of trying to objectify a life into which he had been transported, Bandelier does what he describes. "Language is not simply the novelist's means for representing the world; it is also the world he represents" (Morson 1977:15). And the language of Bandelier's novel *is* carnivalesque discourse. The incongruous and unexpected juxtaposition and confusion of genres, styles, and languages that a Petronious or a Rabelais engages in self-consciously to comic, satiric effect, Bandelier creates naively. It is not without relevance to *The Delight Makers* that Bakhtin's analysis of the origins and history of the novel relies heavily on the novel's debt to folk humor—but that's another essay. If Pueblo clown performances can be summed up in a few words, they are motley or pastiche or bricolage *and* dialogue or translation or mediation—a comic dialogue constructed of bits and pieces of cultural debris. Like the Koshare, Bandelier is attempting to translate and interpret between worlds and to establish a dialogue between the knowns and the unknowns, be they present and past, self and other, or science and art. The novel as a whole is a dialogue, composed of many overlapping and intercalated dialogues, written in a language of motley. Appropriately enough, Bandelier's implicit satire of novelistic conventions and stereotypes, whose title characters are the satirists of Pueblo society, is a *satura,* the Roman word for satire, which is variously translated as "medley," "potpourri," "hash," or "a plate of mixed fruit." Any such parody, either by sacred clown or ethnographer *qua* novelist, "dislocates the union of form and content and thus raises the larger questions of the gap between art and life, artifact and nature, real and irreal" (Zeitlin 1971:648). And, just as a clown performance is an exercise in metacultural commentary and interpretation—"a story they tell themselves about themselves" (Geertz 1973b:448)—so, too, is *The Delight Makers,* and part of that story is a deconstruction of the stereotypes of the Indian and of the fictions of ethnographic interpretation.

D. H. Lawrence once remarked that "white people always, or nearly always, write sentimentally about Indians. Even a man like Adolph Bandelier" ("Indians and Entertainment," quoted in Ceram 1971:67). Perhaps so, for we all romanticize the Other in at least two respects: as the poet Novalis said, "Everything turns romantic as soon as it is moved far away" (quoted in ibid.); and as the philosopher Ricoeur has said "to understand . . . is to be transported into another life" (1974:5). But if, like Bandelier, we temper our imagination with sober facts and "intellectual chastity" and are explicitly reflexive about our enterprise, we *can* have it both ways without "writing sentimentally." Paradoxically, Bandelier undoes the Romantic image of the Indian while simultaneously writing both a "romance" of prehistoric Keresan life *and* a comedy of the ethnological endeavor. Self and Other, after all, are the oldest and most ubiquitous pair of clowns, and Hayoue, ignoring the novelist's excesses, has the last word.

Before concluding with a personal postscript, I would like to end this portion of my text with a statement from Paul Ricoeur that comments both on Bandelier's interpretation of the Koshare and prehistoric Keresan life and on my interpretation of his text (1974:4, 16–17):

All interpretation is to conquer a remoteness, a distance between the past [and other] cultural epoch to which the text belongs and the interpreter himself. . . . It is thus the growth of his own understanding of himself that the interpreter pursues through the understanding of the other. Every hermeneutics is thus, explicitly or implicitly, self-understanding by means of understanding others . . . finally, the very work of interpretation reveals a profound intention, that of overcoming distance and cultural differences and of matching the reader to a text which has become foreign, thereby incorporating its meaning into the present comprehension a man is able to have of himself.

Posttext

The more time I spent in Santa Fe, the more impossible it became to ignore a relatively recent and increasingly popular form of Pueblo pottery, the Storyteller doll. I wanted to know the story behind this unique form of folk art, and by June of 1978 I finally screwed up my courage and went to see its creator, Helen Cordero. Driving through Peña Blanca on the way to Cochiti, I thought of Bandelier's many treks that way and wondered at the coincidence after spending a year reading his prose and residing with his mortal remains. I quickly disregarded my idle musings on the grounds that storyteller dolls had no connection whatsoever with Koshares, drove on to the pueblo, and thereafter immersed myself in a study of Cochiti figurative pottery. One of the first things I discovered was several large standing figures, made between

1875 and 1900, that was, like many clown performances, a caricature of the white man.[4] Who knows if one is not the intrepid ethnographer himself? Needless to say, I revised my opinion concerning the relationship of clowns and clay and later discovered that several of the principal makers of these *monos*[5] were members of the Kushali society. When I began rereading Bandelier's journals for comments both about pottery and about his novel, I learned that one of his Cochiti friends and informants and the model for the Koshare Zashue in *The Delight Makers* was also named Santiago Quintana. As it turns out, Santiago Quintana was Helen Cordero's grandfather, the memorable "wise" and "really good" storyteller who inspired her first and subsequent dolls. He was also one of Ruth Benedict's informants for the collection of Cochiti tales. She described him as follows (1931:ix):

Informant 4 was a very different individual from the others, as can be seen in the material recorded from him. He spoke Spanish fairly, and had been an adventurer all his life. He is very old now, but a leading member of the principales, in great demand in those acculturated Mexican ceremonies in which repartee must be carried on in what is considered to be Spanish [a description of a Koshare performance at a matachine dance]. He liked best to give true stories—accounts of the old days, and his tales of the mythological heroes always emphasized their success in turning the mockery that had been directed against them against those who had mocked them.

I no longer scoff at "magical connections," for I know and I have been told that in the Pueblo world "everything comes together," and you don't have to be blindfolded and whirled around three times for that to happen.

4. Since the coming of the railroad, if not the conquistadore, the Indians of the Southwest have done verbal, dramatic, and graphic imitations of the white man. As these Cochiti figures demonstrate, such behavior is not confined to sacred clowns and ritual occasions. To this day, Rio Grande potters continue to shape tourists, Hopis carve caricature kachinas, Navajos draw cartoons, and Western Apaches verbally re-enact Anglo doctors, schoolteachers, and VISTA workers. For a sensitive description and analysis of the latter, see Basso 1979.

5. Spanish, meaning "monkey; silly fool; mimic; cute little thing."

I commence, with the first of these chapters, a book of travel. . . . I propose to record the result of a journey into a region which lies at our own doors—into a dark continent that is within easy walking distance of the General Post Office.

Sims 1889:3

10 SOCIAL EXPLORERS AND SOCIAL SCIENTISTS: THE DARK CONTINENT OF VICTORIAN ETHNOGRAPHY

CAROL ANN PARSSINEN

So George Sims introduced his account of London slum life, *How the Poor Live,* in 1889. Sims cast himself as an explorer who had journeyed into the unknown and returned to tell his story. But the unknown was not a remote land or an exotic race; rather it was the condition of life among London's urban poor, "a large body of persons of whom the public had less knowledge than of the most distant tribes of the earth" (Mayhew 1861:iii).

From 1850–1910 England produced a body of ethnographic literature written by men best characterized as "social explorers."[1] By profession these men were journalists, like Sims or Henry Mayhew; reformers, like William Booth; or conscious social investigators, like Charles

1. I am indebted to Peter Keating, both for the term "social explorers" and for the suggestive introduction to his selection of their writing, *Into unknown England, 1866–1913* (1976).

Booth; but they shared Sims's determination to make public an alien culture set, paradoxically, right in their midst; and they charted an essential methodology in seeking first-hand knowledge of the poor and, in some cases, living among their subjects for short periods of time.

As Peter Keating has shown, the imagery of exploration is central to the written records of the social explorers: "The paradox of things being at the same time near and far serves to give a genuine exploratory value to what is being revealed while demonstrating that anyone can be this kind of explorer if he will only open his eyes and heart" (1976:15). In the journey pattern both explorer and reader can find a fit representation for their respective roles and their relationship to each other: the explorer's actual movement in time and space; his corresponding development from ignorance to knowledge; and the reader's vicarious experience of the explorer's physical and educational journeys. The logic of chronology becomes the logic of causality in a voyage of discovery: The ways in which one sees become the products of what one has seen already.

This same double journey—in time and understanding—is the basic metaphor for professional ethnographic research; for the ethnographer, too, makes a journey and gathers data about his subjects, developing from innocence to experience and ignorance to knowledge. However inextricable the experience of the ethnographer may be from the products of his research, however individual his interpretive processes in drawing conclusions, his profession as social scientist discourages him from making a portrayal of himself the center of his written account, or perhaps any part of it at all: "There is an inescapable tension in ethnography between the forms, the rhetorical and literary forms considered necessary for presentation (and persuasion of colleagues), and the narrative form natural to the experience of the work, and natural to the meaningful report of it in other than monographic contexts" (Hymes 1973:200). If the ethnographer chooses to present his material topically, the journey may be suppressed altogether, and the fruits of induction wrenched from time into the ethnographic present, to become static, unarguable truths.

The written records of the social explorers, because they did not need to conform to the prescribed format of a professional presentation, reveal a rich variety of narrative strategies and portrayals of the self. Why the explorers went to seek out the poor, how they accounted for their presence, how the poor responded to them, were as much a part of their discoveries as how the poor lived. This essay will examine some samples from the writing of the social explorers, with a particular emphasis on *Life and Labour of the People in London,* by Charles Booth, and *London Labour and the London Poor,* by Henry Mayhew, to see how the form of these works shaped or created their content.

In *A Night in the Workhouse* (1866), the journalist James Greenwood records how he journeyed, disguised as a casual laborer, to Lambeth Workhouse, "there to learn by actual experience how casual paupers are lodged and fed, and what the casual is 'like' . . ." (Greenwood 1866:34). From the outset, however, Greenwood (ibid.:39) finds the disguise difficult to maintain and keeps reminding the reader how alien his own cultural values and personal habits are to the behavior he is obliged to simulate: "In the middle of the bed I had selected was a stain of blood bigger than a man's hand! I did not know what to do now. To lie on such a horrid thing seemed impossible, yet to carry back the bed and exchange it for another might betray a degree of fastidiousness repugnant to the feelings of my fellow lodgers and possibly excite suspicions that I was not what I seemed."

Even more distressing to Greenwood than the violence or disease suggested by the bloodstain, or the cold, filth, and crowded conditions of the sleeping shed, are the obscene language and animal behavior of many of his fellow casuals: "Towzled, dirty, villanous, they squatted up in their beds, and smoked foul pipes, and sang snatches of horrible songs, and bandied jokes so obscene as to be absolutely appalling" (ibid.: 38). Greenwood includes a number of verbal exchanges in dialect, but only hints at those parts he feels unable to record. He does carefully note the objections of a minority of "decent men," clearly relieved to be able to identify with their efforts to restore the ruffian element to order and propriety.

Throughout, Greenwood keeps the reader keenly aware of time, both as it shapes the routine of a workhouse night and as it signals the narrator's eventual release from his ordeal. In the snail-paced hours past midnight, Greenwood indicates (ibid.:46) how even the variety of coughs he hears become a way of reckoning time's passage: "the hollow cough; the short cough; the hysterical cough; the bark that comes at regular intervals, like the quarter-chime of a clock, as if to mark off the progress of decay. . . ." Yet time remains unidimensional, for Greenwood does not conclude the piece with an appeal for better conditions in the workhouse, nor does he establish a causal relationship between what he has experienced and the condition of the poor. Whatever information the reader may have garnered about the operation of the workhouse or the behavior of its inmates is secondary to Greenwood's real subject: the pain of cultural invisibility. Nevertheless, Greenwood's insistent need to separate himself from his experience—and to make the reader aware of the distance—demonstrates the primacy of the portrayal of self in the voyage of discovery.

Jack London also used disguise to gather the material that became *The People of the Abyss* (1903). For London, however, wearing the shabby clothes of the poor was not a prison, but a release: "For the first time, I met the English lower classes face to face and knew them for what they were" (p. 27). He revels in the comradeship, in being "mate," instead of "sir" or "governor," in talking to workmen "as one man to another." Most important, he finds that he has "slipped gently" into the crowd and is now part of that "vast and malodorous sea" he initially feared.

London's repeated appeal to the reader is to recognize the common humanity hidden by material coverings, and he includes many case histories to illustrate the precariousness of good fortune and the nobility and unselfishness of those in want. But perhaps his most telling story is of his own difficulty in getting into the East End. Determined to "see things for myself," London is viewed by his English friends as a cultural embarrassment ("You can't, you know") and by the police with bureaucratic intransigence ("I don't think we can do anything for you"). The travel agent Thomas Cook claims to "know nothing whatsoever of the place at all," and London's cabby, who can think only of Stepney Station as a destination in the East End, requires payment before he will venture any farther. Getting into the East End is, in short, a voyage of discovery in itself for London and an essential preparation for his realization that poor people are ill-nourished rich people in shabby clothes.

In choosing to adopt the disguise of a native, Greenwood and London were obliged to grapple with the paradox that lies at the heart of participant observation. That is, they had to stand both inside and outside their experience and then make what they had discovered coherent for others. By contrast, Charles Booth, who was both a social explorer and a social scientist, began with the formulation of questions that could be answered by empirical inquiry (Simey and Simey 1960:77–79, 246–560). The problem of identity for the investigator was thus a function of how one could best collect data that would answer the questions.

Booth introduces the Poverty Series of *Life and Labour of the People in London* (1902–1903) with a statement of the scope of his investigation and his method of inquiry: "My object has been to attempt to show the numerical relation which poverty, misery, and depravity bear to regular earnings and comparative comfort, and to describe the general conditions under which each class lives" (I:6). To obtain his information, Booth used school board visitors, some sixty-six of whom were assigned to the East London district. These visitors made a house-to-house census of the people, but did not "attempt to meddle" with the "insides of their houses and their inmates" (I:25), nor to gather any information especially for the study.

For three periods of several weeks, however, Booth lodged with East End families whom he classed as "poor" or just above the line of poverty. Despite the difficulty that London and the other explorers had in penetrating the East End or adopting a suitable disguise or explanation for their presence, Booth claimed to have encountered neither problem: "My object, which I trust was a fair one was never suspected, my position never questioned. The people with whom I lived became, and are still, my friends" (I:158).

Booth gives a frankly admiring picture of his friends and their "wholesome, pleasant family life, very simple food, very regular habits, healthy minds and healthy bodies" (ibid.), but at no point does he depict himself as participant with them in any activity, and even the indications of his observation are minimal: "I watched the relations existing between classes E and D [those just above and below the poverty line] in the persons of my landlady and her other tenants. There was the present of a dress altered to suit the hard-worked, ill-dressed child . . . ; the rebuke . . . of the father's drunken ways. . . . In short, there was evinced a keen sense of social responsibility, not unaccompanied by social superiority" (I:159). Booth says that what he has witnessed has "made the dry bones [of his material] live" (I:157–58), but his quantifying mind is clearly at work here, seeing individuals as representative of general categories of behavior and solidly middle-class values. Booth does not seek to capture the life of the discrete individual, in other words, but the principles of anatomical construction.

Yet Booth is aware of the flow of life and the ways in which it blurs his categories. His eight classes of the people of East London are not presented as static entities but as patterns of life which allow for gradations of comfort, subgroups, and changing representation. He is ready to acknowledge different "ways of looking even at mere figures" (I:177) and devotes an entire section to a discussion of point of view. Should the fact that one-tenth of the population of London lives in poverty be cause for optimism or pessimism, Booth asks? Further, what can percentages mean to those who live in "chronic want": "They refuse to set off and balance the happy hours of the same class, or even of the same people, against these miseries; much less can they consent to bring the lot of other classes into the account, add up the opposing figures, and contentedly carry forward a credit balance. In the arithmetic of woe, they can only add or multiply, they cannot subtract or divide" (I:178).

Ultimately, however, Booth's understanding of point of view is of a problem to be discussed, rather than a technique to be used. His resolution to "make use of no fact to which I cannot give a quantitative value" (I:6) does not allow him to give individual voices to the poor, nor to describe the nature of his personal involvement with them or their response to him. Booth is writing about Poverty, not poor people, and in a telling passage, likens his technique to that of a photographer (I:26):

The special difficulty of making an accurate picture of so shifting a scene as the low-class streets in East London present is very evident, and may easily be exaggerated. As in photographing a crowd, the details of the picture change continually, but the general effect is much the same, whatever moment is chosen. I have attempted to produce an instantaneous picture, fixing the facts on my negative as they appear at a given moment, and the imagination of my readers must add the movement, the constant changes, the whirl and turmoil of life.

However naive this passage may be, in its assumption that the camera takes the picture without exercise of the photographer's point of view, or that a single moment may stand for an ongoing flow of activity, Booth does bring together the scientist's commitment to the value of the general, with the explorer's awareness of the "whirl and turmoil of life." In leaving the latter to the reader's imagination, Booth makes clear how form has determined content in his work.

One of the earliest voices of the social explorers belonged to the journalist Henry Mayhew, whose investigatory reports for the *Morning Chronicle* were selected and published in *London Labour and the London Poor* (1861–62). Mayhew announced the novelty of his undertaking in the preface, specifying that his was "the first attempt to publish the history of a people, from the lips of the people themselves . . . in their own 'unvarnished' language; and to pourtray the condition of their homes and their families by personal observation of the places, and direct communion with the individuals" (I:iii).

Consider the following two passages, the first written by Booth and the second by Mayhew, on the topic of London street markets:

1. The neighbourhood of Old Petticoat Lane on Sunday is one of the wonders of London, a medley of strange sights, strange sounds, and strange smells. Streets crowded so as to be thoroughfares no longer, and lined with a double or treble row of hand-barrows, set fast with empty cases, so as to assume the guise of market stalls. Here and there a cart may have been drawn in, but the horse has gone and the tilt is used as a rostrum whence the salesmen with stentorian voices cry their wares, vying with each other in introducing to the surrounding crowd their cheap garments, smart braces, sham jewellery, or patent medicines. . . . Other stalls supply daily wants—fish is sold in large quantities—vegetables and fruit—queer cakes and outlandish bread (I:66–67).

2. Close by is a brawny young Irishman, his red beard unshorn for perhaps ten days, and his neck, where it had been exposed to the weather, a far deeper red than his beard, and he is carrying a small basket of nuts, and selling them as gravely as if they were articles suited to his strength. A little lower is the cry, in a woman's voice, "Fish, fried fish! Ha'penny; fish, fried fish!" and so monotonously and mechanically is it ejaculated that one might think the seller's life was passed in uttering these few words, even as a rook's is in crying "Caw, caw." Here I saw a poor Irishwoman who had a child on her back buy a piece of this fish . . . and tear out a piece with her teeth, and this with all the eagerness and relish of appetite or hunger; first eating the brown outside and then *sucking* the bone (II:92).

The material in passage 1 by Booth is presented with the distance of one who finds Petticoat Lane a foreign and not altogether comfortable place. The sights and sounds are "strange," the goods "cheap" or "sham," the edibles "queer" or "outlandish." The tone of disapproval is hard to miss, as if Booth were warning tourists away from a certain trap. Virtually every noun in the passage is in the plural, whether "smells," "streets," "stalls," "salesmen," "voices," or "garments," giving illustration to Booth's notion that wherever one aims the camera, the result will be the same.

The three vignettes in passage 2 by Mayhew are presented without transition as three individual moments in a flow of experience. The position of the narrator is in the midst of the market activity, "close by" the "brawny Irishman," and near enough to hear the lower cry of the fish vendor and see the poor Irishwoman suck the bones of the fish she buys. Mayhew's attention to the particular—to the red beard and redder neck of the nut seller or the appetite with which the Irishwoman tears her fish—is in sharp contrast to Booth's quantifying plurals. More important, Mayhew tries to capture the peculiar human appeal of his subjects, giving life to the nut seller's incongruous gravity or the deadening routine suggested by the fish vendor's cry. Mayhew does not present a quantity of data, but a way of seeing.

In an essay entitled "Mayhew as a social investigator," Eileen Yeo asserts that Mayhew may rightly be considered an anthropologist, because "he had a sure sense that the opinions of the poor, their evaluation of their lot and life in general were as important . . . as facts about wages" (Thompson and Yeo 1973).[2] Certainly Mayhew's most distinctive contribution to the literature of social exploration was the form in which he cast his interviews. Allowing his subjects to speak in monologue, Mayhew was able to capture the qualities of their speech—the flow of ideas, pattern of associations, emphasis, significant repetition—as well as their opinions about themselves and their lives.

The watercress girl, for example, is most interested in talking about her trade. She details the seasonal variation in price, quality, and expected sale of her "creases" and speaks with authority about how best to prepare and present them for market. Mayhew's unstated but clearly implied questions indicate that the girl might well feel she has a hard lot in life. Instead, her statement reveals a remarkably unsentimental attitude toward herself: "Sometimes I make a great deal of money. One day I took 1s. 6d., and the creases cost 6d.; but it isn't often I get such luck as that. I oftener makes 3d. or 4d. than 1s.; and then I'm at work, crying, 'Creases, four bunches a penny, creases!' from six in the morning to about ten. . . . The shops buys most of me. Some of 'em says, 'Oh! I ain't a-going to give a penny for these'; and they want 'em at the same price as I buys 'em at" (I:151–52).

Mayhew's statement from a young pickpocket reveals a far more self-conscious, but no more sentimental attitude toward life than that of the watercress girl. He offers several explanations for the inevitability of his turning to crime: The corrupting influence of established thieves on innocent boys in low lodging houses; the scorn leveled at beggars, so "a boy is partly forced to steal for his character" (I:411); and, ultimately, the fact that "everybody must look after themselves." The associative pattern of a few sentences catches the principal considerations

2. Using the reports from the *Morning Chronicle,* largely omitted from Mayhew 1861–62, Yeo argues that Mayhew's methodology as a social investigator is clearly superior to that of Booth.

of the boy's life: "I spend chief part of my money in pudding. I don't like living in lodging-houses, but I must like it as I'm placed now—that sort of living, and those lodging-houses, or starving. They bring tracts to the lodging-houses—pipes are lighted with them; tracts won't fill your belly" (I:412).

These samples show Mayhew at his best with qualitative evidence, willing to let people tell their own stories, to surrender point of view in practice, rather than discussing it in the abstract. Mayhew invites the reader to see for himself, to get as close as written re-creation will allow to the experience the monologues represent.

In the preface to *London Labour,* Mayhew refers to himself as a "traveller in the undiscovered country of the poor" (I:iii), and many of his reports are structured to form the double journey of the ethnographer, in time and in understanding. "The London Dock," for example, begins with a guidebook evocation of the sights, smells, and sounds of the dock area. The picture is a paean to material prosperity, an exotic jumble of "tall chimneys vomiting black smoke . . . flaxen-haired sailors chattering German . . . [and] the atmosphere is fragrant with coffee and spice" (III:302). Abruptly Mayhew switches from this romantic picture to the tense group of men at the dock gates, hoping for a day of temporary labor. In contrast to the bustling activity of the opening scene, the men are trapped by need and desperate to be chosen to work. Again Mayhew moves away from the opening picture, as he describes the nature and extent of the work the men are so desperate to get (III:304): "The wheel-work is performed somewhat on the system of the treadwheel. . . . and the six or eight men treading within it will lift from sixteen to eighteen hundred weight, and often a ton, forty times in an hour, an average of twenty-seven feet high." Mayhew calculates the number of men who seek to work, their expected wages for different jobs, and the number of men refused work at one of the docks. He makes "inquiries into the condition of the labourers themselves (III:305), gathering information from men in several lodging houses in the neighborhood.

When, in conclusion, Mayhew expresses horror at the juxtaposition of incomprehensible wealth and incomprehensible poverty at the docks, the reader knows where he started and by what route he has traveled. For Mayhew is writing not only about the docks and dock laborers, but also about his progress in coming to understand them. Point of view dictates the form and becomes the substance of this piece. Like the ethnographer doing fieldwork, Mayhew takes the journey, but does not suppress it in the written record. Instead, he makes clear the inextricable bond between what one learns and how one learns.

Classic and contemporary ethnographers address the problem of translating experience into language. Malinowski's diary of his last year in the Trobriand Islands is particularly valuable for the investigation of the epistemology of ethnography. Because he never intended to publish the diary, it has the special validity of a document that implies no audience other than its author. Certainly Malinowski's revelation of intense self-doubt and his references to the Islanders as "savages" or "pigs" or "scum" may be cited as evidence for its wholly private nature.

Repeated statements in the diary indicate the author's concern with distinguishing "objective" and "subjective" realities. He observes, for example, that ". . . experience in writing leads to entirely different results even if the observer remains the same—let alone if there are different observers! Consequently, we cannot speak of objectively existing facts: theory creates facts. . . . The life that lies behind me is opalescent, a shimmer of many colors. Some things strike and attract me. Others are dead" (1967:114). Later he writes, "I sat on a bench for a while; stars; I thought about objective reality: the stars, the sea, the enormous emptiness of the universe in which man is lost; the moments when you merge with objective reality, when the drama of the universe ceases to be a *stage* and becomes a *performance*—these are the moments of true nirvana" (ibid.:120). At yet another point he speaks of "perceiving colors and forms like music, without formulating them or transforming them" (ibid.).

In the introduction to *Argonauts of the Western Pacific*, Malinowski makes a systematic analysis of the ethnographer's obligations to these competing realities. Although he seeks to crystalize the relationship between the conduct of fieldwork and the generic qualities of the resulting ethnography so that the latter may be susceptible to judgments of scientific rigor, he is ready to acknowledge the inevitable disparity between experience and what one comes to say about it. "In Ethnography, the distance is often enormous between the brute material of information—as it is presented to the student in his own observations, in native statement, in the kaleidoscope of tribal life—and the final authoritative presentation of the results" (1961:3–4).

It is also worth noting that in each of the selections of the diary quoted above, Malinowski tries to capture his immersion in the uninter-rupted flow of experience—what he analyzes as the union of subjective and objective realities—by using a metaphor from one of the arts. Fusion of the self with the other is a "shimmer of many colors," a "perform-ance," or the purest and least programmatic of the three forms, "like music."

Malinowski's use of metaphor is not surprising, for it effectively frees him to concentrate on the distinctive aesthetic properties of his formulation, rather than the uncapturable qualities of his private experi-ence. The result is a creation accessible to the reader because it is complete, concrete, and immediately susceptible to comparison and judgment. One might in fact argue that metaphor lies closer to the "truth" of individual experience than nonfigurative description, since it bears the individuating mark of the experiencing self.

One way to make new sense, and perhaps new claims, about what ethnographers do is to re-examine the process of describing. Of the three traditional rhetorical categories—description, exposition, narration—description calls least immediate attention to its author. Expositors per-suade; narrators tell a story; both have a stake in what and how much they tell. Theoretically, at least, writers of description can choose to detach themselves almost entirely from their material, to record, as Robbe-Grillet claims to do, only the surface reality of things.

But authorial detachment or invisibility should not be confused with its contrived appearance in any form of writing. Only under the most limited circumstances of controlled and absolute predictability is the writer of description freed from answering the same questions ex-positors and narrators must answer: What shall I say? In what order? With what emphasis? What shall I omit? What kind of language will give my choices form? In *The Face of the Fox* (1970), Frederick O. Gearing addresses himself directly to the difficulty of answering these questions: ". . . of the observable goings-on in a community only the smallest fraction can get recorded by the mind, and every description is an artifact composed of a few happenings, which seem to the observer similar in one or another respect to a few other happenings. There is of course a near infinity of options as to what features will determine these similarities and great arbitrariness in their choice. One is accus-tomed to calling these mental gymnastics 'describing' and to calling the resulting artifacts of mind 'descriptions' . . ." (1970:66). And again from Malinowski's diary the words, "Joy: I hear the word 'Kiriwina.' I get ready; little gray, pinkish huts. Photos. Feeling of ownership. It is I who will describe them or create them" (1967:140).

If, in fact, an ethnography is an "artifact"—a created thing—as much as an objective description of real events, then its author is a creator-craftsman, as much as a dispassionate observer and recorder. The difficulty for the ethnographer is, of course, to reconcile these two roles. Initially he must decide how much distance to put between himself and his material. Will he choose a narrative design, in which his own growth and development are the organizing principles? Will he present his conclusions topically, suggesting that his material contains its own animus of organization? Will he attempt to do both and telescope his experience into a preface or a first chapter? Or will he write two books, one that credits his profession as a social scientist, and a second that tells how he came to draw the conclusions presented in the first?

Certainly the most effective way to obliterate the experience underlying ethnography is simply not to admit that it took place or that an ethnographer as subject had any part in it. A non-narrative organization is essential to this end, as is the elimination of references to an "I," whether in parenthetical remarks or interpolated anecdotes. Instead the ethnographer distills his material into such topics as "family and kinship," "social and political organization," "sex and the life cycle," "religion," "economic activities," each organized so as to facilitate comparison with similar topics in other ethnographies. History itself is often denied by a rigorously topical approach, for there is obvious inconsistency in admitting the temporary nature of one's conclusions about a people and not admitting the temporary nature of one's contact with or life among them.

Readers of ethnography are also asked to take quite different roles when ethnographic material is presented as a chronological narrative and when it is presented topically, outside time. The reader of ethnographic narrative, on the one hand, is asked to participate vicariously in the experiences of the ethnographer, to accept the limited knowledge he receives within an allotted time frame and to expect some eventual attempt to answer questions that are raised and issues left unresolved. The reader of topical ethnography, on the other hand, responds to material fully digested and presented outside the restrictions of time and its partial disclosures. He is asked to judge the quality of a logical, rather than chronological development, and quintessential abstracted truths, rather than more immediate circumstantial ones.

Does the ethnographer ask the reader to take the journey with him or to forget that the journey took place? The alternatives, clearly represented by Mayhew and Booth, are in fact competing paradigms of ethnographic realism, as defined as literary genres and as deliberately crafted. But if ethnography cannot claim the documentary accuracy of scientific record, so, too, it cannot claim the creative energy of imaginative literature. Instead ethnography, like the writing of the social explorers, is a genre apart, a union of form and content, of information and unique vision.

The involvement of the person in the field and its effect upon him is of central biographical concern for a reconstruction of anthropological history; few areas in which the individual operates are of greater importance.

Here, among the various experiences in the field, lie uncollected and unexploited data basic to intellectual biography, data whose value for an understanding of the history of anthropology cannot, I think, be overstated.

Jacob Gruber (1966)

11 OCCASIONS AND FORMS OF ANTHROPOLOGICAL EXPERIENCE

DAN ROSE

When in the process of living our lives we have experiences, we have an illusion that we can choose what to do with them. We can write novels, plays, poetry, or social science; if we stick to verbal performance, we can become raconteurs or comedians. There are culturally relevant forms that specific experiences can take, which folklorists call genres. In each culture and in each epoch there are modes for self-expression and for making experiences available to others in socially acceptable ways. Science, for example, in the contemporary period is both a guide for generating experience, as in doing experiments, and for making the results readily available to a scientific community, as in writing articles or delivering papers. The reality of one's experiencing within these cultural forms is encompassed by a taken-for-granted sense of rightness

Poems without citations are by Dan Rose.

during the experiences and when we convey those experiences to others. In literate societies with multiple media, such as print, radio, and television, we have numerous cultural forms in which to cast experiences and multiple channels through which we can consume experiences produced for us by others. With the increase in individual travel and multiple media, the very nature of what we acquire with our senses and its ineluctable reality becomes problematic.

In the social sciences and humanities the problematic quality of experience and reality are for many a topic for analysis and interpretation. I am less concerned with the scientific and humanistic approaches to the problematic of experience and reality than I am with the problem. By that I mean I am not interested in discussing the concepts or the literature that seek to identify, define, and explicate the phenomenon of reality formation; rather, I am more interested in the phenomenon itself, and especially I am concerned with confronting my experiences and exploring their general significance.

The genre that most suits my purpose is autobiography, which serves as the framework for my observations and reflections. Experience is the stuff of our lives, although I would not want to limit experiences to those immediately, physically sensed. The anthropology of experience begins with the public, the semiotic, or, in the terms of our tradition, the social and the cultural.

1. We are socialized by others to the range and types of experiences we can have. This might be called the *legitimacy of experiences,* and we all learn to consider some experiences proper and positively valued and others improper and negatively valued.

2. We are socialized to understand semiotic systems that order experiences and prescribe what we can and cannot do to this order, given our own experiences. This might be called the *allocation of experiences.* Some experiences can be retrieved through language and made public, others cannot. For example, more often than not, it is difficult to explain what is bothering us, because we tend to be inexplicit about the causes of our thoughts and actions.

3. We take up a fundamental attitude toward our experiences, toward the processes of having them, toward the ways we might make them available to others or withhold them from others. The attitude toward our own living processes, what we take in and what we exclude, can be termed the *authenticity of experiences.*

≫

In the period about which I am writing, the year 1969, I tended to legitimize brief experiences, short episodes or events. I wrote poetry, perhaps the briefest genre in our culture outside the ten-second television commercial, and came to consider these poetic harvests from my unconscious life unsatisfying,

for all good poetry is the spontaneous overflow of powerful feelings: and though this be true, poems to which any value can be attached were never produced on any variety of subjects but by a man who, being possessed of more than usual organic sensibility, and also thought long and deeply (Wordsworth 1948 [1800]:5–6).

The spontaneous overflow of powerful feelings was energy I wished to shape in quite different ways. I had a passion as well for social relevance and felt that the emotional life of poetry writing kept me away from the kind of social involvement—the kind of reality—I desired. I wanted to be in a position to have an abundance of nonpoetic experiences, and so I turned away from writing poetry toward the study of anthropology and another way of legitimizing my experiences. My experience was the opposite of the poet Gary Snyder's, whose life provides counterpoint to mine. When Nathaniel Tarn interviewed Snyder for *Alcheringa*, they discussed Snyder's matriculation at the University of Indiana in the anthropology Ph.D. program. Snyder's roommate at Indiana was Dell Hymes, and they often discussed the conflict between the poet and the scholar. Snyder told Tarn:

I decided to quit because it became evident that the things I wanted to do would be better done in poetry than in scholarship. The economic reasons for a scholarly career weren't incentive enough. At the magic-superstitious level, let's say the Muse is jealous. She won't tolerate you having several mistresses. A commitment is required. On the practical level—Dell and I talked about this a lot, Dell was going through the same kind of thing—well if you're going to do a good job it's got to be whole time. I believe in scholarship if that's what you want but it has to be well done. A Ph.D. in anthropology is demanding. I did think about getting the Ph.D. and then quitting, but it seemed to me that the kind of effort one put into getting the Ph.D. was essentially repetitive . . . like proving some sort of point, almost like showing off.
     It wasn't any easy decision. And I'm not sure I've found anyone to do what it was I wanted to do. . . .
     And then the sense that in the world of folklore and mythology there's a . . . wisdom tradition if you like, half buried but that poets can dig it out and anthropologists can't, or aren't allowed to. . . .

Three years out of the field, I think *I realized that I didn't want to be the anthropologist but the informant* (Tarn 1972:109). [*my emphasis*]

For me the situation was reversed. I did not want to be the informant, but I did want badly to be the anthropologist. What follows is part of a story about how I restructured my life in order to disaffiliate myself from one particular cultural form for experiencing the world.

≫

In the spring of 1969, waiting to receive word on proposals I had submitted to underwrite my dissertation fieldwork, I heard about the new Center for Urban Ethnography (CUE) at the University of Pennsylvania, a center that funded research in urban areas among minority groups. Erving Goffman, recently arrived from Berkeley, was one of the directors. As a Ph.D. student at the University of Wisconsin I had become highly politicized by protest activity against the Vietnam War, and was very willing to make my anthropological training relevant to new trends in the discipline as well as to the demands in the country for anthropological contributions to social policymaking. I welcomed the possibility of studying Afro-Americans. As Kluckhohn (1949:229) observed, "Of this culture in the anthropological sense we know less than of Eskimo culture."

I applied through Goffman to the Center and was the first graduate student to be funded by CUE. In the early summer of 1969, my wife, Karen, and I traveled east to visit John Szwed, a director of CUE, and Goffman and to size up the city of Philadelphia where we would be living for at least a year. I had few memories of the eastern United States, because I had not seen the region since childhood, and Karen had never been there. We shared one image of the region: We believed that from Boston to Washington, D.C., there was unbroken city without rural areas in between. We expected to see cement everywhere and rows of uniform tract houses with sparse urban vegetation. The images on television were our major access to the visual layout of the east, and we were more prepared for the conditions of society than the infrastructure.

Unfortunately, we were not prepared socially or visually for eastern cities. We had both grown up on farms and in small towns, comfortably bourgeois by midwestern standards and hopelessly middle class by eastern ones. Her father was a successful businessman and large landholder in a small town; mine was a theologian who taught either in colleges or seminaries throughout my life at home. In the nineteenth century both our families had been homesteaders in the upper Midwest, wresting the soil from the Native Americans whose shadowed presence remained in the place names of towns, streets, and rivers.

In Philadelphia I had lunch with Szwed and Goffman at the University of Pennsylvania Law School dining commons. Two pieces of our conversation on that occasion stayed with me during fieldwork. Goffman asked why I wanted to throw away my career "studying Spades." It was not a racist remark. He was telling me that there were few or no academic rewards in becoming a student of the stigmatized. I felt that I could get beyond institutional—make that academic—racism and responded with the naiveté and hopefulness of the inexperienced. I also felt challenged by adversity because there was much change in the air, and I was perhaps more than a bit stoned by it. There seemed to be great support "out there" for what I would be doing. In retrospect I know I was entirely wrong.

I told them that I was not an Afro-American scholar, that I had concentrated during my doctoral program on culture and personality, complex societies, and general systems theory. Goffman was not disturbed by my ignorance of the literature on Afro-Americans and suggested that it might prove to be an asset. Szwed talked about his perspective on Afro-Americans, with a key reference being Melville Herskovits's *Myth of the Negro Past* (1958).

Herskovits's work impressed me, and I decided to visit his widow, Frances, and tell her of my interest in his ideas and what I intended to do with my fieldwork. She complained bitterly that the anthropology department at Northwestern had "killed" her husband, which I took to mean that his views were more than merely unpopular. What she said complemented the warnings from Goffman about careers, studying the stigmatized, and the inevitable professional ruin awaiting someone in this line of research. I nonetheless resisted the cautionings in favor of socially relevant research.

While reading the literature in Szwed's bibliography, I formulated a working hypothesis for my research in black Philadelphia. My readings suggested that Afro-Americans experienced an all black version of the melting pot upon arrival in the New World from Africa, that is, a melting pot with others of African descent, not primarily with white ethnic groups. In this realm that developed outside the scrutiny of whites, black language and identities were forged to cope with their own diversity of heritages from Africa, and to find mechanisms, codes of strategic conduct, with which to manipulate the whites who enslaved them. The language system evolved to do double duty. Afro-Americans had to develop a set of interaction rituals for polite public contact with one another and with whites: they needed to be able to establish long-term, beneficial relations with one another, such as marriage, friendship, mutual aid, and business; they needed a system of legal mechanisms to deal with internal delicts and grievances; they needed community-wide institutions, performance stages, such as carnival and the church, for purposes of collective integration, the expression of universalistic human impulses, metaphysical explanations, and collective mimesis and transvaluation of white, national culture through story and song where it was in contact with black sensibilities.

I became convinced that the conditions of slavery and Anglo-American racism meant that much, if not most, of black daily life was outside the hearing and seeing of whites, and that deep African sensibilities were preserved in this hidden bubble of sociability. Herskovits made the point well in an illustrative anecdote: "A Charleston planter told his English guest, Captain Basil Hall, in 1827, that he made no attempt to regulate the habits and morals of his people except in matters of police, 'We don't care what they do when their tasks are over—we lose sight of them till the next day,' he said" (Herskovits 1958:117, quoting from Guion G. Johnson, *A Social History of the Sea Islands, with Special Reference to St. Helena, S.C.* [Chapel Hill, 1930], p. 31.). As blacks came in closer contact with white society, new forms emerged while the old were modified and given new meaning. Perhaps the evolution of two cultures in long contact can best be described as a process of creolization, as Szwed believes. The major periods of the processes of fusion and simultaneous protection of self and cultural identity can be roughly indicated in the following chronology:

1. The New World slavery system to 1865
2. Emancipation and marginal agriculture, 1865–1920
3. Migration within the country to urban centers, 1920–70
4. Afro-Americans as citizens in a national system, 1970 to the present.

I have come to believe with Roger Bastide (1974) that there was a major shift in black identity (from 1920 to 1970 in the United States) to what he calls Negritude. This identity retains two poles of internal preference, often culturally and socially opposed: the one seeks to assimilate white culture with some version of the American Dream of material affluence; the other attempts to remove itself from white society and exorcise white society from itself: black separatism. This dialectic is undoubtedly a worldwide postcolonial phenomenon.

≫

Karen and I returned from our vacation to Madison for the summer and anticipated the adventure that violent American cities represented to outsiders. People have often asked me what role my wife played in fieldwork, what she did, and how she made out. I wish she would publish her own story; I do not believe my characterization could escape my biases should I want it to. My comments are based on what she told me, what I observed or felt, and what I overheard her say to others. The first thing to know about her is that she was a musician, not an anthropologist. She played bassoon and piano and taught vocal music for several years. In the summer of 1969 she relished the thought of becoming involved in a field situation. Her image of the way fieldwork ought to be conducted in a potentially dangerous social environment was that we should both get jobs—in black businesses. She was very opinionated, I thought, far in excess of her experiences or her reading knowledge of anthropology and anthropological methods. I resisted her urging, argued against it, and disliked the whole idea, despite the fact that labor in an inner-city neighborhood would presumably have to be taken as a sign of local attachment, if not of total personal commitment. Such a move might reduce any local resentment that an intrusive anthropological investigation might engender.

I much preferred the classic tradition in anthropology, out of comfort, I might add, in which I would talk with people safely shielded behind the tempered English categories found in *Notes and Queries on Anthropology* (Royal Anthropological Institute 1951)—social organization, religion, politics, economics—or the antiseptic *Outline of Cultural Materials* (Murdock et al. 1961). Emotionally I preferred Geertz's gentlemanly conversations with his informants over Goodenough's demanding personal participation.

Our differences over approaches to fieldwork became exaggerated as we entered the field situation; undoubtedly the stress generated by fieldwork has done much to foster the fabled high divorce rate among anthropologists. My passionate sexual involvement with my wife gave our relationship a false sense of reality, and the security I thought I gained through this long infatuation contributed to an instability that was heightened by the move to Philadelphia. In addition to our conflict over approach to fieldwork, I suffered from a growing jealousy. The only other person we remotely knew in the Philadelphia area, outside of Szwed and Goffman, was a man she had met when they were fellow participants in a wedding. He lived with his wife on Philadelphia's Main Line. I thought my jealousy was well grounded because she had invidiously compared me to him on more than one occasion. The fact that he was affluent enough to hang around his house all day on a piece of real estate complete with gurgling brook made him in my eyes something of a competitor; after meeting him, I began to think that the competition was real. In my anxious anticipation about meeting him I wrote the following poem.

THE SUITOR STUDIES THE CHILD BRIEFLY: *while the leg lifts.*

To concentrate on it was to become that palm

gloved hand inside her hose. She pulls the nylon up her calf. The others are waiting in the wings. She prepares, maturely, for what everyone expects. Notice the mouth. The time arrives unexpectedly. Children, although numb, shop at the market. She and the children come together while the womb heals. The split heals. Quite a few wait for her eyes. A number drift loosely; they seem to move at random.

Beneath her on the street things quiet down. Someone uses a ruse to see her. Obviously she prepared for this event although quite independently and still out of reach. The perfume meets him. It continues. Some of these features can't be controlled, although they were checked at the desk. Someone else comes in and the children are reassured. It goes according to plan. There will be minor adjustments as they move their limbs.

As far as I know, what is written here had no counterpart in reality, other than the reality of my imagination.

I haven't said much about Karen, really. Even from this temporal distance and the presumed objectivity it should provide I find it difficult to capsulate her. She was attractive physically, as I have said. I felt claustrophobic with her because she was overly dependent on me (as I in another way was on her). She had no friends outside her parents and sister and disliked, as far as I could discern, all social occasions. She referred to herself as a hermit. In addition, Karen did not like my friends, who tended to be poets, writers, and anthropologists. As a result, the two of us were largely isolated as a couple. We were childless, which blocked us from the inevitable wider social involvements generated by the organization of activities for children of middle-class families. We were consigned to a perennial adolescence, the end of which is marked in most cultures by childbearing.

I feel more than a little ambivalent discussing myself and revealing the autobiographical sources of my professional history. It is all too easy to reduce the work of an author to the biographical items the critic happens to know, and I fear the consequences of that. I press on, not for purposes of revelry but as a sign. I see myself as I see others, as standing for what is developing in this historical period in our lives, in our thought, in our society, and in world societies.

I reveal myself knowing that until very recently, with the exception of Margaret Mead, anthropologists have been colorless commentators upon themselves (Eggan 1974; Murdock 1965). Paul Rabinow has gracefully discussed some of the reasons why anthropologists divulge little, and he has offered us an attractive model—phenomenology and hermeneutics—for recapturing the intimate and problematic aspects of the field experience (1977). My general criticism of anthropologists talking about themselves, however, is that all too often under the guise of self-disclosure, the anthropologist uses the opportunity to talk about his or her own fieldwork one more time. Doing fieldwork is not the same thing as having a reflexive awareness—critical or interpretive—of one's place or of the anthropologist's place in the world.

Once I asked Marvin Harris why anthropologists did not convey more of themselves in their work. He replied that he thought anthropologists had too much to hide. I disagree strongly, for I think we have too little left over to disclose. After satisfying the demands of the actual fieldwork and the tedious task of ordering all the documentation for description and analysis, what do we have of self left over to reveal? There are always Malinowski's diaries, but those were written by a man trapped four years on an island. The sheer quantity of data and the intensity of direct involvement militate against fantasied or fictionalized experiences, the mark of successful novelists who do, unlike anthropologists, speak interestingly about themselves—Laura Bohannan notwithstanding.

We are like novelists, however, in that we deal with everyday reality, and great gobs of it. But we are unlike them in that we do not speak easily and fully about ourselves, and they do. Perhaps the differences lie in that novelists construct stories from the happenings in everyday life while we reconstruct events and transform them into function and structure. The novelist remains closer to the spoken genres of the quotidian, while we break them in order to understand their significance.

My favorite publication is the *Paris Review,* initially published by Sadruddin Aga Kahn and edited by George Plimpton, to which I have a lifetime subscription, and there the craft of fiction is revealed through an impressive series of interviews. No dry manual, these divagations are never divorced in discussion from the subjectivity of the authors who comment on their works and those of others. The subjects of method, of craftsmanship, of author's vision and self-evaluation, of gossip about the well-known, of self-awareness in the act of writing are all played out in a never repetitious music. Anthropologists do not approximate their reflexive interest in themselves.

My experience has been that anthropologists are Jungian *extroverts:* people who love contact with others, gregarious, encyclopedic, knowledgeable, over-extended, quickly absorbing ever more facts on kinship, exotic dress, cuisine, drugs, and arcane practices. Anthropologists have starved with Amazonian savages, dug up clues to earliest human life and civilizations, deciphered the seeming illogic of magic, mythic thought, and rituals. Yet we remain closed to ourselves because we are too busy salvaging the remnants of other ways of life of people who are no longer with us. We have further depersonalized our trade by erecting forms of expression—the scholarly article, the monograph, the site report—that approximate a scientifically reconstituted humanity but not a fully humanized science. Anthropologists, unlike novelists, must not *molest,* to borrow Edward Said's word (1975:83), by fictional re-creation of the world they find. Nor do anthropologists work at finding their voices, to paraphrase Katherine Anne Porter (1963:105), who explained, "I spent fifteen years learning to trust myself." Anthropologists are, upon graduation from their doctoral programs, issued a "voice." It is not the voice one creates to make fictions; it is, rather, a dry but highly disciplined voice, one useful in piecing together regularities from the flux of an overwhelming number of field experiences among people who may be different from oneself and one's culture beyond imagining.

If anthropologists do not have much to look in upon, they will not be used to looking in. If unused to looking in, the autobiographical revelations herein, which I find easy to make, will force the reader into the uncomfortable position of inadvertant voyeur.

≫

Without dramatizing it is impossible for me to convey an adequate sense of my childhood and adolescence, the period of my life that made me receptive to anthropological thought. Anthropology, whatever else it is, is also a world of ideas, and for me the world of ideas began with my father and the burdensome weight of his influence on me. My father was not merely trained in theology, but he erected a Kantian moral edifice that ritualized social behavior in the family and for enactment in public places. He attempted to repress the fleshly, subjective, human side of himself in order to achieve that objective clarity of motive and purpose that characterizes the Kantian notion of the universal. My father would have no quibble with Kant's pronouncement that "The essence of morality is that our actions are motivated by a general rule, that is, that the reasons for the actions are to be found in such a rule. If we make it the foundation of our conduct that our actions shall be consistent with the universal rule, which is valid at all times and for every one, then our actions have their source in the principle of morality" (Kant 1963 [1775–80]:42).

This highly elaborated moral world based on a categorical imperative, erected with the collusion of my mother, if not her heartfelt support, struck me as a highly arbitrary reality. In fact I have thought since leaving home for college that any reality, no matter how intellectually refined or invested with ritual and the trappings of sanctity it might be, is equally arbitrary. This point of view became a marvelous contribution to my thinking about anthropology, for what else is it we study but historically evolved traditions, arbitrary and binding realities.

My wife's deeply felt religious conservatism was no comfort and developed into a source of conflict between us, as I attempted to move beyond the rigidity inherent in such ideal formulations. My poetry reflected my own problems with family religious adherence:

REMARKING TO MY WIFE

into my wildest dreaming
I enter you

coughing the old slowmotion
snails of my confession
to each of your faces

as icons pass through
one another,

and I, falling
through the liturgy
of your mother's church

swim out of your reach
each time you read

the hesitant yes and no from my eyes.

Rearing me became for my father a challenge in religious experimentation, whereby I was to reap all the benefits of his conversion and subsequent devotion; I was to become educated in the ways of God, hopefully gaining, like John Stuart Mill, a head start. This idea of a jump on the rest of my peers was all the stronger in my father's mind because of his rather dramatic religious conversion in late adolescence. His religious experience was rendered more powerful to him because his parents were agnostic from a vast antipathy to any religious observance. My childhood and adolescence were bookish and asocial. I was not encouraged in sports, though my father had won letters in four sports in high school. My feelings toward him were powerfully ambivalent and cut to the center of my being. I shaped some of those accumulated experiences of him in poetry and expressed them this way:

DIRECT DIALING THE ABYSS
FROM A PAYPHONE: FATHER

From a deeper South I felt him pulling
ways he had not tugged before
the voice insistent on a distant line
pulling vaguely at my mouth, numbed cheek,
somehow like a dentist, extracting my voice.

I have entered phonebooths to reach outward
to become real in that other place
even as they die before my speech makes real
someone's face.
                    The whole time after the operator tuned us
it felt as if there was a place where the whole body
turns out sensing someone else,
the way his ear feels against the phone, inside his skin,
his reality unloading and becoming something for me there.

Each watched our distances developing
the teeth disappearing and under whose pillow
are there teeth of buried treasure? Who
believes Lazarus could come forth
on a morning of dimes for a distant child
who'd put faith in darkness at the other end of the line?

We saw each thing grow smaller, even rightly,
voices whispering
growing fainter on the swelling phone
his voice watery down the line
as I faded twisting in the drowning wire.

I was to redeem the time for the days were evil, a New Testament urgency that I never quite felt. To achieve his aim, I was often sent to my room to study, and the first books I remember being given were religious treatises. I did enjoy the magnificent biblical legends that made reading Kierkegaard's *Fear and Trembling* a great delight. Being stashed away in my room in a kind of societyless exile I turned naturally to fantasy that, as Buber noted, occurs to undersocialized minds. I found it easier to make up fantasied responses to catechism than to memorize the lines, a skill that is rather more useful in art class than in memory drills. The catechisms I made up, I at least wrote in those religious tones, with a kind of religious intensity. But the words that came out were an attempt to structure my parents' expectations for me and make sense of them, take command of them:

SOME NOTES ON THE PRESUMED MESSIAH

& the arm shall conceive
& the hand shall bring forth a son
& they shall call his name *Incarcerate*
for he shall hold the people in their chains
though they sing like Dylan Thomas

& the arm shall be swelling like wet wheat
& be bulbous as a gourd
& it shall be reasonable as sponge

& the hand shall choose among its fingers
who shall bring forth
who shall bear the first fruits

& the noise of jets
shall be twisted from the wrist
& the parents cry out in pain,
the trains wailing in the distance
will bring frankincense & more

& under whose star are we caught
by which ray are we pinned
still flapping, to this hour
& bright display

I was sheltered and isolated from much of American culture: movies, comics, television, even some radio, many novels, popular music, and so on. I felt on leaving home like a cultural feral child. I turned to anthropology out of a passionate desire to expand my social awareness, to trade in Kant for David Riesman's *The Lonely Crowd* (1953) and Claude Lévi-Strauss's *A World on the Wane* (1961), the first two social science books that I read. Anthropology was not a window on the social diversity I craved but a doorway, a liberation from self, from locality, from religion, from ritual. Through social science I could embrace otherness, active involvement, travel and adventure, and the politics of competing reality systems; I could embrace society that had been denied me and sponsor my own redemption. For me, anthropology provided the opportunity to take up a new moral position to the world and to my experiences—from renunciation and fantasy to participation in multiple realities.

≫

Before discovering the social sciences, I put my fantasies to use writing poetry, which allowed me to subvert the structure imposed by my home environment, to channel my imagination into a socially acceptable form, and to receive some validation while in high school from English teachers, if not from my parents.

Poetry, like fiction writing, is vastly different from the writing of social science prose. Aristotle captured one aspect of this dissimilarity (McKeon 1947:635–36):

From what we have said it will be seen that the poet's function is to describe, not the thing that has happened, but a kind of thing that might happen, i.e., what is possible as being probable or necessary. The distinction between historian and poet is not in the one writing prose and the other verse—you might put the work of Herodotus into verse, and it would still be a species of history; it consists really in this, that the one describes the thing that has been, and the other a kind of thing that might be. Hence poetry is something more philosophic and of graver import than history, since its statements are of the nature rather of universals, whereas those of history are singulars.

Poetry writing as it is now practiced among American poets is not by any means universal; it is, rather, nicely phrased tropes of personal, almost solipsistically private experience. There is no "universal" poetry, but I don't want to try to clarify what poetry "is." The distinction I want to make is between the writing of social science ("history") and the writing of poetry, two very different acts that require two fundamentally different attitudes towards one's experience of the world.

Anthropology and poetry have, despite their differences, been linked for a long time. For example, Dell Hymes is a peripatetic versifier, Richard N. Adams has published a book of his verse, and Paul Friedrich's poetry has great range and power (1978, 1979). Margaret Mead wrote poetry, but the two most famous anthropological poets have to be Ruth Benedict (who irritated Sapir by using a pseudonym) and Edward Sapir (Mead 1966 [1959]:92–93). I was elated once when my poem *Direct Dialing the Abyss from a Payphone: Father* appeared in *Poetry: A Magazine of Verse*. Benedict and Sapir, Ezra Pound, T. S. Eliot, and Wallace Stevens also had poetry published there. It was the most satisfying publishing event I experienced, and it occurred during the first year of my Ph.D. program. At least I am in the direct poetic line of descent of Sapir and Benedict, if not of Eliot, Pound, and Stevens.

By the time I began fieldwork I had been reading and writing poetry for fifteen years. This generated, as I expected it to, a dissonance between the poetic consciousness and the social science consciousness I was developing. In *Beginnings,* Said sheds light on this dissonance (1978:196):

. . . the author's career is a course whose record is his work and whose goal is the integral text that adequately represents the efforts expended on its behalf. Therefore, the text is a multidimensional structure extending from the beginning to the end of the writer's career. *A text is the source and the aim of a man's desire to be an author, it is the form of his attempts, it contains the elements of his coherence, and in a whole range of complex and differing ways it incarnates the pressures upon the writer of his psychology, his time, his society.* The unity between career and text, then, is a unity between an intelligible pattern of events and for the most part their increasingly conscious transformation into writing. [my italics]

As I came to understand it, my efforts to produce an intelligible pattern of events in writing began with the writing of poems in which the aim was to "imagine the real," as Buber put it. But I did not accomplish this. I found the beginning intention to write poems too limiting, though I was completely serious about writing them. Also I did not identify at all with the life poets lead.

In order to expand my experiential base, it became necessary to replace the poetic unconscious I had cultivated for an anthropological one.

In the beginning, poetry writing was primarily autotherapeutic. I wrote in order to objectify my inchoate feelings and ideas. Once on the page—alienated from myself, in Hegel's strict use of the term—I then examined my work as an objective document while rewriting it. I interrogated each poem for clues to the organization of my mind, my fantasies, and the successes or failures of my social experience. It was a deeply reflexive act, a solipsist's hermeneutics (which may be why the recent resurgence of interest in hermeneutics fails to appeal to me). After this terribly isolated and isolating enterprise, I then thought I could choose among courses of action to remedy or amplify what I perceived needed changing or encouraging in my thought or behavior.

> I sense my wife through a single nostril
> why is it,
> I always lose her in a social space
> she disappears into another room.
> After a door closes
> things collapse into insanity. I
> mole through the house
> take out all partitions to find the single
> carpentered world, she stands with the cat on
> her arm, quietly,
> blonde
>   it sickens me to see the sun dismayed
> the walls laid waste, stairs torn out,
> a second floor on the lap.
> My thinking lies in ruins, except
> for the outer walls;
>   her painting was
> darkened, artificially, you know.

I became almost painfully aware of that subterranean geography of the self that Freud developed the atlas and index for. I refused to apply any pathological models to myself and hence was unattracted to Freudian analysis, though admiring Freud's writings and the enormous task he had undertaken. My own situation I thought of entirely in cultural and experiential terms; I was interested in acquiring greater quantities of experience of whatever kind, rather than in being examined or understood in terms of psychological pathologies, however ingenious the explanatory mechanisms might be.

Over the years I have had two poetic projects, one of which failed, the other of which was merely overtaken by my move to the social sciences.

1. The first scheme was to create an alternative landscape, a fictitious world that, like a painted surreal landscape, would be an interactive complex entity unto itself—a miniature world

SURROUNDINGS OF THE CHROME COUNTRY

the contrivance man in profile land

A peddler in the Chrome Country sells without
A gulley or the valley of green trees whose
Dreamed reflections of green stares at no corner
Of the canvas of this stark unpainted glaze.   ·
A subservient salesman stalks, not seeing
A crucial flaw in flamed steel; but rather
Blank harmonics and dissonances of his
Observation with insurmountable odds:
Fourths of atonality, nor being in a hemisphere
Of apricots. Allover there bled naked country
At the razor of his sight, a provingground
That good is not a subtraction of the clause
From the utter sentence that hung him
Above a reprieve he was stranger to.

A voice like GOD breaks through centuries
Over the battened down ridges of plain plains,
Saying, "If only this cast steel could be
Stunned, roughened with metaphors of sheiks
And streaming camels, sparse onions and
Giraffes: living condolences for the Chrome Country."
But over the edge of the frame,
All out of canvas, screamed a cleavage
From the real with nothing surrounding
But this poem

Unfortunately, modern, or perhaps any, poetry cannot bear the weight of a wholly fictional entity the size of a country; furthermore, such a project pushed me away from an empirical world. The project died from lack of devotion, a poverty of extensive social experience that in the end spells the failure of the imagination.

2. The second project was actually a social-psychological one: I wrote poems about those intimate, hence problematic, to me: my wife, my mother, my father, my brother, and my sister.

OH! GOD

        my sister's children were bleeding
from the throat, the hymns they sang
in soft contralto!
Afraid to die in the paved streets
they lay under the trellis
stretching to become shadow, secret,
their flesh shriveling in a blank stare,
straining to whisper passwords.

They would be found, GOD'S
voice in the rafters was like a leech
an inhaled plastic sack
something soaking up breath like gas;
tears streamed from their mouths,
they fought blindness, my
                    brother fought back.

Darkness fell along the ditches and we looked for him.
My wife cried out his name. The raincoats shot back

SILENCE.

He lay in the alley, sleeping from the way
his brain crinkled under light and rock
                    or the pock
of shot.
      We children were scattered in the infra
red light of the hawk patrols.
                   The owls stood in line on the limbs
forested, silent as snow, shadowed by the large Troll.

They were all looking for the jigsaw puzzle children
which drank for a GOD,
              we thirsted for Him and the abstractions
of righteousness.
We rang bells for His death while fearing something like
His voice, the skinny voice, or what we thought, afraid
we would find someplace outside childhood on a burning deck,
the blown lights from the Second Coming, and we had not yet
come at all.

Only on the back porch lay our chances,
the screen door sang as it slammed, something secular,
a salvation, the airraid over, the warning that
some green would come, the new tree; sheets in
the wind from a stifling fresh wash.
Grandmother lit up like a sign,
her apron common as coffee. The spiral spring
that pulled the screen door hummed. Light lay
a great deal like rain,
over everything children see.

The nuclear family is a terribly cramped space, I discovered, and the majority of my poems reflected that realization.

My concern with interpersonal relations from my family life was the existential concern that served as the basis for my scientific interest, the study of what Goffman termed face-to-face interaction. The literature that attracted me was derived from Buber, Simmel, G. H. Mead, Sartre, Goffman, Schutz, and Garfinkel. These authors constructed models of the actor and the situation that could contain the scale of experiences I had inside my family and inside the other intimate locales associated with middle-American, small-town life. When I began my fieldwork, I turned away from poetry as a futile task of self-revelation and toward experience-within-a-scientific-body of knowledge. By engaging the world in this way I achieved a personal success and the infusions of the social world I had set about apprehending.

My involvement with poetry, while serious, was always secondary. I published two books (Rose and Renner 1967; Rose 1970) and submitted poems on occasion to literary journals. I was poetry editor for several years of the university literary magazine and won several university-sponsored poetry prizes. My writing was such a private activity that I did not pursue publications very avidly, and friends submitted at times for me. I chose with great care the poets I liked, leaning toward those whose voices spoke directly and vividly to me. They were, in chronological order, Emily Dickinson, Gerard Manley Hopkins, and Wallace Stevens. Pound gave me more moments of pleasure than any other but Stevens. Eliot reminded me of what I wanted to get beyond. I never really emulated any of them except once I tried to write a poem the way I thought Wallace Stevens might have. I felt for Stevens first a kinship with his poetry of the imagination, then with him as a person. Mentioning him, I do not mean to compare his poetry and mine; there is no basis for it. I admired his turning down a career in poetry to remain an executive in the New England insurance industry—undoubtedly a wise choice. I too eschewed influence: influence from other poets, either pater or peer. The literary critic Harold Bloom calls the avoidance of influence in poetry writing, *kenosis:* "For, in *kenosis,* the artist's battle against art has been lost, or the poet falls or ebbs into a space and time that confine him, even as he undoes the precursor's pattern by a deliberate, willed loss in continuity"

(Bloom 1973:90).[1] Kenosis gives the name to the social isolation of my writing experience.

Bloom's theory of poetic influence is a neo-Freudian one, certainly revisionist, but nevertheless oedipal in its main dimensions: "Poetic history in this book's [*The Anxiety of Influence*] argument, is held to be indistinguishable from poetic influence, since strong poets make that history by misreading one another, so as to clear imaginative space for themselves" (ibid.:5). Bloom has argued, and I think few would disagree, that as poetry has become over the last century more subjective, the preceding generation has exerted greater weight and can dominate a practitioner's creative consciousness. Bloom claims, "Poetry is the anxiety of influence, is misprision, is a disciplined perverseness. Poetry is misunderstanding, misinterpretation, misalliance" (ibid.:95). And he adds, "Poetry (Romance) is Family Romance. Poetry is the enchantment of incest, disciplined by resistance to that enchantment" (ibid.). Like Stevens, I was a poor family member of the circle of poets and resisted all too successfully, never embracing that enchantment of incest that Bloom identified at the very heart of poetic sensibility.

Stevens's attraction for me was based on his delicious use of language—not so much musical as palpable—visually and verbally gustatory. But equal to that sensual attraction was his foregrounding of human imagination, that legacy from the Symbolists; it was thematic to everything he wrote. For him it was the supreme epistemology, the way we grasp the world. Imagination was the way we experience, and, paradoxical as it sounds, it was the basis of reality to him. My favorite

---

1. Even while quoting him, I am compelled to disagree with Bloom's easy typifications of the poet's relations to other poets, because Bloom does not capture what poets do. Bloom, in order to make poetry understandable to critics, fails to link poet and reader, a more vital, if elusive, relationship. I prefer the view of Cid Corman, who, jousting with other windmills, nevertheless clarifies the point at which I would differ with Bloom's characterization of poetic families in incestuous relations: "Art is never concerned with attaining any 'truth.' Or 'falsehood' either, though Plato and Picasso repeating him assert otherwise. Art is man realizing his experience in such a way (via some medium) that it may be realized by others too" (Corman 1976:no page). Or, to put it in anthropological terms, the poet's main concern is not to relate to other poets, though poets relate to poets, but to be an artificer of the world of his or her own experiences that evoke in the reader (who may or may not be another poet) a semblance of grasping and illuminating of experiences of the world. Not being a poet or not being a native makes Bloom miss the reason for poetry. He captures a sense of its sociology but cannot uncover why it should exist at all. He fails to take the emic view. In the end, poets relate not only to one another, but to one anothers' experiences of the world, and these are not the same thing at all.

statement of his was *Tea at the Palaz of Hoon,* written in 1921 (Stevens 1955:65), and it was solipsistic enough to call forth my most immediate response.

> Not less because in purple I descended
> The western day through what you called
> The loneliest air, not less was I myself.
>
> What was the ointment sprinkled on my beard?
> What were the hymns that buzzed beside my ears?
> What was the sea whose tide swept through me there?
>
> Out of my mind the golden ointment rained,
> And my ears made the blowing hymns they heard.
> I was myself the compass of that sea:
>
> I was the world in which I walked, and what I saw
> Or heard or felt came not but from myself;
> And there I found myself more truly and more strange.

For many years I was like Stevens's hero of the poem who in the act of writing verse found myself more truly and more strange. However, I can only agree with Bloom, who observed, "A poem is not an overcoming of anxiety, but is that anxiety" (Bloom 1973:94). Poetry kept me anxious and resolved nothing, so that when I chose anthropology and when I began fieldwork, I was attempting rationally to retrain my unconscious, to develop a different way of becoming in the world, an alternative way of experiencing the social, in sum, initiating a search for a new range of human experience.

Underlying this struggle to retrain was a deep, perennial conflict between art as expressed in poetry and politics as manifest in the inherently political nature of experience. *Tea at the Palaz of Hoon* was a hymn to the self-sustaining, imaginative acts of the self. One cannot find anything comparable to this in the works of Marx, Weber, Durkheim, or Parsons—Boas, Kroeber, Geertz, or Hymes.

What constitutes a legitimate experience for anthropological purposes may not have much meaning for the poet. Novelists, poets, and anthropologists each have different beginnings, different sets of original intentions. In each case, the relation of author to experience is different, and in each case the symbolic forms used to cast experience into text make different kinds of demands on the writer. In becoming a social scientist, this orienting attitude to experience and to public text is what one must first of all accept.

Anthropology requires a willful giving up of the self in order to capture another type of understanding of human life:

> While remaining human himself, the anthropologist tries to study and judge mankind from a point of view sufficiently lofty and remote to allow him to disregard the particular circumstances of a given society or civilization. The conditions in which he lives and works cut him off physically from his group for long periods; through being exposed to such complete and sudden changes of environment, he acquires a kind of chronic rootlessness; eventually, he comes to feel at home nowhere, and he remains psychologically maimed. Like mathematics or music, anthropology is one of the few genuine vocations. One can discover it in oneself, even though one may have been taught nothing about it (Lévi-Strauss 1974 [1955]:55).

The psychological maiming, the rootlessness, is one basis of anthropological reality. The selves of the anthropologists are caught up in description, analysis, and model building of ways of life, codes, and symbol systems that remain entirely outside themselves and that they cannot much affect. Anthropologists cannot imagine freely: their loyalties are to the discipline; to canons of fidelity; to truth and fact finding; and to the current paradigms that sweep the field on occasion, that collectively pose the problems and channel the thoughts that anthropologists take to the field and later to the office in order to develop the prized texts based on extensive fieldnotes.

I had to face the dialectic tension between the personal symbolism of poetry and the creation of public, established, conventionally presented scientific knowledge. It grew to be less of a dialectic as I sublimated the poetic. With the shift to the kind of mind set necessary for fieldwork, my attitudes toward my own modes of experiencing changed: I no longer captured minute experiences for the poetic phrase. Nor did I dredge up anything from over the wall of the bubbling, active dreamlife of the unconscious for later objectification onto the page. In the process a part of myself was repressed, deliberately lobotomized, freely and wittingly.

The transition from poetry to anthropology was demanding and not without pain, but the continuity between lives was unsurprisingly there. I continued to be interested in the organization of interpersonal relations, in holism, but in the anthropological rather than the Kantian variety, and in events and social encounters. While I did not realize in advance all the changes fieldwork would bring to my life, I wanted to be able to think, feel, and act like an anthropologist, and I never wavered from this goal despite an almost uncontrollable fear for my life.

≫

When I arrived in Philadelphia for fieldwork, I was alone with a car and trailer loaded with household goods and books. I stayed in a youth hostel in Fairmount Park and spent some time exploring the area I had decided to study. I then returned to Wisconsin for Karen, and we moved into an apartment in a house dating from the Federal period on an exquisite chestnut-lined street near my proposed fieldwork site. The whole neighborhood exuded a sense of history and gentle Philadelphia affluence. I was much taken with the intimacy of center-city Philadelphia, including Society Hill, the restored area next to the river.

The city was designed by the colonial proprietor William Penn to rival London. But Philadelphia no longer rivals London, or for that matter New York, which has passed both of them as the most cosmopolitan of world cities. Philadelphia is the aging core of dying Quaker culture, where a belief and behavior system of libertarian ideals is coupled oddly with a renunciation of public, political, and social involvement in favor of a pursuit of private economic or leisurely interests (Baltzell 1980). It is a city of nearly two million inhabitants, a figure which is more than doubled if those living in the suburbs of the surrounding counties are counted.

William Penn appointed Captain Thomas Holme to plan the city of Philadelphia in 1682. Holme laid out the city on the fashionable, familiar, and eminently rational, if tedious, grid pattern with the 100-foot-wide Market Street (originally High Street) stretching east and west between the small Schuylkill River and the great Delaware River estuary (Reps 1965:162–63). Today the downtown stores follow this east-west pattern and comprise the central business district. Just a few blocks south of Market are rowhouse residences where white people live. A bit farther south, exactly six blocks below Market, is Lombard Street, the beginning of a black neighborhood.

There is a tiny alley between Pine and Lombard called Waverly Street. Tiny rowhouses, shoulder to shoulder, face a narrow way, wide enough originally for only a horse-drawn cart. At the turn of the twentieth century, when W. E. B. DuBois walked through these quarters for his study, *The Philadelphia Negro* (1967 [1899]), these shadowed passages were squalid—the homes of black porters, domestics, drivers, barbers, cooks, caterers, whores, and derelicts.

Although I would never have admitted it to myself at the time, I was beginning to feel a pervasive disorientation, because I did not know what to expect from the city or from Afro-Americans. I had DuBois's book under my arm, and I began using it as a badly needed prop to talk to the black people who still lived there. I say "still lived there" because the area was becoming gentrified. The tiny rowhouses inhabited by Philadelphia Afro-Americans for a century were being renovated by young, affluent white people who were part of the burgeoning service economy in Philadelphia and the rest of the country, the result of postwar economic prosperity. Pockets of black residences remained, and there were a few bars frequented by blacks in their thirties or older, but it was no longer a predominately black area.

To the Afro-American of Philadelphia there were three main black living areas in the city: North, West, and South Philadelphia. South Philadelphia was thought to be made up of the old and tired, North Philadelphia of the unemployed and gangs of teenagers, and West Philadelphia of the black middle class, with a number of nice neighborhoods and homes. I arrived in Philadelphia with a map drawn by a friend of the family who was teaching school in Minneapolis. He had grown up in black North Philadelphia but had visited the other two sections of the city. He used a couple of sheets of paper to make the map of the three areas. The spaces he drew were filled with Xs. He marked an X in areas I was to avoid. As I examined the map more closely on arriving, I realized that there were not many places I could safely go. His one piece of advice to me had been, "Don't go into these parts of town without a *brother.*" It was superb advice and I followed it. Wherever I went, I followed or took a colleague, a sponsor, an interlocutor, a guide, a defender.

An example. Once I was playing pickup basketball with young black men on a public court just bordering South Street. When we took a break I wanted to buy some soft drinks, and the nearest place to do it was a corner grocery on South Street. I started out alone, taking my trip as a challenge, and soon one of the basketball players fell in beside me, letting me know it was in my best interests if he accompanied me. Unaccompanied white males are fair game for a hustle designed to part them from the large quantities of money they are presumed to have. When black and white men are seen together in the black areas, it is believed that the black man has a prior claim on the white and has already or is about to score on the mark. Most situations are much more complex, the motives and assumptions about behavior much more tangled, but in brief, this is how in poor neighborhoods the system works.

I chose black South Philadelphia as a study site because it had the reputation for being tired: the poor and the old lived there, not the militant younger people who would give me trouble. The men I met in bars told me South Philadelphia was the *jungle,* not a reassuring metaphor. Their name for it stood for the difficulty of surviving there. I listened to them with anxiety because their faces bore the scars of successful campaigns. I say successful, because they were not dead. *Survival* was a word that cropped up often in bar talk, and increasingly I appreciated why.

Everyone I met was armed; men, women, children, and the very old.

I also came to understand this: the great scarcities in the poor sections of the city were startling. I knew people within a block of where we later lived who had neither electricity nor running water. The tragedy was that it was not all that uncommon. The absence of money made money visible. People always seemed to have a little change in their pockets, but often that was all they had. Partially as a response to the scarcity, there was an extremely deep running economic and social involution. People preyed on one another in order to make out. My drinking partners referred to the area as a jungle rather aptly, for the scarcities provoked great hardships, animosities, and incredible lifelong nervous disorders. The arms, guns, knives, small clubs—borne in fear —were carried in order to maintain one's material possessions and one's dignity in the face of potential loss of one or both. The involution intensified competition, and the story was told of two brothers on South Street who were eating together. One left gravy on his plate and the other reached over with his bread to sop it up. The brother with the gravy killed the other. Whether the story is apocryphal or not I do not know.

After Karen and I had settled in, I began to make daily contacts with black people who were living along Lombard Street just south of our Clinton address. Mostly I made contact with men my own age who drank at the 410 bar and who were native to Philadelphia and not recent immigrants.

In the middle of October, the second month of our stay, Goffman invited us over to his house. We discussed what Karen and I each were doing. Karen was going to finish her master's degree by writing a thesis on the use of percussion in the music of Béla Bartok. I discussed my growing involvement in the networks of men I drank with at the bar and my interest in the history of blacks in that part of Philadelphia since

DuBois's study in the late nineteenth century. Goffman heard me out, listened to my observations on black behavior, and then suggested quite a different direction for my research. He said why don't you get a job in a black neighborhood and move into the area as a sign of good faith. He thought I should not mention that I was an anthropologist or that I was working on a doctoral dissertation but should adopt an identity that would hide that fact. I would then be in a better position to observe everyday life unencumbered by academic identities and the distance such identities put between the fieldworker and the people being studied. He said I could claim I was laying out of school for a while and had followed Karen to the city because she was studying music here.

My immediate reaction was negative: I preferred to play the role of anthropologist. Goffman said that undoubtedly we would be perceived as hippies, a benign identity of the period. Karen claimed, rightly, that she had advocated all along that I get a job and go native in a black neighborhood. I felt outnumbered, and I was angry, furious—I was livid with rage. In a moment of self-destructive hostility, directed ultimately against myself, I said I would do it. Goffman's reputation, incisiveness, and persuasiveness neatly folded into Karen's heartless urging, and I reacted badly to the weight of it all. In addition I saw her thesis go out the window as she claimed that she, too, could help with the fieldwork if we lived in a black area; she might even take a job. I could no longer claim I was living outside the area to protect my wife's interest in completing her thesis. She was not a colleague, yet was now to be a fieldworker.

Some of my hostility was well founded. She was completely untutored in anthropology, and she did not finish her thesis on Bartok, as I figured she would not. She was important in the fieldwork we were to conduct, although she disliked taking notes and mostly did not, and I don't think we worked at all well together. My anger did not really subside but migrated to some part of my brain in the form, no doubt, of resentment over my loss of agency and, ultimately, over my loss of identity as an anthropologist.

Karen felt completely at home with the duplicity our field stay now demanded. I hated it. It went against everything the political evolution within anthropology had achieved in the 1960s, I felt. I would have been completely comfortable with full disclosure of my methods and myself. I felt that Goffman and Karen celebrated a way of life I couldn't command. But self-destructively, I went along and tried to sustain it. Later that same week I drove into South Philadelphia, obtained a job, and proceeded to look for housing near work. Just as Goffman predicted, we were seen as hippies, or I was taken for a draft dodger, or the both of us were thought to have abandoned families in Wisconsin and to be hiding out in a childless love nest in the anonymity of South Philadelphia. No one asked because it was not proper—or safe—to do so, but opinion in the guise of practical speculation flew about.

The upshot of the suggestions Goffman made and the statuses he had us build for ourselves was that I was not to conduct the type of fieldwork that had typified whites studying blacks up to that time. Elliot Liebow (1967) and Ulf Hannerz (1969) both spent days with their subjects but not as participants in the daily and nightly round. We became trapped inhabitants of that South Philadelphia street world, and our only escape was to movies or to visit her friend and his family in Bryn Mawr. We were locked together in faked identities, undercover agents for science, and we suffered cabin fever as if we had been snowed in for nearly two years. It was a situation I could only wish on KGB or CIA agents; unfortunately they are partly self-selected for such trickster roles; I was not.

≫

After our momentous chat with Goffman, I made plans to do two things: to find a place to live in a black neighborhood and to find a job. From a trolley ride to become acquainted with the city, I saw a hole-in-the-wall *jackleg* mechanic's auto repair shop. Since I was manually dexterous, if not highly experienced, I figured I could do that sort of work. Fighting like cats and dogs over the details of finding housing, Karen and I looked through some of the city's most devastated landscape for adequate shelter and facilities. One enterprising real estate agent who heard our request for housing with blacks offered to rent us an empty church cheaply. Perhaps he figured that if we wanted to live in the neighborhoods in which he owned real estate we would need an ecclesiastical base, since it appeared we would have one foot in eternity and the other on a banana peel.

I found the job first. That garage I saw from the trolley turned out to be the locus of my fieldwork for two years. When housing became available, we moved in. As a matter of fact, we moved in next door to the auto repair shop. For the first couple of months, I walked or rode the trolley to work from our Clinton address. In the winter we moved to Fourteenth Street and lived there for more than eighteen months.

I drove to the shop with my disintegrating Chevrolet, a marvelous ghetto car, and I was going to ask the proprietor to repair it; a noise was emanating from the clutch housing. I parked the car, got out, and approached a man wearing a mechanic's uniform who was sitting on the stoop next to the open garage. I found out later that his name was Boycie. He became in time a good friend. I asked if he were the owner; he shook his head no and directed me inside. Inside I met a man named Telemachus, who wore a greasy porkpie hat pushed back on his head. He had grey eyes in a soft brown face, and he was in his late forties. The day was hectic, but I noticed right away that he had an eighteen-year-old man named Raymond—I could tell because it was written on his shirt—working for him. I was disappointed, for I figured that Raymond, of all people, would be the reason I would not get hired. If he had a shirt with his name on it, he was full time; if he was full time, it did not seem to me that the gutted first floor of a rowhouse made into a repair shop would absorb all that labor. The place only held three cars, and by ordinance it is illegal to work on the street. I had no intention of putting anyone out of a job, but I figured that I would at least ask if Telemachus needed part-time help. I would much rather have worked part rather than full time—I wanted to do anthropology, not repair battered Pontiac LeManses.

Later when it was not quite so busy, Telemachus ran my car into the opening of the shop, its rear end ungraciously hanging over the sidewalk, raised the front end with a compressed air jack, and, taking a tinshears, snipped a bit of offending metal from the clutch housing. The circumcision cleared up the noise, he charged me three dollars, and after the painless operation, he and I chatted for a moment. I said I was looking for part-time work and that I had no wish to put anyone else out of a job. He squinted into the street and said cryptically to come in on Monday morning about eight o'clock. I drove away feeling at least that there was some progress being made in donning the apparel for the new role.

Telemachus' repair shop was one of many in the area. South Philly is redolent with mechanics who believe that if they open a garage and tell their friends, they will have numerous customers and grow affluent by repairing automobiles. It is by no means that easy. South Philly has a lot of repair shops because the majority of automobiles there need them; they are old cars, nearly worn out, and migrate to the area via used car lots from the more affluent sections of the city. The inherent problem of making a living from one of these operations is that the repairs may cost more than the car is worth, so the shop owner is placed in the intolerable position of working for a slim or imaginary margin of profit. If the repairman charges too much, he will have an automobile on his hands that cannot be resold because he does not have title to it and cannot be given back to the owner without a complete loss of investment in time and replacement parts. This enduring dilemma confronted Telemachus daily, and he was unable, because of other critical variables, to solve the problem.

The operation was completely illegal, which means it was not licensed by the city. As a result, Telemachus did not qualify for a state tax number, which would have enabled him to buy parts without paying the 6 percent sales tax. Without the tax number, parts wholesalers did not recognize him as a legitimate business, so he could not benefit from wholesale prices on replacement parts. As a result he attempted to acquire parts from friends who were mechanics in other repair shops. They would steal parts from their shops and sell to him for cash. This system did not work well, because custom theft from a fixed position inside a shop is at best a rather restricted enterprise. Those who thieved for him had to be circumspect and thus could not provide him with the flow he needed. He was forced to rely on purchasing parts at retail prices.

Telemachus was also unskilled and remained that way during the two years I worked there. He could not read a manual and had not been trained in transmission repair. He would open a transmission after I had spent an hour under a car lying on my back on the stinking oily floor pulling it out, and if he could visually identify what was bad or broken, he would replace it. As often as not, such insensitive surgery was ineffective, I would have to pull it out again, and the same biblical method— seek and ye shall find—was used once more to repair it. I pulled and replaced some transmissions as many as eight times before he gave up and had someone else rebuild it or went scavenging in the junkyard to find a replacement.

In addition to the owner's lack of skill and the costly illegality of the operation, Telemachus' customers were hopelessly poor and often could not pay or could pay only partially. Payment would sometimes stretch over a year. Customer poverty, while a key problem, was matched by labor difficulties. Telemachus' own labor was technically inadequate and those of the people he hired equally so. As a result, time was lost, and as any capitalist knows, time is money. Although there was always a customer at the door needing repair work done, and although Telemachus always hired another person full or part time, he could not keep helpers for long, because his cash flow was in constant jeopardy, and he simply could not pay them.

As a result of the capricious payday system, Telemachus' relations with Raymond were constantly strained. Telemachus viewed Raymond as a charity case because he had been in prison on armed robbery charges and was unskilled, which made him relatively unemployable. Telemachus felt that the lack of a consistent payday was offset by his hiring Raymond; or, some money is better than no money. Raymond, for his part, worked when he wished to, which was when a job was big enough so that he could be sure of hitting Telemachus for a portion of the proceeds. This meant not only that Raymond was often not in the shop as a regular hired hand ought to be, but also that he refused to work on jobs if he perceived that there was nothing immediate in it for him. These two conflicting perspectives on work expectations engendered inherent conflicts, and this is what I walked into.

Telemachus, I believe, saw me as a source of easy exploitation. He knew that if I *wanted* a job with him, I was exploitable, plus he knew that my expectations about labor were that I would work as I said I would, which is how he stereotyped white men who worked with their hands. His ploy was to replace Raymond's arbitrary, unskilled, and hence undependable work with mine, which, at least to his mind, would be no worse. Quite expectedly I did not perceive this matrix of definitions of the situation, and I blithely blundered directly into the middle of some ongoing action. I got caught up in the plot, but I had not been issued the script. I did keep track of as many of the economic transactions as I was privy to, and I documented and analyzed at the end of the day the exchanges and the litigations I had heard.

Following Goffman's role-playing suggestions, I never mentioned that I was studying Telemachus or anyone else in the area. As a result, all note taking was from memory. I never asked any questions except the ones that natives or ignorant foreigners, such as myself, might ask, which turned out to be not many. With such a high degree of illicit activity, asking questions tended to reduce not only one's credibility but also one's longevity. I had no intention of losing either.

There were boundaries in South Philly, visible and invisible. One of these boundaries existed between blacks and whites on the interpersonal level as well as on the business level—as it does in the rest of the country. Telemachus rented his hole-in-the-wall garage from an Italian-American, Tony Antonini. They did not converse much, and there was no business cooperation between them. There may have been a hint of competition, because Tony also had a transmission repair shop, as well as other businesses. There was, however, a clear division of customers: Telemachus had black customers, Tony had white ones. I stayed on the black side of the boundary, for it was obvious that with a simple move, like renting around the corner from the garage on Thirteenth Street (an Italian-American block), I could be caught up in a white world, duplicating the situations of most other white fieldworkers who have studied blacks.

This area for both black and white was the kind of place an entrepreneur might begin. Transitions could be made, threshholds crossed. One could begin an illegal business and with success turn it into a legal one. One could start out small, gain business experience, and grow. Like parts of the rest of the city, the space adjacent to Fourteenth Street was in a slow process of decay and rebuilding.

Tony was one of those young Italian-American entrepreneurs who was just starting out and who did not find it necessary to discriminate sharply between legitimate and illegitimate or legal and illegal enterprises. Tony worked nights as a forklift operator, and during the day he oversaw his businesses. He owned the rowhouse that Telemachus' shop was in, as well as four others. Above the shop was an apartment, which he rented out to a welfare recipient with her five children. His office and, behind it, his whorehouse were on the first floor, and Karen and I rented the second and third floors. Needless to say, as the partying got underway on the weekends, the rear bedroom of our apartment was unusable. We thought of creative ways of retaliating for our high rent and limited use of the apartment. One fantasy was particularly attractive: We would invite a troupe of flamenco dancers over Saturday, about 1:00 A.M., and ask them to perform in the back bedroom. This would have brought the ceiling mirrors in the room below crashing onto the rapt partiers. But it was not to be; it remained a fantasy.

Tony's businesses included an automobile glass shop. The social organization that he put together resembled a Mafia in that he tried to get others to run businesses for him while he kept them indebted to him economically and personally. His attempt, however, proved futile, and perhaps was not well thought out. The glass shop was run by an Irish-

American, while the transmission repair shop was run by a black man. To operate a successful family business, I should think one ought to stick with family, but Tony was not a racist, or perhaps he had no family interested in his businesses. The glass shop went under, and the black man refused to run the transmission shop after a spat over money. Tony had to replace the transmission shop manager, so he hired Dave, a repairman from a nearby transmission rebuilding outfit. Dave was a very competent mechanic and did an excellent job of repairing in general. He had no time for small talk or socializing.

Tony's illegal activity, while it included providing the services of women to a network of friends and to friends of friends, was not his only illegal activity. He also dealt in hijacked stolen goods, though he was not the hijacker. He made a point of telling me that if I had something on the side, he wanted a part of it, and he made a big deal of showing me he had influence with the local police precinct. I never revealed to him that what I had going would be of little interest to him and of even less remuneration. I was now a full-fledged spy for anthropology, a voyeur for social knowledge. It was a role I loathed, was no good at, felt alienated within, acted inauthentically all through, and recovered from slowly. I'm not sure why I kept trying to pull it off for the two years I was there.

≫

> *Wild dogs bark far away. Look the loop of the figure is beginning to fill with time; it holds the world in it. I begin to draw a figure and the world is looped in it, and I myself am outside the loop; which I now join—so—and seal up, and make entire. The world is entire, and I am outside of it, crying, "Oh, save me, from being blown for ever outside the loop of time!"*

> Virginia Woolf, *The Waves* (1931:189)

And thus it was that I awoke very early Monday morning to walk to South Philly, down Fourteenth Street, to greet a new life, to work in the garage, to acquire a whole new self. My emotions remained flattened. I felt nothing as I began the day by drinking coffee alone in the early yellow light of the Philadelphia fall.

As I walked, the only parts of my body I inhabited were my eyes. I couldn't feel, but I could see, as if I were watching in pedestrian time a newsreel of a city to which I was a total stranger, as if I were in the dark theater alone watching the street unwind.

The streets at ten minutes to eight were alive, people everywhere, traffic strong and the screech of steel wheels on steel rails as the trolleys passed me on Fourteenth Street heading into south Philadelphia. The overhead wire hummed a high-pitched metallic note as the trolleys rapidly approached and rocked away.

On the left as I walked there was a blasted space between the standing rowhouses on either side, full of rubble, piss, bottles, and the jagged ends of the red brick the city is constructed of. At Fourteenth and Bainbridge I passed a pawn shop open, unbelievably, at this hour, men outside talking loudly and joking, the biggest of them with a .38-caliber pistol stuck in his belt, the blunt handle with brown wooden grips showing. I heard him say how he took the young boys with their knives, how he had a whole trunkful of knives he had taken off *jitterbugs*. I set my face like cement and walked by them looking straight ahead.

The sign above the street in front of a brick warehouse announced

ROSE AUTO

black letters on a sign such a tasteless color of yellow I thought it needed lab tests. A man was standing outside, staring across the street toward the Martin Luther King, Jr., housing project. He looked toward me as I approached, revealing that one eye always looked straight ahead, for it was made of glass. I remained unseen as he glanced away uninterested. People were out at the Projects wading through invisible breezes made apparent by the blowing scraps of paper and particles of dust that filled the gutters and that nicely offset the clear and green shattered shards of glass. At the corner of Christian and Fourteenth I stepped into a luncheonette for another cup of coffee.

Welcome to the jungle, I thought, but actually it didn't seem so bad, at least not terrifying, because there was ordinariness hanging heavily in the deliberateness of peoples' movements and in the sense of decay that touched each façade.

The luncheonette did not look quite complete. It was the first floor of a rowhouse on the corner. There was a counter that ran down the wall, with stools in front of it. A black truckdriver was blowing his steaming coffee, impatient to get underway. Along the counter were racks of Tastycakes, potato chips, boxes of fresh, unappetizing, jelly-filled pastries; toward the back there were display racks with children's toys on them, smiling pink panda bears, plastic-wrapped dolls that could cry and evacuate tap water into their diapers. Food and toys and radios.

There were about six different kinds of portable radios. The place could have been Taiwan or Mexico: it had the half-finished look and odd combinations of things I associate with other countries. There were three black women standing in a ragged queue with their hair under bandanas waiting to pay for pastries. I looked at them, they looked at me as I walked in. Joe, who owned the place, an Italian-American who lived above the store with his parents, did not look at me. I later came to know that he had a black girlfriend who sometimes minded the cash register and who bore children by him.

I passed a dusty real estate agency on the opposite corner, saw what appeared to be an aging candy store. It was, in fact, a large and successful numbers bank that I later saw firebombed. One night a year later I heard the crash of plate glass and the crackle of rushing flames. I ran up to the third floor of the apartment, loaded my Bolex movie camera with black and white 400 ASA film, and shot from the window on the top floor the scene on the street: the blaze flickering, the red lights of the fire engines flashing and lighting up the three-story rowhouses on either side of the street in a regular, visual rhythmic beat as the firemen doused the fire. The numbers bank had been bombed, but it was later rebuilt.

Telemachus' shop was in the next block, and I sat in front drinking coffee until he arrived five minutes later. He drove up in a wine-colored Catalina Pontiac, four-door hardtop without hubcaps, a smile wrinkling his face. We exchanged greetings, he opened the garage door, threw the power switch, and the shop began its daily electronic life. The radio and the air compressor simultaneously took off making a competitive racket. The compressor was old, its parts had been patented in the nineteenth century, and it erratically banged with an oily gurgle, stuffing air into a tank that would power tools, lift cars, take bolts off and spin them on, clean the dirt off aging transmissions with hard blasts of stale air. Telemachus noted my coffee and asked if I could use another one. My addiction was such that I said yes. He left the shop in my charge and walked the opposite way I had come, to a restaurant a block away for coffee, and, as it turned out, Tastycakes.

The shop he rented was the first floor of a rowhouse. The floor had been removed, the basement filled in, and a concrete pad poured for the garage floor. There were three cars parked in the shop, that being all it would hold. They were set extremely close to one wall. On the other wall were storage benches full of old parts, generators, transmissions, ignitions, the flotsam and jetsam of junkyards, where anything awaits rebirth in the hands of the bricoleur-repairman, who, on demand, can turn a part from car A into one for car B—maybe.

I stood in the open doorway and looked up and down the street. Young Raymond was not around. I speculated that maybe he did not work full time and comforted myself with the thought. At least he did not arrive early in the morning, whatever that meant. I did not worry about it but put my attention to figuring out where I was and how I was going to navigate these waters.

I could hear people moving around upstairs above the din of the radio. Surely their apartment would become intoxicating from the fumes of the garage. I could see through the cracks in the boards up, into the apartment. The compressor full of air sighed to a stop, and the Moments were singing on WDAS, "Somebody Loves You, Baby."

> *Somebody loves you, Baby, and it's me*
> *Somebody loves you, Baby, and it's me*
> *I've given you all I possess*
> *True love and so much happiness*
> *So why don't you believe me when I say*
> *Somebody loves you, Baby, and it's me*
> *Yeah, Yeah*
> > *and it's me.*

A man moving out of middle age stood close to me, ignoring me, looked up to the apartment windows above the shop and screamed out, "I'RY, I'RY." He was trying to rouse the woman upstairs. He wanted to ask her to go for a drink with him. He already had a sheet or two to the wind.

Telemachus returned with two coffees and two Tastycakes, one a French apple, the other a cherry pie. He set his lit Pall Mall cigarette on the back of the car nearest the door of the shop, and we stood there eating Tastycakes and drinking the steaming coffee. Telemachus began a long monologue about race and discrimination. It was not a real monologue. Out of the corner of his eye, using peripheral vision, he would talk about people and situations and then watch me for my reaction. He was measuring me, testing; I was tested a lot that way, by everyone at first, until people came to know me. His disguised dialogue ended with his statement that he had a white girlfriend, and I was to treat her and blacks all the same.

I didn't know it, but Telemachus' white girlfriend called him every day at work, in the morning usually, in the slack early morning minutes before customers came in. The phone rang, and Telemachus told me that it was probably Angela—Angie—and he wasn't there, would I please answer it. He instructed me to tell Angie that he had gone out to get parts for a car. I went over and answered the phone. I did as I was told; it was another test. She wanted to hang on the line, but I discouraged her, telling her that Telemachus would be gone for a while, that he had to go across town. She told me to tell him to call her back, that it was an emergency. When I hung up, Telemachus was in the cloth bathroom. I yelled to him and told him what she had said. Telemachus grunted something unintelligible. When he came out, he made no effort to call Angie, and I wondered why not. We went back to the doorway. No business had come in, and Telemachus was not making much effort to work on the three cars parked in the shop. He continued his mono- logue, touching on his brother's speakeasy in New York City. I didn't know what a speakeasy was, but after Telemachus finished that part of the story, I had the idea that it was an illegal gaming house where cards, craps, roulette, drugs, booze, and women were to be had in any combi- nation or singly. They were little casinos, and Harlem was as active as Vegas, in just the same way.

It might have been last on the agenda, Telemachus might not have really cared, but he finally got around to asking me if I had had any experience fixing automobiles. I began my string of lies by replying that I had worked on my father-in-law's school buses doing everything except major overhauls. The truth was nearer to the fact that I had done minor repairs on my English sports car, and that no matter what I did, the damn thing always needed more.

Then, that seemingly settled, Telemachus continued to talk, his topic drifting back to his family. Apparently he felt some pressure to get his son out of jail. Aston, his youngest boy, about twenty-four-years old, was in prison for narcotics possession. Telemachus said that Aston had already cost him three thousand dollars, but that this time he could get him out for only sixty dollars. He wanted to leave him in prison because he knew he'd just be put back in again, but his wife cried and begged him to pay. Two of his girls were at home; one of them, the baby, was in her last year of high school. His two other sons both worked, one as a professional gambler, the other for his brother in Harlem who had the anything-goes speakeasy. His wife, he told me, was religious, and that really got to him. She was always off to church for this or that. Ever

since her operation, she had become more and more religious. It was just
a waste of time and money.

Telemachus said, "Let's put these cars on the street," and we drove
the two cars out and parked them, leaving only Telemachus' daughter's
car up on stands at the very back of the shop. His timing was good,
because a white man, tall and thin, about forty, wearing cheap cotton
slacks and a cotton shirt, drove an old Pontiac into the doorway. The
man was obviously poor and very nervous and asked Telemachus about
a transmission repair job. He worried over the money, the down payment, whether he should leave the title to his car with Telemachus or
not. Telemachus was gentle and tried to calm him down.

I watched the whole thing, and it brought back memories of my
years as a teenager in Kentucky at the edge of the Bluegrass region
where I attended public school. My high school had been divided between the town kids, whose parents taught at the college or seminary,
and the most-often-poor country kids, whose parents were dirt farmers
or worked on the horse estates painting white fences or grew tobacco.
This nervous, poor white man reminded me of those years and those
people. He was the kind of guy who went to the Salvation Army store
in Minneapolis once when he was stuck there, bought used shirts, and
drove that ragged Pontiac to Florida in search of a job, selling the shirts
at gas stations along the way to pay for gas. The man was evocative for
me of the violence of my grade school-high school peers in Kentucky;
the country boys whom I had physically feared, even though I had to
fight them, the hillbillies who grew up to drift, join the Army, or fight
over women at some hillbilly music hall on Saturday night in one of the
backroad shack towns along the palisades of the Kentucky River. It was
only an evocation, for the man was pitiful, and in his anxiety to pay for
the job Telemachus would do, had worked himself into a dither. He
probably would be too nervous to go to his job as a dishwasher that
afternoon.

Another customer came in for a tuneup while I was under the
Pontiac, trying to find the bolts that held the transmission onto the
engine. I was lying on my back on a flat mechanic's creeper, using a
trouble light and jointed socket wrenches. Telemachus had been under
there with me, on his own creeper, patiently explaining and showing
me what to do. Despite the interruptions and other things Telemachus
wanted to do, we had the transmission out by midmorning and on the
back bench under two fluorescent lights, ready to be washed off with

gasoline and taken apart for diagnosis and repair. About eleven that morning I went to the door, wiping my grease-stained hands on a mechanic's rag, and tried to get the nasty taste of transmission fluid out of my mouth and nose. Across the street in front of the check-cashing place was a bench with advertising on it where people sat to wait for the trolley. Raymond was sitting on the bench with his uniform on, his arm casually over the back of the bench. He was watching the door of the shop. As I was looking up and down the street, I saw Raymond, recognized him immediately, and before I had a chance to react, Raymond called across to me, "Are you working for Telemachus now?"

I said, "Yeah, I guess so."

Raymond answered, "You're gonna hafta take a lot of shit!"

I was extremely curious about why Raymond, who had prior right to the shop, should be sitting across the street rather than coming in to work. The whole encounter lent an air of uncertainty and ambiguity to the work situation, and my expectations became a little rubbery. An increment of anxiety was added to an already spicy dish. I could only wonder and remember to write it all down in my field notes at the end of the day.

The time was crawling toward three o'clock, and we had not stopped for a lunch break. I was starving. WDAS was selling hair conditioner and playing the hits. Curtis Mayfield was in the middle of a definite hit, singing:

> *day or night,*
> *Which would you prefer to be right?*
> *How long have you hated your white teacher*
> *Who told you you loved your black preacher?*
> *Do you respect your brother's woman friend*
> *And share with the black folks not of kin?*
>
> *People must move to the people*
> *A better day is coming for you and for me*
> *With just a little bit more education*
> *And love for our nation will make a better society.*

It began enigmatically, but the themes were there in the soul of the music pulling at consciousness: themes of women and sex, blacks getting themselves together, and there were the moral urgings for education and for inclusion of blacks as a part of the nation. The song was attracting attention everywhere it was heard. Every radio in black South

Philly and West Philly and North Philly had it on, it was a hit, and everyone knew the words by heart the second time through. Every black-owned car that came into the shop had its radio dial set to WDAS. I know because I checked. He sang:

> *Now some of us*
> *Would rather cuss*
> *And make a fuss*
> *Than to bring about a little trust*
> *But we shall overcome, I believe, someday,*
> *If you'll only lissen to what I have to say.*

And then back to the chorus, changed slightly,

> *If you had a choice of colors,*
> *Which would you choose, my brothers?*

I was in the shop alone now, trying to listen to the unfamiliar music to catch the words. I had to listen hard because the music wasn't like what I listened to on FM or the white hit parade, not even like rock and roll according to Presley from my early high school memories.

When Telemachus left the shop, he gave me an assignment. As he left he said, "I'm going over to the gas station on Christian and take that tire from my daughter's car. I'll be back in a minute. See if you can get some bolts from that box of odds and ends and stick those Buick valve covers back on."

I said I would do it. I bent over the cardboard box with forsaken leftovers from a hundred other jobs and searched for bolts with the proper threads that would keep the valve covers in place. I didn't hear Raymond come into the shop. Raymond was next to me when I looked up, startled. Raymond had changed from his uniform to street clothes. He was over six feet tall and the clothes looked good on him. He had on close-fitting black slacks, hard shoes, a well styled shirt. Raymond would liked to have been a model. He had the build for it, and he had never been cut in the face, but he was not handsome. Raymond asked, "Where's Telemachus?"

"He's over at the gas station getting a tire fixed," I replied. I didn't know what to make of Raymond's appearance and did not particularly link it with Telemachus' absence. Raymond seemed jittery at the same time, agitated or something.

He said, "I'm going to get my shit together," and with that he

walked around me and moved toward the back of the shop. I figured
Raymond was pulling himself out of the job for his own reasons, and
that he was going to pick up whatever personal effects he had around.
To me it seemed plausible that Raymond was angry at Telemachus and
had decided to take his things home. I turned back to the box and kept
rummaging through the greasy assortment, looking for the elusive,
usable bolts.

I looked once to see what Raymond was doing out of an idle
curiosity as to what a person would leave in a garage that he might need
to come back for. Raymond had a little cloth sack and was squatting in
front of the tool chest toward the back, quickly putting gleaming metal
things into it. I watched more closely, and Raymond reached into the
bottom drawer and pulled out a short pistol. He stuck it into his waist-
band. I had an immediate flash of myself being between Raymond and
the door and Raymond having to shoot his way to get to the door. But
fantasy was no sooner projected on the mental screen than Raymond
rushed by me out the door. I was afraid now that Raymond had a gun,
was angry at me for taking his job, would find some excuse to use the
gun, and I would be the target.

It was no consolation that I had no experience dealing with these
sorts of situations. I had no idea what to do next and absolutely no clue
as to what the gun meant. It was the image of the gun, not Raymond's
being there, or timing his presence with Telemachus' absence, that filled
the screen.

Telemachus returned in a few minutes as he said he would, and I
told him that the Buick was ready to go and that Raymond had come
into the shop looking for him. Telemachus was surprised. He exclaimed,
"Raymond! Looking for me? What'd he do?"

"Well, he said he came to get his shit together. He went there and
took some stuff out of those drawers. He took out a gun, and it really
scared me."

"That's my gun," Telemachus said.

"I was afraid he was going to shoot me," I added.

"He couldn't shoot you with that; it's just a starter pistol, a cap
pistol."

I knew that Raymond could make a zip gun out of it, and I was
uncertain enough about the turn of events to imagine that. Telemachus
seemed deflated and said, sighing with disgust, "Well, let me go back
there and see what he stole this time."

Telemachus began his inventory, and I stood in a pool of dread and uncertainty. Telemachus looked on his workbench with the Slim Jim disemboweled on it, opened up the wardrobe against the far wall with the pinups on the door and checked the shelves, then walked back to the tall tool chest, and, starting at the top, went from drawer to drawer. He walked back to where I was standing and said that Raymond had taken chrome wrench sets, the .22 starter pistol, two impact hammers, a Chrysler wheel puller, and a set of miniature wrenches. He looked pained and acted disgusted. He said his children had given him the starter pistol, and that all those things mounted up, maybe four hundred dollars worth. The impact hammers were expensive, and now every bolt would have to be removed or tightened by hand. The impact hammers were like drills. They fastened and unfastened bolts and ran on compressed air.

Telemachus looked me full in the face and told me, "When I leave, you're in charge and nobody can come in and take anything. Do you understand?"

I replied that Raymond worked there, and that I didn't know any different than to let him into the shop to get his things. I was curious as to what being in charge meant. Did it mean if I were in charge and Raymond came in, I would have to physically stop him from taking things? I had no idea how to go about that.

Telemachus finished the short lecture saying, "Boy, this is your place when I'm gone; you run it then; treat it like it was your own place."

Telemachus was soft with me and did not belabor the point. The lecture was also over because a man walked past the front of the shop, and Telemachus walked quickly to the door and called out, "Hey! Come here a minute."

I could overhear them talking. Telemachus asked, "You're Raymond's brother, aren't you?"

"Yeah," the man answered flatly.

"You tell Raymond to bring back the things he took or I'm going to call the police," Telemachus said, then repeated it. The brother was noncommittal, said he would tell Raymond, and left after that brief exchange. It wasn't five minutes before another person Telemachus knew stopped in and told him that Raymond was already trying to sell the items he had taken.

From that point on Telemachus did no more work for the day. He stood in the doorway the rest of the afternoon and talked to people. Everyone he knew he told of Raymond's theft. He would tell what a bad worker Raymond was, how he had tried to pick his own work on the cars, usually the easiest things. He would not pull a transmission out or learn to repair them. He said that Raymond left at noon on Friday and did not come in on Saturday until after lunch.

An old man drove an aging and scarred Ford into the shop. He and Telemachus talked, and he told him the Raymond incident. After Telemachus got through, the man turned to me and said, "You should never do that. You should never steal from a man who is trying to help you up. Telemachus was trying to teach him a trade."

I thought that he had heard the official version from Telemachus, but I wanted to clarify my own new and uncertain position by becoming involved in this role. I said to the customer, "Raymond probably stole from him because he hired me." At least I would see how this explanation flew. The man turned away and had nothing further to say, so my comment clarified nothing for me.

Not for Telemachus either. He kept standing in the doorway, looking up and down the street with a worried expression on his face, his body tense. At the needed times he would instruct me in something, and I worked on, aware of Telemachus' growing apprehension and all too aware of my own. As if my own feelings weren't bad enough, I had to see how worried Telemachus seemed to be. After all, he, not I, knew how the system worked. I finally spread my lunch on the fender of the man's Ford and ate it without anything to drink, standing up. Telemachus continued to look up and down the street. He didn't speak to the children on the way home from school unless they demanded his attention. At 7:30 P.M. we called it quits, and Telemachus said goodbye, see you in the morning. I said goodnight and walked over to Thirteenth Street to catch the trolley up to Clinton. I was shaken by Telemachus' depression, lack of ease, and preoccupation. I brooded about the day's events on the trolley. The question was in both our minds: What would Raymond do next? With this kind of fieldwork I knew I'd be in the action, that much was already pretty clear. I would have to let people define their own situations; my way of doing things was impossible to force on others.

That evening I narrated the day's events to Karen, and we discussed whether or not I should return the next day. I said I thought I should. I don't know whether or not I was driven by a deep anger or what. I knew I did not tend to quit what I set out to do. The events of the day and their unfolding were a unique challenge to my understanding.

The next morning I returned, again arriving about eight o'clock. Telemachus arrived about ten after. There was something new that morning: I noticed it in the right hip pocket of Telemachus' blue pants; it was a long hunting knife in a leather holster and the handle stuck up out of the pocket within easy reach. Weapons were kept in the right back pocket when they weren't stuck in the belt like the pistol the guard of the pawnshop had. So, Telemachus' preoccupation yesterday afternoon was turning into something; he was expecting Raymond to show. There could be a bloody, maybe deadly scene. I figured then that there was a real reason for me to be worried. I asked Telemachus about it, but he would say nothing about Raymond. He had a distant look in his eyes all morning and seemed to be brooding. Telemachus set me to work immediately and again he toyed with things, not doing much, the white man's Slim Jim lying in pieces on the back bench. Telemachus either stood at the door or worked just inside the doorway, watching the street.

A black man about sixty with a sporty straw hat walked slowly into the doorway of the shop. Every move he made was consummately casual and deliberate. He walked up one side of the street and down the other every day, stopping at places of business, knocking on the doors of the rowhouses. He moved so laconically he seemed invisible. It was Juice, the numbers runner. Everywhere he stopped someone would give him a number and some money. He never wrote the number down. He could remember the most perverse combinations, and because he never wrote the numbers down, he had never been busted for numbers running. Plus he was almost invisible. I looked at him with his sport shirt, his straw hat, his slacks, and his shoes. They were black leather shoes, and everywhere he had a corn or bunion the leather was cut out in a square. The white socks underneath made his shoes look like a surrealist's checkerboard. Telemachus played the number of his street address, 369. He usually put a couple of dollars on the number. If it came in he would get about eight hundred dollars, he said.

While Juice was still there, a beefy black man drove a red Oldsmobile to the space on the street in front of the door. He came slowly into the shop, and when Juice left he told Telemachus he had a valve problem. The man's name was Moe, he played bass in a jazz band in Atlantic City, and his younger brothers were bassists in the Philadelphia jazz scene. Telemachus took Moe's owner's card for the car. He told Moe what the job would cost him and asked for a twenty-five-dollar downpayment. Moe gave him the money and his keys, and Telemachus told him he could come back and pick up the car at the end of the week. Moe stood around and they talked casually for a while in front of the shop with Telemachus continuing to look nervously up and down the street.

Moe left and Telemachus kept standing there at noon in the cool October air, looking up and down the street. I was halfway back in the garage, close to the radio where I couldn't hear enough. If I was to be a professional snoop, at least I ought to get in on more of the strategic conversations Telemachus had. It was frustrating not to hear everything said. James Brown was singing "The Popcorn," and nearly half the people in Philadelphia knew how to dance it. I was jerked alert when I heard Telemachus yell, "Hey! Hey Raymond! I want to talk to you for a minute."

I had no idea what would happen next, but I pretended to lean under a hood while keeping my eyes on the front of the garage. Maybe Raymond would keep right on going, maybe he would come in and get mad and pull a gun. Raymond edged just inside the door of the shop and stood etched against the light, and Telemachus said to him, "I want the things back you took yesterday and I won't say anything more about it."

At this Raymond leaned over a little toward Telemachus and began to talk intensely, very fast and very low. I could catch nothing of what he said. Telemachus telegraphed his intense wariness and readiness for fast action; it took no training to read it in the stiff poise of his body. I, not sorting out my growing paranoia from the realities of the situation, had the overwhelming feeling I was deeply implicated in the mess. In a kind of final voice Telemachus asked Raymond, "You aren't bringing the things back, then?"

Raymond said, "No, I'm not."

Telemachus, looking him directly in the face and with an even, unhurried voice, said, "I'm going to have to get out a warrant for your arrest. With your record you might have a rough time. If you'll bring back the stuff, I won't call the police. Will you bring it back?"

"No," Raymond responded, turning his head so that he was looking over the street, "go ahead and get your warrant. Do whatever you want to do. I'm not bringing the stuff back."

Raymond left, and I walked with dread up to where Telemachus was standing. Telemachus just gave a forced wry grin and shook his head. I asked him what Raymond had said when he was talking low and fast. Telemachus said he didn't even catch all of it. He didn't want to talk to me about it, and this did nothing for my sense of impending doom. Neither of us said much the rest of the afternoon.

By 5:30 Telemachus had functionally called it a day. He and I were sitting next to the garage on the stoop where Boycie had been sitting the first day I drove up to get my car repaired.

The two of us sat there, both pulling on Pall Malls, when a round-faced black man named Russ pulled his Mercury into the doorway. He called a familiar greeting to Telemachus, came over, and sat down, filling the stoop. He began complaining about President Nixon, whom he referred to as "your President," and then he looked at me. None of the black men who mentioned politics in the shop liked Nixon, and none of them felt that they had elected him. Nearly every black house in South Philadelphia had a calendar picture or glossies of Jack and Bobby Kennedy and Martin Luther King. They were heroes and had in common their deaths and their death-defying rhetoric. The phone rang, and Telemachus got up to answer it. Russ and I talked a bit, and the conversation drifted around to the fact that I was new there. What happened to Raymond, Russ wanted to know? I explained that he had been there last week but had quit this week. I mentioned the theft and how Telemachus had told everyone what Raymond had done. I figured that telling the details in the way that Telemachus had done was, in anthropological terms, "culturally acceptable." I felt as if I were doing as Telemachus had done, and I wondered if I by my talk were reaching out to those still hidden, very real gossip networks and linkages that could galvanize a whole black neighborhood instantly with newsworthy events. I knew from the press during the rioting that black areas in cities could ignite almost instantaneously, and I had the feeling that news traveled like light on the street. There was a readiness for instant news, too, because the common greeting among men who came into the shop or met at the 410 Bar was, "Hey, what's happening man?" Or, more telegraphically, "S'appenin?"

If the anthropologist could act like a native and get the appropriate response from the person, he knew he had the rules of the society right. If the natives laughed at him, for example, he had done it wrong. In my case it might be a more dangerous game, I was sure. If I didn't act like a native, I might end up visiting the coroner, and I might even if I did.

I felt I had no choice. I was in it now, and I might as well play it for all it was worth.

Russ didn't react to the news of Raymond's quitting or theft in any remarkable way. He asked if I knew what Raymond was going to do, and I said I hadn't heard and didn't know. Telemachus had been on the phone, laughing and joking with Angie, and he came back and said he and his girlfriend were going on a date Thursday night. He and Russ began talking about women, and the conversation drifted from women back to the reason Russ had come. The left rear blinker light on his Mercury didn't work and could Telemachus take a look at it. Telemachus told him that Danny (the name I got stuck with) was a good mechanic and would look at the wires first thing in the morning. They said their goodbyes and dispersed.

I took the trolley home, not feeling any more certain about anything than before. That evening Karen wanted to hear about the day. I was nearly too depressed to talk about it but sketched in the day and the details.

The next morning I again got there before Telemachus. At ten minutes after eight he arrived. He unlocked the garage door and told me he would be back in a minute. He walked up to the luncheonette and bought two regular coffees. In Philadelphia that meant with cream and sugar. If one wanted nonregular coffee or black coffee, one had to ask for it specially. I set my sack lunch down on the tall wooden cabinet in the back of the shop. Telemachus' mood had been no better that morning, and as I looked about the shop I noticed tools lying around (by design?) that could become the implements of aggression, of defense, and of death. There was a brass hammer on Telemachus' back bench. Halfway down, on a bench near the blanketed bathroom, lay another ballpeen hammer. Near the front of the shop, on another bench was a claw hammer with one of the claws broken off. These were not comforting sights. The advice I had heard—never pull a gun unless you know how to use it—applied to hammers, too. If one picked up a hammer, one had better have a good reason and be prepared to use it.

Telemachus returned to the shop carrying a brown paper bag with the coffee. He opened the bag on the end of the car next to the open door and we stood in the doorway, as on Monday, drinking our coffee and chatting. Again Telemachus gave a little monologue on not discriminating along racial lines, perhaps obliquely referring to Raymond; I didn't know. Since the week was wearing on, Telemachus finally decided to tackle the Slim Jim he had torn down on the back bench and get the skinny white man's Pontiac back into running order. He told him he'd have it by the end of the week. He told me to come to the back bench and he would show me how to work on transmissions. He was interrupted by the inevitable phone call from Angie, and he took it and joked with her. When he came back to the bench, he told me he liked to joke when he was feeling bad, and he felt a lot better. He was obviously referring to the war of nerves Raymond was escalating. He showed me the scorched clutch bands of the transmission and said he would have to call his friend over at TRANSCO and ask him to bring over some new clutches. He went on to explain the special tools and showed me the basic parts of the transmission. The only thing I knew about them was that Lee Iacocca, president of Ford Motor Company, had a Ph.D. in transmissions. They must be pretty complicated.

Telemachus' friend from TRANSCO showed up complaining that Telemachus owed him money. He said he would not give him the transmission clutches for the Slim Jim unless Telemachus paid cash right then. Things were getting hot for him at TRANSCO, and it was less and less possible to sneak off and sell TRANSCO parts. If Telemachus didn't pay him right away, it wouldn't be worth it for him to bring parts over because he was taking the risk, doing it for money, and he needed the money or he wouldn't be doing it. Telemachus made sounds of disgust with his mouth, pulled some soiled bills from his right pocket, and paid the man. Then they began talking about other things; he wanted to borrow some of Telemachus' smokers for the weekend. Telemachus said he could, went over and opened the wardrobe with the pinups, took out the 8mm porno films, and handed them to him. The man set down Telemachus' porno magazine he had been reading and said the boss was out of the shop and he had better be getting along. Telemachus walked him to the door, telling him about Raymond on the way. Telemachus did not introduce the man to me, and we had said nothing to each other, barely exchanging glances. After he left, Telemachus and I went back to the bench, and Telemachus showed me how to reassemble the clutches. It was painstaking work. Telemachus' tools were worn and not up to the job, particularly on the seals and rings.

Telemachus walked from the back bench against the rear wall to the tall toolbox for a pair of needlenose pliers. He was pawing through the drawer when Raymond came walking into the shop. Raymond edged around Telemachus and as he was doing it, Telemachus, caught by surprise, said to him, "This isn't between you and him, this is between you and me."

Raymond responded with a curt, "I just want to talk to him. Stay out of this." Then he stood facing me.

I was caught in a cul de sac. The workbench was against the wall. My back was to the wardrobe. And Telemachus' daughter's Valiant was up close to the back bench. I had nowhere to go except through Raymond, and he was not moving. He was too close for comfort, and I felt the implicit menace in his closeness. Telemachus had turned to watch what was happening and was close behind Raymond. Raymond didn't even turn around to check where Telemachus was. The thought of weapons crossed my mind, but they weren't that close. There was a more critical problem, which was knowing when they were called for; and that took split-second timing. I was beginning to think that this was a situation for words, and I hoped they would not fail me. They usually didn't.

Raymond asked, "How do you like working for Telemachus?"

I paused before answering him and thought, *How can I cool him out*, and I reached for a familiar mode of address, figuring that might do it. "Oh, I don't know, Babe, you know; you get your hands dirty and all. I don't mind it."

Raymond just turned around, not saying anything to that, and left me hanging there, but we all knew that it had only begun. Telemachus had moved back to the tool chest and Raymond walked up to him. Before Raymond could say anything, Telemachus began complaining about all the things Raymond had stolen and how much they cost. He told Raymond that he had taken even more than he had first thought.

I stood and watched them in an icy fear. Raymond reached into his shirt pocket and pulled out a pack of Pall Malls. I pulled a lighter from my jeans and thought it might help if I seemed willing to communicate and be amicable. Raymond had his eyes on me and said, "I didn't ask you for a light."

Telemachus motioned me back, and I made the strategic blunder of walking back to the bench and into the corner where the pinups grinned at me from the metal wardrobe. Raymond dropped into the mode of talk that was rapid and low, and I could not pick out one word. As they talked, Raymond picked up a linoleum knife that had the hook taken off and the end sharpened into a point. It had been lying on top of the wooden cabinet. Then he asked Telemachus for *his* knife.

Telemachus, in a completely flat voice, asked, "What do you want to see my knife for?"

"Just let me see your knife," Raymond said. "I'm not going to do anything with it."

Telemachus pushed his hand into his right pocket where the money had seemed to come from and pulled out his pocket knife. He handed it to Raymond. I thought, *Now why did he do that?* I felt like my life had just been thrown away from a tall bridge, and already the spirit was looking for the shortest route to the hereafter. Raymond opened the knife and held it loosely in the palm of one hand. In the other he held the modified linoleum knife. Both palms were up with the knives in them, and his thumb held them securely in place. I noticed this in the infinite slow motion that seems to accompany so many fateful situations. With his hands poised in front of him, he walked to the corner where I was standing weaponless. Telemachus drifted in quietly behind Raymond then and casually placed his hand next to the handle of the brass hammer. I did those rapid calculations always done in last agonizing minutes and figured if Raymond wanted to use the knives and put his hands in motion that Telemachus, with all the speed in the world, would not have time to bash Raymond's head in with the hammer before I fell to the floor.

Raymond, who had his hands poised, the knives lying dormant but ready to burst into weapons of death, asked me, "Why did you have to answer me smart like that, using words like 'baby,' when all that I asked you was how you liked working here?"

I replied that I did not know I was answering smart when I answered the question. I went on, "I didn't know why you asked me how I liked working here in the first place because I've only been here two days and I really don't know yet. I didn't know what kind of answer you expected. I'm confused by this whole business."

I was beyond registering shock but was not prepared for Raymond's next move. Raymond placed both the knives next to me on the workbench in no particular fashion. It was not like he was suddenly going to pick them up again. He continued, "Maybe you won't be so nervous now, and you will feel more free to talk. I'm talking to you now; I'm being honest with you."

"I'm being honest with you, too," I replied.

But Raymond was not through; he was about to pull the rug out from under the assertions of honesty I had made.

"Why did you tell a man last night that they were looking all over for me?"

A new terror made my mind go blank. Even with the knives down on the bench it was more terrifying now than when he had held them. I felt in that split second that I had an option, and only one. I had to explain—no—deny I said anything last night to Russ.

"I never said anything to a man about you," I replied, lying smoothly. I couldn't believe that what I had told Russ last night was around here already this morning. *This is what I get for acting like a native of this place,* I thought. I continued, "I haven't said anything to anyone. Besides, what would I say?"

"Then the man must have lied," he said.

I hurried on, enjoying the moment of dishonesty: "Since we're being honest with each other, I want to ask you something," I said. Nice bit of irony.

"Okay," Raymond replied.

The question I wanted to ask was for me the crux of the matter, "I figured out that you think I asked Telemachus for your job and he gave it to me."

Raymond replied, "I told my mother that's probably what you thought. But that's not it. I like to see a man work. I can go out there and get me jobs. I have nothing against you working here."

He turned away then, leaving me to recover in the alcove made of car, workbench, and wardrobe. Raymond picked up his conversation with Telemachus and again they discussed returning the tools and getting out the warrant on Raymond. Raymond pulled another cigarette from his rumpled pack and turned back to me.

"Do you have a light?" he asked neutrally, without rancor, or even much thought, it seemed, to the incident.

I brought out my lighter and lit his cigarette. Raymond turned away without a word and started for the door with Telemachus trailing along after him. They talked for ten more minutes in the doorway. I decided to eat my lunch and so picked it up and walked to the front of the shop and past them across the street to Tony's Transmissions. He had a coke machine in the back. I figured I might as well die on a full stomach as an empty one, but really it was all over. If I had known more, I would have understood the meaning of the cigarettes. Those little gestures with lighting a cigarette were profound, and it would take me another year to put that piece of the puzzle into place.

≫

After eating, I was in the shop alone while Telemachus went to Tartack's around the corner for lunch. A black woman cooked platters there, and the food was down home and excellent. When Telemachus returned, I wanted to know what Raymond was going to do next. As usual, Telemachus was not reassuring. He asked me where he could buy a gun. So it was going to escalate again. I did not know what to think. I told him I knew some people at a bar where I drank, and maybe they would sell me a gun. I also thought, *if I find a gun, I'm going to buy it for my own damn self.* We worked through the afternoon in silence. The shop was busy; I worked in front with Telemachus at the back bench. When I started for the trolley to go home, Telemachus said he would give me a ride. I agreed but would not let Telemachus take me to Clinton Street. It would just have precipitated another kind of crisis. I would have to explain why we lived on an elegant street, and then at some point why we wanted to live in a ghetto, and neither Telemachus nor anyone would have bought any kind of line that we had developed with Goffman's guidance. I asked Telemachus to let me out on Lombard Street. Telemachus said he could take me all the way home. I said no, that I lived just around the corner and thanks for the ride.

Telemachus was worried about Raymond and the incident of the morning. He knew Raymond could start a lot more shit than he had already. He figured the scene with Raymond and the knives was enough to scare me off, that I was too inexperienced to go up against someone like Raymond, who was street-wise. He asked me, "Do you need any money?"

I replied, "Thanks, no. As long as I have a dollar in my pocket I'm okay."

Telemachus figured he owed me something for the three days, and he also thought he would never see me again. He stopped the car and said goodnight. I said, "See you in the morning."

When I got home, before cleaning the grease off, I turned on the tape recorder and taped my account to Karen of the day's events. We talked it over whether I should go back the next day; I knew Telemachus would be surprised to see me. I decided to go back, and I didn't know why.

A piece of the puzzle of black life was beginning to fall into place; at least I had seen it happen, it had happened to me. When a person had a grievance about something, it was directly between you and that person, even if the outcome was a long knife wound. No one can stand, safely, in the middle.

Before falling asleep in the darkness, I had an almost involuntary daydream-fantasy. I was replaying Raymond standing in front of me with a knife in each hand. It was humiliating to be backed up in a corner like that, a loss of face. In my replay I pulled out a gun and said to Raymond, "You son of a bitch, no one pulls a knife on me." I shot the gun into Raymond's guts and watched him collapse onto the oil-slickened floor of the shop. My unreleased anger kept me awake as I replayed the events and fantasied other outcomes; in some I died, in others I was the angry and successful killer.

I had discovered firsthand that everyone was armed, men, women, and children, in defense of their possessions and honor. My fear, my ignorance of norms, and my realization that I was not an equal before the local law of the streets prompted me to call my father. I asked him to buy me an automatic pistol. Our family had never had a gun in the house, and I was very surprised when an Italian automatic pistol arrived in the mail. I put a bullet in the chamber, filled the clip, kept the safety off, and wore it in my right front pocket every day for the next twenty-two months. Some have expressed surprise that I did not shoot off my own vital parts carrying the weapon so ready for the kill.

Because of my social location in the garage with Telemachus and our customers and my episodic travels with Boycie to various establishments, I had to find methods of analysis for the data I was able to generate. Economic exchanges became the most important central feature, while litigations and face-offs, such as the rather traumatic one with Raymond, became the second most ubiquitous element (Rose 1974; 1977). There is an interior connection, however. People who exchange never do so perfectly, and grievances arise. While this is an obvious fact, one is hard pressed to find where in the literature of anthropology the economic exchange-litigation relationship is adequately modeled. I came to understand an economic exchange as a strip of behavior and the litigations arising over economic exchanges as other strips of behavior that are articulated and do the work of bonding people to one another, changing the grounds of that bond, and sometimes terminating the bond. There is a third aspect of the exchange-litigation phenomenon and that is the way in which it is modeled and sanctioned —commented upon—in the art of the people (Rose 1975). Certain exchanges in the culture are preserved in stories, folklore, songs, and poems. The symbolic forms are thus not neutral toward the way mundane exchanging is done. The deep impact of Raymond's litigation with me, and his more extended one with Telemachus, set the stage for a problem in everyday black South Philadelphia life that I carried with me as an experience I needed to make scientific sense of. Event analysis —the arguing event or the exchange event—became the metaphysical basis on which I did my analysis and built my models (see Rose, forthcoming).

≫

Although my *beginning intention* in becoming an anthropologist had been to trade in my poetic unconscious experiences for an anthropological public life, I did not acquire in advance the emotional or scientific competence necessary to deal adequately with the unusual circumstances of my field experiences in South Philadelphia. Raymond, in challenging me physically and rhetorically, set up a trial by fire and a ceremony of passage. As a result my unconscious life has been forever, I suspect, backgrounded by the powerful impact that our encounter provided. I have no urgings to write verse.

By deciding to become, say, a member of a profession, we place ourselves in situated activity systems, in occasions and institutions, that legitimize and constrain what is considered proper to think, feel, and do. By becoming a member of a recognized category of human existence, a member of a status with role responsibilities, we also assume the canons of appropriate expression for the experiences we have. By becoming an anthropologist, I gain access to certain literate forms— writing accredited articles and books—through which I express myself and authenticate my identity.

I make these obvious observations against the realities of our times, times of phenomenally rapid change and uncertainty. In all this I see myself as a symptom, as a marker, as a token of fundamental shifts in the field of anthropology as the object of our inquiry—"natives"— disappears by being absorbed politically into the nation states and economically into the world economy. Anthropologists are faced with becoming, as a result, antiquarians, or autobiographers, or historians, or theoreticians who seek to explain the phenomena of preindustrial humanity that has vanished before our eyes. The changing status of native peoples has altered forever the field of anthropology, the status of beginning intentions, and, as this volume reveals, the forms in which anthropologists cast their experiences. For me the standard monograph or article could not be made to fit the mode through which I experienced life among the impoverished Afro-Americans of South Philadelphia. My experiences were narrative experiences. I could not, because I did not reveal my professional identity, break the flow of everyday life with direct questions concerning kinship or behavior, I could issue no questionnaires, take no censuses, tap no gifted informants for their stock of knowledge, and I could not taperecord speech explicitly for sociolinguistic purposes. I could not do *Notes and Queries* fieldwork, so I did not fill my fieldnotes with that sort of data. Not having that sort of data, I was unable to manufacture or synthesize the proper scholarly articles. I was alienated, trapped really, within the discipline I had chosen, but which structurally I could not perform adequately within.

My search for a meaningful way to combine anthropology and social concern has in retrospect proved futile, a futility brought about by the almost total refusal of anthropologists to establish a political base at the heart of the discipline or to reward those who study Western as opposed to non-Western social systems. Thinking back, there was minimal institutional, intellectual, or collegial support for what I did, reflecting, perhaps, a deeper racism in our society and its scholars than we want to consider.

After having gone native in a black world for two years, I re-emerged powerfully distressed and with a lingering disorientation. I felt completely untouched by any magic muse that might have brought some enlightenment to the racial question, structure to my brain-bending experiences, coherence and explanation to the politics of our racially polarized cities, or even profound insight into the fabled sexuality of blacks (or natives in general) that a voyeuristic public demands of those adventurers who cross the forbidden cultural boundaries. I came away with pockets and hands full of fragments, shattered shards of another way of life, of ways of making do in America; I emerged from the deep debris of the highly piled bottom of United States society with an armful of random samples that it became my job to make sense of.

≫

I have chosen to place my experiences in South Philadelphia in the *story form*, a mode of communication that anthropologists have for the most part studiously avoided and that the journals do not honor. Stories are for talk over coffee or at cocktail parties or at the annual meetings in the halls or at the bar. Stories for social scientists are sublimated in the scholarly report and are displaced as the analysis of social organization where the flow of lived experience has no place. This sublimation and displacement, wholly legitimate within the aims of a science of humans, has, nevertheless, obscured the symbolic forms that we as practicing anthropologists use. As a result, the hidden rhetoric of the article and the monograph has not been much questioned and the tacit, formal dimensions of the field have dominated our thought. All this now is changing, and we are presently confronting ourselves and our discipline in new ways as the whole of anthropology evolves. We are currently entering a second academic phase or post-academic phase, away from the discipline as it was authored prominently by Franz Boas.

BIBLIOGRAPHY

Alland, Alexander
1975   *When the spider danced: Notes from an African village.* New York:
        Doubleday.
Andrews, Dudley
1976   *The major film theories.* New York: Oxford University Press.
Antin, David
1975   Video, the distinctive features of the medium. In *Video art,* Institute
        of Contemporary Art, University of Pennsylvania, pp. 57–72.
Babcock, Barbara
1980   Reflexivity: Definitions and discriminations. *Semiotica* 30(1–2):
        1–14.
Bachnik, Jane M.
1978   Inside and outside the Japanese household *(Ie):* A contextual ap-
        proach to Japanese social organization. Ph.D. dissertation, Anthro-
        pology Department, Harvard University.

Bakhtin, M. B.
   1968   *Rabelais and his world.* Trans. Helen Iswolsky. Cambridge: The
           M.I.T. Press.
Baltzell, E. Digby
   1980   *Puritan Boston and Quaker Philadelphia.* New York: Free Press.
Bandelier, Adolph F. A.
   1889–   Original journals (typescript). Library, Museum of New Mexico,
   1890   Santa Fe.
   1890–   *Final report of investigations among the Indians of the southwest*
   1892   *United States, carried on mainly in the years from 1880 to 1885, parts*
           I and II. Papers of the Archaeological Institute of America, Ameri-
           can Series III. Cambridge: Harvard University Press.
   1933   Kin and clan [1892]. *New Mexico Historical Review* 8(3):165–75.
   1966   *The southwestern journals, 1880–1882.* Ed. and annotated by Charles
           H. Lange and Carroll Riley. Albuquerque: The University of New
           Mexico Press.
   1970   *The southwestern journals, 1883–1884.* Ed. and annotated by Charles
           H. Lange and Carroll Riley. Albuquerque: The University of New
           Mexico Press.
   1971   *The delight makers* [1890]. New York: Harcourt Brace Jovanovich.
   1975   *The southwestern journals, 1885–1888.* Ed. and annotated by Charles
           H. Lange, Carroll Riley, and Elisabeth M. Lange. Albuquerque:
           The University of New Mexico Press.
Bandelier, Adolph F. A., and Hewett, Edgar L.
   1937   *Indians of the Rio Grande Valley.* Albuquerque: The University of
           New Mexico Press.
Barnes, Will C.
   1914   Adolph F. A. Bandelier, tribute and reminiscence. *El Palacio* 2(2):
           5–6.
Barthes, Roland
   1975   *The pleasure of the text.* New York: Hill and Wang.
Basso, Keith H.
   1979   *Portraits of "the white man": Linguistic play and cultural symbols*
           among the western Apache. New York: Cambridge University Press.
Bastide, Roger
   1974   *African civilizations in the New World.* New York: Harper and
           Row.
Bateson, Gregory
   1936   *Naven: A survey of the problems suggested by a composite picture of the*
           culture of a New Guinea tribe drawn from three points of view.
           Cambridge: Cambridge University Press.
   1972a   Experiments in thinking about observed ethnological material. In
   [1940] *Steps to an ecology of mind,* pp. 73–87. San Francisco: Chandler.
   1972b   *Steps to an ecology of mind.* New York: Ballantine Books.
Benedict, Ruth
   1931   *Tales of the Cochiti Indians.* Bulletin of the Bureau of American
           Ethnology 98. Washington, D.C.: U.S. Government Printing
           Office.

ben Jelloun, Tahar
  1976 *La reclusion solitaire.* Paris: Editions de Noel.
  1977 *La plus haute de solitude.* Paris: Editions du Seuil.

Berger, Peter L., and Luckmann, Thomas
  1966 *The social construction of reality.* New York: Doubleday.

Berreman, Gerald D.
  1962 Behind many masks. *Society for Applied Anthropology, Monograph no. 4.*

Bingham, Hiram
  1914 Bandelier. *The Nation* 98:328–29.

Bloom, Harold
  1973 *The anxiety of influence: A theory of poetry.* New York: Oxford University Press.

Bolinger, Dwight
  1968 *Aspects of language.* New York: Harcourt Brace and World.

Booth, Charles
  1902– *Life and labour of the people in London.* 17 vols. (Poverty Series, IV).
  1903   London and New York: Macmillan.

Bowen, Elenore
  1954 *Return to laughter.* New York: Doubleday.

Brody, Samuel
  1930 A lecture on principles of the new Russian cinema by Sergei Eisenstein. *Close Up* 6(4).

Byers, Paul
  1966 Cameras don't take pictures. *Columbia University Forum* 9(1):27–31.

Bywater, Ingram, trans.
  1954 Poetics. In *The rhetoric and the poetics of Aristotle,* ed. Friedrich Solmsen. New York: Modern Library.

Capote, Truman
  1965 *In cold blood.* New York: Random House.

Ceram, C. W.
  1971 *The first American: A story of North American archaeology.* New York: Harcourt Brace Jovanovich.

Chagnon, Napoleon, and Asch, Timothy
  1970 *The feast.* 30 min., 16mm.
  1973 *Magical death.* 28 min., 16mm.

Chagnon, Napoleon, and Irons, William, eds.
  1979 *Evolutionary biology and human social behavior: An anthropological perspective.* North Scituate, Mass.: Duxbury Press.

Chilungu, Simeon W.
  1976 Issues in the ethics of research methods: An interpretation of the Anglo-American perspective. *Current Anthropology* 17(3):457–67.

Corman, Cid
  1976 *The act of poetry.* (Sparrow 44). Santa Barbara: Black Sparrow Press.

Degerando, Joseph-Marie
   1800   *The observation of savage people.* Trans. F. C. T. Moore. Berkeley: University of California Press.

Derrida, Jacques
   1976   *Of grammatology.* Trans. Gayatri Chakravorty Spivak. Baltimore: Johns Hopkins University Press.

Descartes, René
   1968   *Discourse on method.* Trans. F. E. Sutcliffe. London: Penguin Books.

Diamond, Stanley
   1974   *In search of the primitive.* New Brunswick, N.J.: Transaction Books.

DuBois, W. E. B.
   1967   *The Philadelphia Negro: A social study.* New York: Blom.
   [1899]

Dumarest, Father Noel
   1919   *Notes on Cochiti, New Mexico.* Trans. and ed. Elsie Clews Parsons. Memoirs of the American Anthropological Association 6(3):137–236.

Dumont, Jean-Paul
   1976   *Under the rainbow: Nature and supernature among the Panare Indians.* Austin: University of Texas Press.
   1978   *The headman and I: Ambiguity and ambivalence in the fieldworking experience.* Austin: University of Texas Press.

Duvignaud, Jean
   1973   *Le langage perdu.* Paris: Presses Universitaires de France.
   1977   *Change at Shebika.* Austin: University of Texas Press (first published by Editions Gallimard, 1968).

Edgerton, Robert, and Langness, Louis
   1974   *Methods and styles in the study of culture.* Corte Madera, Calif.: Chandler and Sharp.

Eggan, Fred
   1974   Among the anthropologists. In *Annual review of anthropology,* ed. Bernard J. Siegel, Alan R. Beals, and Stephen A. Tyler, pp. 1–20. Palo Alto: Annual Reviews.

Else, Daniel F.
   1967   *Aristotle's poetics.* Cambridge: Harvard University Press.

Erikson, Erik, ed.
   1978   Reflections on Dr. Borg's life cycle. In *Adulthood,* pp. 1–31. New York: W. W. Norton.

Fabian, Johannes
   1971   Language, history and anthropology. *Journal of the Philosophy of the Social Sciences* 1:19–47.

Firth, Raymond
   1974   Society and its symbols. *Times Literary Supplement,* 13 September, pp. 1–2.

Fox, Robin
    1967   *The Keresan bridge: A problem in Pueblo ethnology.* New York: Humanities Press.
    1973   *Encounter with anthropology.* New York: Harcourt Brace Jovanovich.

Freud, Sigmund
    1965   *Death, grief and mourning.* New York: Doubleday.

Friedländer, Paul
    1969   *Plato,* vol. 3. Princeton: Princeton University Press.

Friedrich, Paul
    1978   *Poetry and anthropology.* Chicago: Benjamin and Martha Waite Press.
    1979   *Bastard moons.* Chicago: Benjamin and Martha Waite Press.

Frye, Northrop
    1957   *Anatomy of criticism: Four essays.* Princeton: Princeton University Press.

Gearing, F. O.
    1970   *The face of the fox.* Chicago: Aldine.

Geertz, Clifford
    1965   Religion as a cultural system. In *Anthropological approaches in the study of religion,* ed. M. Banton, pp. 1–46. New York: Praeger.
    1973a   *The interpretation of culture.* New York: Basic Books.
    1973b   Deep play: Notes on the Balinese cockfight. In *The interpretation of culture,* pp. 412–53. New York: Basic Books.
    1980   Blurred genres: The refiguration of social thought. *The American Scholar* 49(2):165–79.

Gelb, I. J.
    1952   *A study of writing: The foundations of grammatology.* Chicago: University of Chicago Press.

Gluckman, Max
    1977   On drama and games and athletic contests. In *Secular ritual,* ed. Sally Falk Moore and Barbara Myerhoff, pp. 227–43. Assen, Holland: Van Gorcum.

Goad, Edgar F.
    1938   Bandelier's early life. *The Historian* 1(1):75–82.

Goffman, Erving
    1959   *The presentation of self in everyday life.* New York: Doubleday.

Goldfrank, Esther S.
    1927   *The social and ceremonial organization of Cochiti.* Memoirs of the American Anthropological Association, No. 33.

Goldman, Albert
    1974   *Ladies and gentlemen, Lenny Bruce!* New York: Ballantine Books.

Goody, Jack
    1977   *The domestication of the savage mind.* Cambridge: Cambridge University Press.

Greenwood, James
  1866   *A night in a workhouse.* London: Office of the *Pall Mall Gazette.*

Gruber, Jacob
  1966   In search of experience. In *Pioneers of American anthropology: The uses of biography,* ed. June Helm, pp. 3–28. Seattle: University of Washington Press.

Hannerz, Ulf
  1969   *Soulside: Inquiries into ghetto culture and community.* New York: Columbia University Press.

Hareven, Tamara K.
  1978   The search for generational memory: Tribal rites in industrial society. *Daedalus* 107(4):137–49.

Harris, Marvin
  1968   *The rise of anthropological theory.* New York: Crowell.

Hawkes, Terence
  1977   *Structuralism and semiotics.* Berkeley: University of California Press.

Hendron, J. W.
  1940   *Prehistory of El Rito de los Frijoles.* Southwestern Monuments Association, Technical Series 1. Coolidge, Arizona.
  1946   *Frijoles: A hidden valley in the New World.* Santa Fe, N.M.: The Rydal Press.

Henry, Jules
  1964   *The jungle people.* New York: Vintage, Random House.

Herskovits, Melville
  1958   *The myth of the Negro past.* Boston: Beacon Press.

Hess, Irwin
  1974   *America's historic villages and restorations.* New York: Arco.

Hobbs, Hulda
  1942a   The story of *The delight makers* from Bandelier's own journals. *El Palacio* 49(6):109–24.
  1942b   Addenda to *The delight makers.* *El Palacio* 49(8):163–66.

Hodge, F. W.
  1916   Bandelier obituary. *American Anthropologist* 16(2):349–58.
  1932   Biographical sketch and bibliography of Adolph Francis Bandelier. *New Mexico Historical Review* 7(4):353–70.

Hodges, H. A.
  1952   *The philosophy of Wilhelm Dilthey.* London: Routledge and Kegan Paul.

Honigman, John J.
  1976   The personal approach in cultural anthropological research. *Current Anthropology* 17(2):243–61.

Hornby, Richard
  1977   *Script into performance.* Austin: University of Texas Press.

Hymes, Dell
   1971   The contribution of folklore to sociolinguistic research. *Journal of American Folklore* 84:42–50.
   1973   An ethnographic perspective. *New Literary History* 5(1):187–201.
   1978   The grounding of performance and text in a narrative view of life. *Alcheringa: Ethnopoetics* 4(1):137–40.

Hymes, Dell, ed.
   1969   *Reinventing anthropology.* New York: Random House.

Jay, Robert
   1969   Personal and extrapersonal vision in anthropology. In *Reinventing anthropology,* ed. Dell Hymes, pp. 367–81. New York: Random House.

Kaberry, Phyllis
   1957   Malinowski's contribution to field-work methods and the writing of ethnography. In *Man and culture: An evaluation of the work of Bronislaw Malinowski,* ed. Raymond Firth, pp. 71–91. London: Routledge and Kegan Paul.

Kant, Immanuel
   1963   *Lectures on ethics.* New York: Harper Torchbooks. (Originally published 1775–80)

Keating, Peter
   1973   Fact and fiction in the East End. In *The Victorian city: Images and realities.* 2 vols., ed. H. J. Dyos and Michael Wolff, pp. 585–602. London: Routledge and Kegan Paul.
   1976   *Into unknown England, 1866–1913: Selections from the social explorers.* Glasgow: Fontina/Collins.

Kelley, David Humiston
   1976   *Deciphering the Maya script.* Austin: University of Texas Press.

Kidder, Alfred V.
   1928   Adolph F. A. Bandelier. In *Dictionary of American Biography* 1: 571–72.

Kluckhohn, Clyde
   1949   *Mirror for man.* New York: Whittlesey House.

Konrad, Herman
   1977   Review of *Ethics and anthropology,* by Rynkiewich and Spradley. *American Anthropologist* 79(4):920.

Krader, Lawrence
   1968   Person and collectivity: A problem in the dialectic of anthropology. *Transactions of the New York Academy of Sciences.* Series II, 30(6): 856–62.

Kuhn, Thomas S.
   1962   *The structure of scientific revolutions.* Chicago: University of Chicago Press.

Kyriazi, Gary
   1976   *The great American amusement park.* Secaucus, N.J.: Citadel Press.

Labrot, Sharon
    1977   Two types of self-reflexiveness. Unpublished paper, Center for Humanities, University of Southern California.

Lange, Charles H.
    1968   *Cochiti: A New Mexico pueblo, past and present.* Carbondale, Ill.: Southern Illinois University Press.

Langer, Suzanne K.
    1960   *Philosophy in a new key.* Cambridge: Harvard University Press.

Lasch, Christopher
    1978   *The culture of narcissism: American life in an age of diminishing expectations.* New York: W. W. Norton and Company.

Lawrence, D. H.
    1936   *Phoenix: The posthumous papers of D. H. Lawrence,* ed. Edward D. MacDonald. New York: The Viking Press.

Leroi-Gourhan, André
    1964   *Le geste et la parole.* Vol. 1: *Technique et langage.* Paris: Albin Michel.

Lévi-Strauss, Claude
    1961   *A world on the wane.* New York: Criterion Books. [1955]
    1963   *Structural anthropology.* New York: Doubleday.
    1969   *Tristes tropiques.* Trans. John Russell. New York: Atheneum.
    1971   *L'Homme nu.* Paris: Plon.
    1974   *Tristes tropiques.* Trans. John and Doreen Weightman. New York: Atheneum. [1955]
    1976   Jean-Jacques Rousseau. Founder of the sciences of man. In *Structural anthropology,* vol. 2, trans. Monique Layton, pp. 33–43. New York: Basic Books.

Lewis, Oscar
    1967   *Five families.* New York: Mentor Books.

Liebow, Elliot
    1967   *Talley's corner.* Boston: Little, Brown.

Lifton, Robert Jay
    1967   *Death in life: Survivors of Hiroshima.* New York: Simon and Schuster.

Linde, Charlotte
    1978   The creation of coherence in life stories. *Structural semantics.*

London, Jack
    1903   *The people of the abyss.* London and New York: Thomas Nelson.

Louch, A. R.
    1966   *Explanation and human action.* Berkeley: University of California Press.

Lummis, Charles F.
    1952   *The land of Poco Tiempo.* Albuquerque: The University of New Mexico Press.

McKay, Patricia
    1977   Theme parks. *Theatre Crafts* 11(4):27.

McKeon, Richard
  1947   *Introduction to Aristotle.* New York: Modern Library.

Malinowski, Bronislaw
  1922   *Argonauts of the western Pacific.* New York: E. P. Dutton (paperback edition 1961).
  1926   *Crime and custom.* London: Kegan Paul, Trench, Trubner.
  1932   *The sexual life of the savages.* London: George Routledge.
  1967   *A diary in the strict sense of the term.* Trans. Norbert Guterman. New York: Harcourt, Brace and World.

Mannheim, Karl
  1969   The problem of generations. In *Essays in the sociology of knowledge,* ed. Paul Kecskemeti. London: Routledge and Kegan Paul.

Martin, Samuel E.
  1972   Nonalphabetic writing systems: Some observations. In *Language by ear and by eye,* ed. James F. Kavanagh and Ignatius G. Mattingly, pp. 81–102. Cambridge: M.I.T. Press.

Mastai, M. L. d'Ortange
  1975   *Illusion in art: Trompe l'oeil.* New York: Abaris Books.

Maybury-Lewis, David
  1965   *The savage and the innocent.* Boston: Beacon Press.

Mayhew, Henry
  1861–   *London labour and the London poor.* 4 vols. London: Griffin, Bohn,
  1862   and Company.

Mead, Margaret
  1966   *An anthropologist at work: Writings of Ruth Benedict.* New York: Atherton Press.
  1973   *An anthropologist at work: Writings of Ruth Benedict.* New York: Equinox Books.
  1976   Towards a human science. *Science* 191:903–9.

Mendilow, Adam A.
  1952   *Time and experience.* London: Peter Nevill.

Miller, Ben
  1977   Reflexivity in ethnography: An annotated bibliography. Unpublished paper, Temple University.

Moran, Maurice J., Jr.
  1978   Living museums: Coney Islands of the mind. Unpublished Master's thesis, New York University, School of the Arts, Department of Drama.

Morson, Gary Saul
  1977   The heresiarch of Meta. Unpublished review of Bakhtin and Vološinov.

Murdock, George Peter
  1965   *Culture and society.* Pittsburgh: University of Pittsburgh Press.

Murdock, George Peter et al.
  1961   *Outline of cultural materials.* New Haven: Human Relations Area Files, Inc.

Myerhoff, Barbara G.
    1979   *Number our days.* New York: Simon and Schuster.
Myerhoff, Barbara G., and Moore, Sally Falk
    1977   Introduction: Forms and meanings. In *Secular ritual,* ed. Sally Falk
            Moore and Barbara G. Myerhoff, pp. 3–24. Assen, Holland: Van
            Gorcum.
Myrdal, Gunnar
    1969   *Objectivity in social research.* New York: Pantheon.
Nabokov, Vladimir
    1966   *Speak memory: An autobiography revisited.* New York: G. P. Put-
            nam's Sons.
Nancy, Jean-Luc
    1977   Larvatus pro Deo. *Glyph* 2:14–37.
Nash, Dennison, and Wintrob, Ronald
    1972   The emergence of self-consciousness in ethnography. *Current An-
            thropology* 13(5):527–42.
Ortiz, Alfonso, ed.
    1969   *The Tewa world: Space, time, being and becoming in a Pueblo society.*
            Chicago: University of Chicago Press.
    1972   *New perspectives on the Pueblo.* Albuquerque: University of New
            Mexico Press.
Parsons, Elsie Clews
    1939   *Pueblo Indian religion.* Vols. 1 and 2. Chicago: University of Chi-
            cago Press.
Paul, Robert A.
    1978   Gardner: Altar of fire. *American Anthropologist* 80:197–99.
Plato
    1974   *The republic,* Book VII. Trans. G. M. A. Grube. Indianapolis:
            Hackett Publishing Company.
Porter, Katherine Anne
    1963   The art of fiction XXIX (Interview). *Paris Review* 8(29):87–118.
Powdermaker, Hortense
    1966   *Stranger and friend.* New York: Norton.
Rabinow, Paul
    1975   *Symbolic domination: Cultural form and historical change in Morocco.*
            Chicago: University of Chicago Press.
    1977   *Reflections on fieldwork in Morocco.* Berkeley: University of Califor-
            nia Press.
    1979   The interpretive turn. In *Interpretive social science: A reader* (with
            William Sullivan). Berkeley: University of California Press.
Radin, Paul, ed.
    1942   *The unpublished letters of A. F. Bandelier concerning the writing and
            publication of* The delight makers. New York: Charles P. Everitt.
Ramos, Tony
    1979   Catalogue notes in *Videthos,* ed. Eric Michaels. Long Beach, Calif.:
            Long Beach Museum of Art.

Reisman, David
    1953   *The lonely crowd: A study of the changing American character.* Garden City, N.Y.: Doubleday Anchor Books.

Reps, John W.
    1965   *The making of urban America: A history of city planning in the United States.* Princeton: Princeton University Press.

Ricoeur, Paul
    1962   The hermeneutics of symbols and philosophical reflection. *International Philosophical Quarterly* 2:191–218.
    1974   *The conflict of interpretations: Essays in hermeneutics.* Evanston: Northwestern University Press.

Rose, Dan
    1970   *The abyss.* Madison: Cynthius Press.
    1974   Detachment: Continuities of sensibility among Afro-American populations of the circum-Atlantic fringe. *Journal of Asian and African Studies* 9:202–16.
    1975   An economy of scarcity: Adaptive strategies in Afro-American exchanges. Paper read at the annual meeting of the American Anthropological Association.
    1977   A public argument in an Afro-American urban locale. *Journal of the Steward Anthropological Society* 8:137–53.
    n.d.   *Events* (forthcoming).

Rose, Dan, and Renner, Bruce
    1967   *Poetry: 1967.* Milwaukee: University of Wisconsin, Cheshire.

Rouch, Jean
    1978   On the vicissitudes of the self: The possessed dancer, the magician, the sorcerer, the filmmaker, and the ethnographer. *Studies in the Anthropology of Visual Communication* 5(1):2–8.

Royal Anthropological Institute
    1951   *Notes and queries on anthropology.* 6th ed. London: Routledge and Kegan Paul.

Ruby, Jay
    1975   Is an ethnographic film a filmic ethnography? *Studies in the Anthropology of Visual Communication* 2(2):104–11.
    1976   In a pic's eye: Interpretive strategies for deriving meaning and signification from photographs. *Afterimage* 2(9):5–7.
    1977   The image mirrored: Reflexivity and the documentary film. *The Journal of the University Film Association* 29(4):3–13.
    1980   Exposing yourself: Reflexivity, film, and anthropology. *Semiotica* 30(1–2):153–79.

Sack, Leeny
    1979   Untitled work-in-progress presented at New York University seminar "Performance and Anthropology," conducted by Richard Schechner.

Said, Edward W.
    1975   *Beginnings: Intention and method.* Baltimore: Johns Hopkins University Press.

Sartre, Jean-Paul
  1968   Search for a method. New York: Vantage Books.
Schaefer, Jack Warner
  1966   *Adolph Francis Bandelier.* Santa Fe: The Press of the Territorian.
Schieffelin, Edward L.
  1976   *The sorrow of the lonely and the burning of the dancers.* New York: St. Martin's Press.
Scholte, Bob
  1972   On defining anthropological traditions: An exercise in the ethnology of ethnology. In *The nature and function of anthropological traditions,* ed. Stanley Diamond. Philadelphia: University of Pennsylvania Press.
Sebeok, Thomas A., ed.
  1977   *A perfusion of signs.* Bloomington: Indiana University Press.
Segall, Marshall H.; Campbell, Donald T.; and Herskovits, Melville J.
  1966   *The influence of culture on visual perception.* New York: Bobbs-Merrill Company.
Sekula, Alan
  1975   On the invention of meaning in photographs. *Artforum* 13(5): 36–45.
Silverstein, Michael
  1979   Language structure and linguistic ideology. In *The elements: A parasession on linguistic units and levels,* ed. Paul R. Cline et al., pp. 193–247. Chicago: Chicago Linguistic Society.
Simey, T. S., and Simey, M. B.
  1960   *Charles Booth: Social scientist.* London: Oxford University Press.
Simmons, Leo W., ed.
  1942   *Sun chief: The autobiography of a Hopi Indian.* New Haven: Yale University Press.
Singer, Milton
  1972   *When a great tradition modernizes.* London: Pall Mall Press.
Sontag, Susan
  1977   *On photography.* New York: Farrar, Straus and Giroux.
Staal, Frits
  1979a   Comment: *Altar of fire. American Anthropologist* 81:346–47.
  1979b   The meaninglessness of ritual. Unpublished paper.
Steinberg, Leo
  1978   Introduction: The glorious company. In *Art about art,* ed. Jean Lipman and Richard Marshall. New York: E. P. Dutton.
Stent, Gunthar
  1975   Limits to the scientific understanding of man. *Science* 187:1052–57.
Stevens, Wallace
  1955   *The collected poems of Wallace Stevens.* New York: Knopf.
Swearingen, James E.
  1977   *Reflexivity in Tristram Shandy: An essay in phenomenological criticism.* New Haven: Yale University Press.

Tarn, Nathaniel
  1972   Interview with Gary Snyder. *Alcheringa* 4:104–13.

Tedlock, Dennis
  1978   *Finding the center: Narrative poetry of the Zuni Indians.* Lincoln: University of Nebraska Press.
  1979   The analogical tradition and the emergence of a dialogical anthropology. *Journal of Anthropological Research* 35(4):387–400.
  1980   The spoken word and the work of interpretation in American Indian religion. In *Myth, symbol, reality,* ed. Alan M. Olson, pp. 129–44. South Bend, Ind.: Notre Dame University Press.

Thompson, E. P., and Yeo, Eileen, eds.
  1973   *The unknown Mayhew: Selections from the Morning Chronicle, 1849–50.* Harmondsworth, Middlesex: Pelican Books.

Turnbull, Colin
  1972   *The mountain people.* New York: Simon and Schuster.

Turner, Victor
  1957   *Schism and continuity in an African society.* Manchester: Manchester University Press.
  1968   *The drums of affliction.* Oxford: Clarendon.
  1969   *The ritual process.* Chicago: Aldine.

Vatsayan, Kapila
  1968   *Classical Indian dance in literature and the arts.* New Delhi: Sangeet Natak Akademi.
  1974   *Indian classical dance.* New Delhi: Ministry of Information and Broadcasting.

Vonnegut, Kurt, Jr.
  1972   Preface. *Between time and Timbuktu or Prometheus-5.* New York: Delta Books.
  1974   *Wampeters, foma and granfalloons.* New York: Delta Books.

Weiner, Annette
  1978   Epistemology and ethnographic reality: A Trobriand Island case study. *American Anthropologist* 80(3):752–57.

White, Hayden
  1973   *Metahistory: The historical imagination in nineteenth-century Europe.* Baltimore: Johns Hopkins University Press.

White, Leslie A., ed.
  1940   *Pioneers in American Anthropology: The Bandelier-Morgan letters, 1873–1883.* Vols. 1 and 2. Albuquerque: The University of New Mexico Press.

Wiesel, Elie
  1973   *Messengers of God: Biblical portraits and legends.* Trans. Marion Wiesel. New York: Vintage Books.

Winnicott, D. W.
  1971   *Playing and reality.* London: Tavistock Press.

Wissler, Clark
  1914   Bandelier obituary. *El Palacio* 1(6–7):8.

Wolfe, Tom, and Johnson, E. W.
    1973   Introduction. In *The new journalism*, ed. Tom Wolfe. New York: Harper and Row.

Woolf, Virginia
    1931   *The waves.* New York: Harcourt, Brace and World.

Wordsworth, William
    1948   *The prelude.* New York: Rinehart and Company.
    [1800]

Worth, Sol, and Adair, John
    1972   *Through Navaho eyes: An exploration in film communication and anthropology.* Bloomington: Indiana University Press.

Worth, Sol, and Gross, Larry
    1974   Symbolic strategies. *Journal of Communication* 24(4):22–29.

Yff, George; Whitener, Carroll H.; and Natewa, Rex, trans.
    1941   *Jesus Christ an penan' qok'shi John tsinan yaakyakowa.* Zuni, N.M.: privately printed.

Young, Michael, ed.
    1979   *The ethnography of Malinowski.* London: Routledge and Kegan Paul.

Zeitlin, Fromma
    1971   Petronius as paradox: Anarchy and artistic integrity. *Transactions and Proceedings of the American Philological Association* 102:631–84.

CONTRIBUTORS

BARBARA A. BABCOCK is an associate professor of English at the University of Arizona. Her principal research interests are critical theory, narrative theory, modes of reflexivity and inversion, especially Pueblo ritual clowning, and ethnoaesthetics and folk art. Her publications include "The Novel and the Carnival World" (1974); "A 'Tolerated Margin of Mess': The Trickster and His Tales Re-considered" (1975); "The Story in the Story: Metanarration in Folk Narrative" (1976); "Introduction" and " 'Liberty's a Whore': Inversions, Marginalia, and Picaresque Narrative," in *The Reversible World: Essays in Symbolic Inversion* (1978, ed.); "Too Many, Too Few: Ritual Modes of Signification" (1978); "Reflexivity: Definitions and Discriminations," in *Signs about Signs: The Semiotics of Self-Reference* (1980, ed.); and "Arrange Me into Disorder: Fragments and Reflections on Ritual Clowning" (1981). She is presently writing a book on the life and work of the Cochiti potter Helen Cordero.

GEORGE E. MARCUS is an associate professor of Anthropology and chairman of the department at Rice University. He holds a B.A. in politics and economics from Yale University and a Ph.D. in anthropology from Harvard University.

On a Henry Fellowship, he read social anthropology at Cambridge University. After a long period of research and writing on the modern Kingdom of Tonga, he has recently been doing firsthand research on the viability of dynastic family formations in contemporary capitalist societies. Through attempts to write ethnography and also to teach its value to students, who generally have a firm humanities/social science dichotomy in mind, Marcus became interested in the genre characteristics of ethnography. Additional stimulation from colleagues interested in a revival of the teaching of rhetoric and in the field of historiography led Marcus to write the short paper in this volume, which is the prelude to a planned longer work.

ERIC MICHAELS is a researcher in Anthropology and social communication at the University of Texas, Austin. Born in New York, he has alternated between academic life in Texas and at Temple University in Philadelphia, and practical involvement in media and the arts in New York and New Mexico. His publications include accounts of communal societies, applications of ethnographic techniques to media research, and critical articles on video. The videotapes discussed in "How to Look at Us Looking at the Yanomami Looking at Us" were included in "Videthos: An Anthology of Cross-cultural Video," produced for the American Anthropological Association and remounted for the Long Beach Museum of Art. Currently Mr. Michaels participates in a study group on the application of linguistic models to communication research at the University of Texas and is designing video installations for New Wave discos.

BARBARA MYERHOFF is a professor of Anthropology at the University of Southern California. She received her Ph.D. from the University of California, Los Angeles, and her dissertation research was on the Deer-Maize-Peyote Symbol Complex among the Huichol Indians. Her publications include *Number Our Days* (Dutton, 1979), which was translated by the author and Lynne Littman into an award-winning short film; *Changing Images of the American Family: A Multidisciplinary Perspective,* with Virginia Tufte (Yale University Press, 1979); *Secular Ritual: Forms and Meanings,* co-editor with Sally Falk Moore (Royal Van Gorcum Press, 1977); *Life's Career: Cross-Cultural Studies in Growing Old,* co-editor with Andrei Simic (Sage Publications, 1977); *Symbol and Politics in Communal Ideology: Cases and Questions,* co-editor with Sally Falk Moore (Cornell University Press, 1975); and *Peyote Hunt: The Sacred Journey of the Huichol Indians* (Cornell University Press, 1974).

CAROL ANN PARSSINEN received her Ph.D. in English and American Literature at Brandeis University in 1971. She was associated with the Center for Urban Ethnography (University of Pennsylvania) from 1972–74 and developed an approach to ethnographic writing using the techniques of literary analysis. Currently she is Publications Coordinator for INA Service Company in Philadelphia.

PAUL RABINOW is an associate professor of Anthropology at the University of California, Berkeley. He received his B.A., M.A., and Ph.D. degrees from the

University of Chicago. His publications include *Symbolic Domination: Cultural Form and Historical Change in Morocco* (University of Chicago Press, 1975); *Reflections on Fieldwork in Morocco* (University of California Press, 1977); *Interpretive Social Science: A Reader*, with William Sullivan (University of California Press, 1979); and *Michel Foucault: Beyond Structuralism and Hermeneutics*, with Hubert Dreyfus (forthcoming, 1981).

DAN ROSE teaches ecological anthropology at the University of Pennsylvania, and is associate professor of Landscape Architecture and Regional Planning with a secondary appointment in the Department of Anthropology. His extensive fieldwork has been conducted largely within the middle-Atlantic region of North America, and his professional interests include theoretical and aesthetic anthropology. His book entitled *Energy Transition and the Local Community* was published by the University of Pennsylvania Press in 1981, and *Events*, an autobiographical account of field research and intellectual influence, is forthcoming. His current projects include a review of integrative theories in the biological and behavioral sciences from 1950 to 1980.

JAY RUBY is an associate professor of Anthropology at Temple University; Co-editor of *Studies in Visual Communication;* and President of the International Film Seminars (Robert Flaherty Film Seminar). He has been a visiting faculty member of the University of California, Santa Barbara; University of California, Davis; University of Pennsylvania; Princeton University; and Livingston College, Rutgers. He has done fieldwork in the southwestern United States, Mexico, Sudan, and rural central Pennsylvania. He is the author of archaeological site reports and articles on film, music and 1960s popular culture.

RICHARD SCHECHNER, a professor in the Department of Performance Studies, School of the Arts, New York University, is a theater director and author. His productions include *Dionysus in 69, Commune, The Tooth of Crime, Mother Courage, Oedipus* (Seneca), *Cops,* and *The Balcony,* all with The Performance Group, which he founded in 1967 and led until 1980. Also he has directed Michael McClure's *The Red Snake* in 1981 at the New York Shakespeare Festival. His books include *Environmental Theatre* and *Essays on Performance Theory.*

DENNIS TEDLOCK received a B.A. from the University of New Mexico, and a Ph.D. in Anthropology from Tulane University. He has done archaeological field research in New Mexico and Utah, followed by linguistic and ethnographic research among the Koasati of Louisiana, the Zuni of New Mexico, and the Quiché Maya of Guatemala. He has taught at Iowa State, University of California (Berkeley), Brooklyn College, Wesleyan, The New School for Social Research, and Yale; he is currently Associate University Professor of Anthropology and Religion at Boston University. He was co-founder and editor of *Alcheringa: Ethnopoetics,* an experimental periodical, and his books are *Finding the Center: Narrative Poetry of the Zuni Indians* (Dial, repr. by Nebraska) and (with Barbara Tedlock) *Teachings from the American Earth: Indian Religion and*

Philosophy (Liveright). Currently he is working on a new English translation of the Popol Vuh, sacred book of the Quiché Maya, and on a book tentatively titled *Mythography and Mythopoesis.*

VICTOR TURNER was born in Scotland and obtained his doctorate from the University of Manchester in 1955. He was chairman of the African Studies Committee at Cornell from 1964 to 1968; chairman of the Committee on Social Thought at the University of Chicago in 1976 and 1977; and chairman of the Advisory Council to the Anthropology Department of Princeton from 1973 to 1977. He is presently the William R. Kenan, Jr., Professor of Anthropology at the University of Virginia. He has done fieldwork in Zambia, Uganda, Mexico, Ireland, Italy, and France. He is the author of *Ndembu Divination* (1961); *Chiamba, The White Spirit* (1962); *The Forest of Symbols* (1967); *The Drums of Affliction* (1968); *The Ritual Process* (1969); *Dramas, Fields, and Metaphors* (1974); *Image and Pilgrimage in Christian Culture* (1977); and *Process, Performance, and Pilgrimage* (1980).

INDEX

art: as reflexive communication, 12–13; self-portraits, 12; self-reference, 12
Artaud, Antonin, 84
Asch, Timothy, 135, 137
Ashton, Martha, 78
autobiography, reflexivity in, 5–6, 9
Autobiography of Malcolm X, The, 9

Baal Shem Tov, 113
Babcock, Barbara, 2–3
Bachnik, Jane, 166
Bakhtin, M. B., 196, 201
Balinese cockfight, 17, 19
Baltzell, E. Digby, 241
Bandelier, Adolph, 187–203
Barthes, Roland, 174–75, 185
Basso, Keith H., 203
Bastide, Roger, 224–25
Bateson, Gregory, 21, 75–76, 130, 169
Bellow, Saul, 17
Benedict, Ruth, 233
ben Jelloun, Tahar, 178–83, 185
Berger, Peter L., 7
Bergman, Ingmar, 9
Berreman, Gerald D., 21
Bharatanatyam, 43, 53–56, 60
Block, Mitchell, 16
Bloom, Harold, 237–39
blurred genres, 8, 16
Boas, Franz, 273
Bohannan, Laura, 227
Bolinger, Dwight, 156
Booth, Charles, 205–6, 208–12, 217
Bowen, Elenore, 22
Brecht, Bertold, 40, 68–69, 72
Brook, Peter, 85, 95
Brown, James, 262
Browne, Sir Thomas, 106
Bureau of Indian Affairs, 188
Burke, Kenneth, 167
Byers, Paul, 125

Cage, John, 11
Campbell, Donald T., 15
Carpenter, Edmund, 50
Castenada, Carlos, 8
Ceram, C. W., 188–89, 195, 201
Chagnon, Napoleon, 135, 137, 170
Chilungi, Simeon W., 26
Chomsky, Noam, 154–55

Christ, 44
clowns: demystification of, 193–94; description of, 191–92; performances by, 201; persecution of, 188; as ritual personages, 192; role of, 192; and storyteller dolls, 202–3
Conference on Visual Anthropology, 29, 135
Cordero, Helen, 202–3
Corman, Cid, 238
cultural relativity, 8
cultures: consequences of, 103; interpretation of, 103; as mirrors, 103; self-awareness of, 18–19; self-presentation in, 103; as stages, 104
Curtis, Edward, 63–65

dance-drama: Balinese, 40–41; Kerala Indian, 68; in literature and art, 53; Yakshagana, 78
definitional ceremonies, 114; as interpretation, 105
Degerando, Joseph-Marie, 26
de Menil, Adelaide, 47
Derrida, Jacques, 156, 158
Descartes, Rene, 173, 183–85
Devi, Rukmini, 54–55
Diamond, Stanley, 174, 177, 185
Die Koshäre (The Delight Makers), 188, 193–94, 196, 200–201, 203
Dilthey, Wilhelm, 107
Dinka (of Africa), 3
Dionysus in '69, 87
Discourse on Method, 173, 183–84
divine order, for social scientist, 184
Doll's House, 88–89
Downey, Juan, 135, 137, 139, 141–42
drama, 100; aesthetic, 84–85; culturally defined roles in, 89; definition of, 86; ethnodramatics, 95–96; historical, 100; hypokrisis, 154; poesis, 154
Dramaturg/Ethnodramaturg, 95
Du Bois, W. E. B., 241, 244
Dumont, Jean-Paul, 165–66
Duvignaud, Jean, 175–78, 183, 185
Dylan, Bob, 10–11

Edgerton, Robert, 16
Eggan, Fred, 227
Eisenstein, Sergé, 121–22, 129

Indian clowns *(continued)*
(Ku-sha'li), 191; Zuni (Koyemci), 192
interpretive strategies: folk models, 125; inference/attribution, 5–6, 122–25, 128, 130
Irons, William, 170

Jackson, Mahalia, 10–11
Jacobs, Sue-Ellen, 26
Jay, Robert, 17
Jesus Christ An Penan' Qok'shi John Tsinan Yaakyakowa, 158
Jews: chosen people status, 107; cultural/ethnic identity and values, 101–2, 115; dispersion, 107; Eastern European immigrants, 33, 101, 115; Hasidism, 112–13, 115; Holy Land, 107; oral tradition of, 115; *shtetls*, 101; Yiddish, 101; *Yiddishkeit*, 101; Zionism, 102
Johnson, E. W., 13–14
Johnson, Guion G., 224
Jung, Carl, 157

Kaberry, Phyllis, 164
Kant, Immanuel, 229, 232
Karanth, K. S., 78
Keating, Peter, 206–7
Kenny, Anson, 12–13
Kerala Indians, 48, 50–51, 62–63
Kierkegaard, Soren, 231
King, Carol, 11
Kluckhohn, Clyde, 222
Knorozov, Yurii, 157
Knowles, Christopher, 64–65
Konrad, Herman, 26
Krader, Lawrence, 128
Kuhn, Thomas S., 7–8, 126
Kwakiutl Indians, 64

Labrot, Sharon, 18, 126
Langer, Suzanne, 104
Langness, Louis, 16, 23
Lasch, Christopher, 7
Lawrence, D. H., 83, 201
Leroi-Gourhan, André, 155–56
Lévi-Strauss, Claude, 8, 19, 22, 153–54, 157–58, 170, 175, 232, 240
Lewis, Oscar, 9, 13
Liebow, Eliot, 245
life histories, 103; in ethnography, 114–17;

life histories *(continued)*
impact of, 116; uses of, 101
Lifton, Robert J., 107
Linde, Charlotte, 104
linguistics: codification, 159; model for myth, 153
London, Jack, 208–9
Louch, A. R., 164
Luckmann, Thomas, 7
Lummis, Charles, 190

McBride, Jim, 16
McKeon, Richard, 232
McLuhan, Terry, 64
Mailer, Norman, 8
Makbeth, 87
Malcolm X, 9
Malinowski, Bronislaw, 20–21, 30, 87, 164, 168, 214–15, 227
Mannheim, Karl, 99
Marcus, George E., 16, 23
Mastai, M. L. d'Ortange, 129–30
Maybury-Lewis, David, 21–22
Mayfield, Curtis, 256
Mayhew, Henry, 205–7, 210–14, 217
Mead, Margaret, 9, 20, 28, 127, 134, 227, 233
Me Generation, The, 7
membership, 99; collective behavior in, 105–6; common/generational cohort, 100–101; cultural/ethnic identity, 101–2
Mendilow, Adam A., 109
meta-communications, 4
meta-levels, 2
Michaels, Eric, 19
Miller, Ben, 21
Moments, The, 253
Moran, Maurice J., Jr., 56–57
Morgan, Lewis Henry, 189
Morson, Gary Saul, 201
Mother Courage, 73, 87
Murdoch, George Peter, 225, 227
music: lyrics as symbolic system, 10; reflexiveness in, 10–11; reflexive performances in, 11; songs as storytelling, 10–11
Myerhoff, Barbara, 65
Myrdal, Gunnar, 18, 127
myths: "authors" of, 154; synchronic and diachronic dimensions of, 158; syntagmatic chain, 158; tellers of, 154, 158–59